Recent Titles in Contributions in Sociology

The Mythmakers: Intellectuals and the Intelligentsia in Perspective
Raj P. Mohan, editor

The Organization-Society Nexus: A Critical Review of Models and Metaphors
Ronald Corwin

The Concept of Social Structure
Douglas V. Porpora

Emile Durkheim: Ethics and the Sociology of Morals
Robert T. Hall

The Development of a Postmodern Self: A Computer-Assisted Comparative Analysis
of Personal Documents
Michael Wood and Louis Zurcher

The End of Conversation: The Impact of Mass Media on Modern Society
Franco Ferrarotti

Rural Sociology and the Environment
Donald R. Field and William R. Burch, Jr.

Democracy in the Shadows: Citizen Mobilization in the Wake of the Accident at
Three Mile Island
Edward J. Walsh

American Ritual Dramas: Social Rules and Cultural Meanings
Mary Jo Deegan

Multiculturalism and Intergroup Relations
James S. Frideres, editor

Homelessness in the United States. Volume I: State Surveys
Jamshid A. Momeni, editor

EXPLORATIONS IN THE UNDERSTANDING OF LANDSCAPE

Explorations

IN THE Understanding OF Landscape

A Cultural Geography

WILLIAM NORTON

Contributions in Sociology, Number 77

GREENWOOD PRESS
NEW YORK • WESTPORT, CONNECTICUT • LONDON

Library of Congress Cataloging-in-Publication Data

Norton, William, 1944–
    Explorations in the understanding of landscape : a cultural
geography / William Norton.
        p.   cm. — (Contributions in sociology, ISSN 0084–9278 ; no.
77)
    Bibliography: p.
    Includes index.
    ISBN 0–313–26494–5 (lib. bdg. : alk. paper)
    1. Landscape assessment—Methodology. 2. Human ecology—
Philosophy. I. Title. II. Series.
    GF90.N66   1989
    304.2—dc19   88–21340

British Library Cataloguing in Publication Data is available.

Library of Congress Catalog Card Number: 88–21340
ISBN: 0–313–26494–5
ISSN: 0084–9278

First published in 1989

Greenwood Press, Inc.
88 Post Road West, Westport, Connecticut   06881

Printed in the United States of America

The paper used in this book complies with the
Permanent Paper Standard issued by the National
Information Standards Organization (Z39.48–1984).

10 9 8 7 6 5 4 3 2 1

Copyright Acknowledgments

The author and publisher are grateful to The Canadian Association of Geographers for granting
the use of Tables 1 and 2 from *Humans, Land and Landscape: A Proposal for Cultural
Geography* by William Norton, Copyright 1987.

For Pauline

Contents

EXHIBITS   ix

PREFACE   xi

1. INTRODUCTION   1

2. VIEWS OF HUMANS AND NATURE: RELATED
   DISCIPLINES   11

3. DEVELOPMENT OF CULTURAL GEOGRAPHY   27

4. CONTEMPORARY CULTURAL GEOGRAPHY   45

5. UNDERSTANDING LANDSCAPE: BEHAVIORAL
   APPROACHES   67

6. UNDERSTANDING LANDSCAPE: EVOLUTIONARY
   EMPHASES   87

7. UNDERSTANDING LANDSCAPE: SYMBOLISM AND
   SOCIAL PROCESSES   113

8. UNDERSTANDING LANDSCAPE: ECOLOGICAL
   EMPHASES   141

9. RETROSPECT AND PROSPECT   161

   BIBLIOGRAPHY   169

   INDEX   193

Exhibits

Figure 1	The Central Theme	4
Table 1	Humans and Land: Evolution of Concepts	63
Table 2	Humans and Land: Geographic Emphases	65
Figure 2	The Lewin Field Concept	71

Preface

I have written this book because of a firm conviction that some signposts are needed to help direct the continuing growth of North American cultural geography, to clarify aspects of the much needed convergence with an essentially European social geography, and finally, to provide a broad intellectual context for both of these developments. The result is an intellectual and historical discussion of material and symbolic landscape. Methodology dominates, but this does not disguise a concern with region delimitation, group delimitation, and human decision making in landscape. Combined, these three concerns represent a means of analyzing landscapes. This book argues for acceptance, or at least consideration, of a wide range of methodologies, but the central theme, or subject matter, remains the traditional concern of landscape.

Landscapes are created and given meaning as a result of human groups, or cultures, occupying and making decisions in particular areas on the surface of the earth. We are, then, concerned both with culture and landscape. The focus on the culture concept is vital for geographers, and this book reviews and comments on the concept from a variety of perspectives, anthropological and sociological as well as geographic. This is argued to be a most positive aspect of the work. The focus on landscape maintains a conventional geographic emphasis but recognition of both cultural and social content broadens that conventional emphasis in a much needed fashion. The discussions of culture and landscape thus contribute to the ongoing fusion of cultural and social geography.

Necessarily, this is not a definitive volume. It reviews and comments on relevant literature and concepts via a novel organization that I believe provides important insights. The early chapters review the culture concept on the basis of a wide-ranging literature and explain the emergence, development, and current character of cultural geography. The later chapters exploit and continue these methodological debates in a series of four somewhat unconventional discussions. Within the general framework of understanding landscape, the four themes emphasize evolution, behavior, symbolism, and ecology. A more conventional organization into region, landscape, diffusion, and so forth was considered and rejected. The blending of cultural and social literature required a fresh approach. Unavoidably, the conventional themes are scattered throughout this book. This is not only necessary because of the organization employed, it is in fact desirable. Regional, ecological, and human decision-making issues belong everywhere in a book of this type and not in neatly demarcated sections. It is hoped that the organization of this book will be a stimulus to others to continue this intellectual exploration.

This book does not purport to be a text in the usual sense. Nevertheless, it provides a useful framework for a variety of human and environment, cultural, social, and methodology courses. This point requires some clarification.

The initial stimulus for writing this book resulted from teaching cultural geography to second-year students in a Canadian university. The lack of a suitable text at a post-first-year level, which was initially a minor heuristic inconvenience, resulted in the eventual, three- to four-year evolution of the structure evident in chapters 5 to 8 of this book. I gradually realized that it was necessary to teach much more than conventional cultural geography. Given a central theme of landscape, I was prompted to turn to the other disciplines, to understand the character of geography as a discipline, and to incorporate both cultural and social material. This book is a result of those prompts. It suggests a course structure but does not, quite deliberately, offer all of the necessary content. At this time, I do not believe that such a text is appropriate. Divergent views as to course content prevail. The framework presented in this book can accommodate a wide variety of such content. Hence, my belief that this book will prove a valuable source of ideas and inspirations for both instructors and students.

I am firmly committed to a revitalization of cultural geography, and I believe that a fuller appreciation of intellectual origins and a convergence of cultural and social work can combine to facilitate such a revitalization. Analyses of the cultural landscape have a long and illustrious heritage in geography and these explorations are intended to contribute positively and constructively to that heritage.

This work has benefited from conversations with numerous students, who often proved to be excellent teachers. More particularly, this book owes most to Pauline; without her concern, interest, and love it would not have been written.

1

Introduction

PRELIMINARY COMMENTS

The concern in this book is with the branch of geography typically labeled cultural geography in North America and social geography in Britain. This branch of geography is diverse in content and method. Indeed, it is commonplace to assert that cultural and social geography are separate areas of research. In a developmental sense this is quite correct, but it is argued here that largely separate intellectual histories cannot disguise a basic unity. This book strives to emphasize the desirability of regarding the two as one with their shared interest in region delimitation, group delimitation, and landscape. No attempt is made to argue for total unity as any such attempt would be intellectually stultifying; rather the theme of cultural geography is broadened to include much social geography. One aim of the volume, then, is to attempt a clear articulation of content and methods—a difficult aim because the differences between the two are not mere dilettantism but are often deep-seated differences rooted in the notion of human geography as a discipline and in underlying philosophies.

The material in chapters 3 and 4 leads to the conclusion, or rather the suggestion, that one central theme can be identified. This is a focus on the evolution of the cultural landscape and on relevant variables. The substantive empirical discussions contained especially in chapters 5 to 8 reflect this theme. Thus, a second aim is to provide a critique of the literature of cultural and social geography that is focused around the suggested theme. It is hoped that this critique will provide a useful framework for future research and an indication of the relative merits of different methods for different problems.

The contemporary status of this branch of geography is such that a review and critique of this type is urgently required, because recent literature indicates a proliferation of work in North America, Britain, and elsewhere. In the United States, a new journal, the *Journal of Cultural Geography*, emerged in 1980 under the auspices of the Popular Culture Association and the American Culture Association; a major atlas of North American society and cultures was published (Rooney, Zelinsky, & Loudon, 1982); a cultural ecology working group was established within the Assocation of American Geographers and a newsletter published; and a theme issue of *Antipode* dealing with radical cultural geography appeared in 1983. In Britain, the journal, *Progress in Human Geography*, provides a clear indication of the increasing concern with cultural or social geography with a series of review articles that address, for example, cultural concerns in specific regions (Spencer, 1982), specific geographic problems (Harriss & Harriss, 1982), and specific methodologies (Gold & Goodey, 1983). In an important sense, the North American and British literature complement each other with the former focusing largely on methods and issues of landscape and the latter focusing largely on methods and issues of cultural and social relevance (Cosgrove & P. Jackson, 1987).

Having suggested the appropriateness of a critique and appraisal of cultural geographic literature, this introduction will now provide the rationale for the general framework around which this book is organized. It is suggested that a legitimate realm for cultural geography is the analysis of cultural landscapes and relevant variables. At this time, the term *landscape* is not carefully defined. Various uses of the term emerge throughout the book, and a restrictive definition would not prove useful. Suffice it to say that landscape is both material and symbolic. It is material in the sense that it comprises such things as settlements and it is symbolic in that it has a meaning to humans. The suggestion that variables are analyzed refers to those factors involved in landscape evolution. Relevant variables include language and religion, which can be responsible for the emergence of landscape in both its material and symbolic aspects. Useful approaches to landscape analyses include the full array of contemporary methodologies such as those of the positivist, Marxist, idealist, structuralist, and phenomenologist. Fortunately, an acceptance of such diverse approaches is not necessarily a hindrance to identification of a common subject matter. This point is tellingly made by Leonard Guelke (1983) in a comparison of human geography and history that acknowledges that human geographers of differing methodological persuasion have failed to interact with one another even when dealing with essentially similar subjects. Historians, on the other hand, "have been able to maintain some kind of meaningful dialogue amongst themselves" at least partly because they "have focussed their energies on definite historical questions" (Guelke, 1983, p. 85). The lesson is clear. A concern with common issues is crucial to that meaningful interaction that is so important to the development of knowledge. For the cultural geographer, then, the first task is to articulate a set of issues that are, in principle, amenable to all approaches. Issues ought not to be defined by approaches although, of course, different approaches do result in different specific questions.

The diverse character of cultural geography that is suggested above is relatively recent in origin. Traditionally and certainly prior to the 1960s, the subject focused on "differences from place to place in the ways of life of human communities and their creation of man made or modified features" (NAS–NRC, 1965, p. 23). Until recently, there has been little concern about this unchanging character, and it is only since circa 1970 that various philosophies, largely nonpositivistic, have been advocated. Ronald Johnston (1983a, p. 90) suggested that cultural geographers were little concerned with the increasing gap between themselves and other human geographers emphasizing a positivistic spatial analysis, and that this was perhaps a result of the fact that anthropology was not exhibiting similar developments. Certainly, recent emphases appear to support this assertion, with new interests in nonpositivistic ideas that, although related to cultural geographic literature, might be more closely related to anthropology. This is one reason why this book pays close attention to both anthropology and human geography.

THE CENTRAL THEME

One central theme is suggested and pursued—a concern with the emergence of landscape and the variables responsible for landscape change. This is a traditional theme with origins in early twentieth-century European and U.S. geography, but it has recently been subject to major reinterpretation. Regardless of the methodological emphasis, the following framework is advocated (Figure 1).

Figure 1a distinguishes the prehuman from the human landscape, a somewhat artificial distinction in that for most areas of the world no date can be determined for this transition. Nevertheless, the rationale for recognizing a prehuman landscape is sound in principle, because it represents the stage on which human activity takes place. Typically this landscape has been called the physical or natural setting. The evolving human landscape is depicted as a continuum rather than as a series of stages emphasizing the likelihood of continuous rather than discrete development. This evolving landscape is acknowledged to be a consequence of both previous landscapes and of the ongoing processes prompting change. The basic framework depicted in Figure 1a also serves to highlight the purpose of cultural geographic research, namely to describe, analyze, and explain the evolving human landscape.

Figure 1b delimits a series of stages from the initial prehuman landscape through the prehistoric, historic, and contemporary landscapes through to the future landscape. These divisions are based largely on the type of data: the prehistoric stage requiring archaeologic data, the historic and contemporary stages utilizing conventional geographic sources, and the future stage relying on predictions.

This evolving human landscape has a variety of characteristics as shown in Figure 1c. The visible, material landscape is a traditional area of interest and might be approached as a whole or in terms of particular components such as

Figure 1
The Central Theme

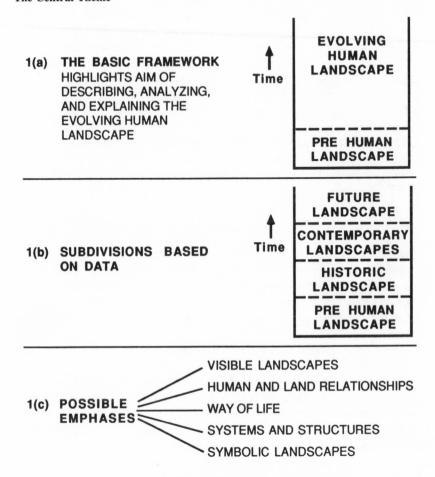

1(a) **THE BASIC FRAMEWORK**
HIGHLIGHTS AIM OF
DESCRIBING, ANALYZING,
AND EXPLAINING THE
EVOLVING HUMAN
LANDSCAPE

Time

EVOLVING
HUMAN
LANDSCAPE

PRE HUMAN
LANDSCAPE

1(b) **SUBDIVISIONS BASED
ON DATA**

Time

FUTURE
LANDSCAPE

CONTEMPORARY
LANDSCAPES

HISTORIC
LANDSCAPE

PRE HUMAN
LANDSCAPE

1(c) **POSSIBLE
EMPHASES**

VISIBLE LANDSCAPES
HUMAN AND LAND RELATIONSHIPS
WAY OF LIFE
SYSTEMS AND STRUCTURES
SYMBOLIC LANDSCAPES

house styles. Frequently, a distinctive relationship between humans and the land can be identified, with emphases ranging from forms of determinism such as environmental, superorganic, or Marxist views to views emphasizing individual decision making and behavior. Each of these concepts is explained more fully, both conceptually and empirically, in subsequent chapters. At this stage, it is only necessary to note that deterministic approaches typically assume one-to-one cause-and-effect relationships. Thus, environmental determinism assumes that the physical enviroment is cause, the superorganic sees culture as cause, and some Marxist views assume an economic determinism. In each of these three cases, human landscape and way of life are effects. Closely related to these ideas is the establishment of a distinctive way of life, or *genre de vie*. Way of life can be seen as including the usual cultural universals such as language, religion, politics, society, and economy. The human landscape can also be viewed in structural terms, emphasizing the interaction of variables and the relation of objects. For the positivist, this may be a systems approach; for the Marxist, a structuralist approach. Finally, it is possible to focus on the meaning of landscape, that is, on landscape as symbol. This is a relatively recent emphasis and can be regarded as an alternative to the more traditional study of visible, material landscapes. Each of these five emphases is one way of viewing the content of, and approach to, cultural geography. Each emphasis implies a particular content and particular approach. But for all five, the common denominator is the general purpose noted in Figure 1a. Thus, the framework is sufficiently tight to allow for a definition and, at the same time, sufficiently broad to encompass the necessary diversity of content and method.

SOME WORDS OF CAUTION

One possible reaction to the above theme is to assert that it is both overly simple and needlessly broad and hence, of limited value. This is not true. There are likely to be difficulties in any attempt to delimit a subject and identify key ideas. This section identifies seven difficulties that this book encounters and strives to overcome.

1. The question of accepting diverse approaches represents a difficulty. For many social scientists, the primary commitment is to approach and the secondary commitment is to subject matter. Thus, the inclusion of more than one approach presents a problem. This book removes this difficulty by arguing for the primacy of subject matter, problems, and aims, and the relegation of method. In this way, diverse approaches become an advantage, not a disadvantage. Problems are defined and relevant approaches employed rather than limiting the range of problems to those prompted by a specific method. The resultant range of problems is stimulated by earlier empirical work and by the inspiration of specific methods. It is this need for a catholic view of cultural geography that plays a major role in identifying the key theme of the subdiscipline.

2. A major difficulty in much contemporary research concerns the degree to which the results of empirical work are legitimately comparable to earlier empirical work. This point is explicitly debated by Glenn Carroll (1982, p. 37) in regard to the rank-size rule, a basic principle of urban geography. "We do not suffer from a lack of empirical research but instead from a lack of consistent findings . . . these differences arise because the empirical research is often not comparable. Vastly different samples, research designs, measures and analytical techniques are employed." One possible solution is to use a common framework that imposes at least some uniformity on empircal work and encourages comparisons.

3. Emphasizing the need for unity does not detract from the importance of incorporating the results of work from other disciplines. The cultural geographer

has traditionally been linked to anthropology and occasionally history, but has largely ignored psychology and sociology. Indeed, even the ties to anthropology have been highly selective, as is evident from the discussion of the superorganic by James Duncan (1980), and the links to history have been evident principally in British and European research. A catholic approach is advocated here. The cultural geographer might turn to anthropological literature focusing on cultural systems; sociological literature focusing on territoriality; psychological literature focusing on learning, personality, and perception; and historical literature focusing on social and cultural change. At present, the interest in such work is limited, and this represents another difficulty that cultural geography needs to overcome. The cultural geographer needs to become a full partner in contemporary developments in the social sciences and humanities. One partial means of accomplishing this is to further integrate the traditional cultural and social interests. By employing relevant work from other disciplines, it becomes increasingly possible to contribute research that goes beyond the necessarily narrow confines of a particular specialty and to elevate cultural geography to a stature comparable to that of related disciplines. The need, then, is to formulate key questions, notably those implied by the already identified central theme, and to approach these questions by reference to the most appropriate method. Questions about cultural and landscape change are indeed important and can be profitably tackled by the cultural geographer.

4. Given the considerations noted in the previous paragraph, it is important to ask if it is necessary, viable, and worthwhile to delimit and define cultural geography. Is it necessary, viable, and worthwhile? In terms of subject matter, the answer is yes. But in terms of method, a somewhat more nebulous consideration, the answer is no. Cultural geography is as distinguishable from anthropology, for example, as sociology is from psychology. There are important differences but, at the same time, major overlaps in methods and content. The important distinctions, other than those rather irrelevant ones perpetuated by institutions, are those of subject emphasis. Both the sociologist and the psychologist, for example, tackle issues of abnormal behavior and share conceptual and empirical work, as an appraisal of relevant texts clearly demonstrates. The differences are long established in the respective disciplines, and center on the emphases on individuals and societies. In a similar vein, the cultural geographer and the anthropologist share a great deal of conceptual and empirical work. The differences of emphasis in this case have traditionally included a greater interest by geographers in environmental causes, region delimitation, and, more recently, spatial behavior. However, these relatively distinct geographic emphases have not proved sufficient to establish cultural geography as a research area comparable to that of cultural anthropology. Distinguished scholars in cultural geography who are well known outside their discipline constitute a much shorter list than a comparable one for anthropologists. Similarly, there are few popular books by cultural geographers and there are many by anthropologists. These considerations suggest that cultural geography has failed to make a

mark comparable to that of other disciplines. At least two responses are possible. First, cultural geography does indeed lack a focus and it is more properly included as one aspect of anthropology. Second, cultural geography has failed to exploit its distinctiveness—the emergence of landscape. This book argues for the latter response in the succeeding pages and thus argues for a viable subdiscipline of cultural geography. It is worthwhile to note here that the complaint of a lack of impact is by no means restricted to cultural geography. The 1980s have been characterized by a general concern with the failure of geography as a whole to generate a vigorous and effective public image. The limitations of cultural geography are also the limitations of the parent discipline.

5. Asserting a role for cultural geography promptly introduces another difficulty: the presence today of distinctly different types of cultural and social urban studies. This also emerges as a difficulty in anthropology. In both fields of study, the traditional focus has been on rural topics with only limited excursions into urban work. The occasional urban emphasis has, indeed, often assumed a distinctly sociological appearance. This has not always been the case and need not be the case. The principle of landscape change is applicable equally to rural and urban issues. It seems likely that future research will increasingly demonstrate this point, and the specific convergence of cultural and social geography is already achieving this goal.

6. It is not necessary to argue the relative merits of individual and societal foci at this time. The relevant emphasis is likely to be evident from the research question. Nevertheless, recent work has found it necessary to argue this issue in some detail, and it is a topic that is pursued on several occasions in this volume. The basic question is: What is the appropriate scale for analyzing human activities—individual, small group, large group, or state? These are not, of course, discrete entities, rather they are specific scales along a continuum of possibilities. A current trend in human geography is to argue for some group scale. Andrew Sayer (1982, p. 80), for example, noted that human agents are more than individuals; Ernst Griffin and Larry Ford (1980) argued for close consideration of social differences for the exercise of developing models of internal city structure; and Simon Leonard (1982, p. 190) pursued recent sociological ideas concerning the constraints placed on individual behavior. In principle, however, any scale is acceptable.

7. The final observation in this section relates to the possible problems that can result from imposing a framework, however loose, on research. Following the earlier arguments, it is suggested that, rather than serving as a mental straitjacket, the suggested framework might actually allow for the convergence of theoretical positions. Successful application of initially divergent concepts to various studies of landscape change might contribute a clearer appreciation of alternative conceptual positions and to initial reconciliations. Establishment of a key theme is more likely to lead in this direction than it is to restrict the range of research.

CONCLUDING COMMENTS

This introduction has attempted to prepare the reader for the chapters to follow, which attempt a close analysis of the conceptual and empirical content of cultural geography. It has been suggested that cultural landscape evolution is a meaningful central theme, which can be approached from a variety of perspectives and can serve to elevate cultural geography to greater intellectual rigor and popular appreciation. It needs to be noted at this stage that it is not the intention of this book to criticize earlier work in a wholesale manner. The criticisms being made are not of specific work, but rather of the conception of cultural geography as necessarily diverse in method and content. Diversity can be healthy, but at the same time it spells out the need for some central focus. The suggested emphasis on landscape change does not necessarily imply a need to seek origins or to contemplate futures. The specifics of the time scale need to be a response to the specific research issue. The important principle is the concern with change and the causes and consequences of change.

It is important to emphasize that the field of cultural geography as discussed in this volume is both narrower and broader than is characteristic. First, it is narrower in that the term *cultural geography* is often used as a synonym for human geography and thus taken to include such major themes as population, agriculture, and industry. This is the interpretation made by Terry Jordan and Lester Rowntree (1986) in their standard text. This broad view is rejected here because it is felt that the incorporation of all human geography into cultural geography creates a weakened *cultural* geography, lacking a clear central purpose. Thus, the current volume elects to restrict cultural geography by interpreting it as one of the subdisciplines of geography, along with, for example, population geography, agricultural geography, and industrial geography.

Second, the cultural geography of this volume is broader than some traditional views in that it actively attempts to incorporate social geography within the cultural label. The reason for consciously adding social geography is that cultural and social geography are indeed very similar. They have been taught and researched separately for reasons of historic circumstances and academic convenience, and this has partly hidden their fundamental conceptual similarity. Thus, this volume introduces a cultural geography with a strong social content.

The contents of this volume are organized as follows. Following this introduction, chapter 2 considers the complex issue of human and land relations from the perspective of disciplines other than geography. This is essential material because cultural geography did not arise in an intellectual vacuum, rather it was intimately bound up with more general humanistic and social science developments. Clearly, it is not possible to do full justice to the diversity of ideas, but it is necessary to introduce and appraise key material. This chapter content is nongeographic in that it is not conventionally seen as a part of geography, but it is basic to an understanding of geography. Chapter 3 continues the methodological discussion of chapter 2 with a focus on the history of cultural geography;

a history that should be easier to interpret as a result of being preceded by the discussion of related disciplines. The emphasis here is on North American cultural geography, although the European heritage is also incorporated in some detail. Chapter 4 concludes the methodological chapters, focusing on contemporary cultural geography and recognizing the cultural-social convergence. Radical and humanistic methodologies and the issue of social scale are discussed. Combined, chapters 2, 3, and 4 provide a methodological statement about cultural geography.

Chapters 5 to 8 combine methodology and a critique of substantive research. The sequence of chapters might be a little surprising at first sight. Chapter 5 acknowledges at the outset that cultural geographers are confronted with a fundamental subjective-objective dichotomy. Different human beings "see" identical landscapes differently. This basic fact has to be tackled before much of the conventional literature can be evaluated. The behavioral approach is closely related to some work in psychology, and this is incorporated as appropriate. Chapter 6 pursues the central theme of landscape evolution. Landscapes and regions are both concerns here, and a massive literature is narrowed down in order to permit a discussion of changes. This chapter comprises much of the conventional content of cultural geography.

Chapter 7 proceeds to focus on social matters and on the symbolic landscape. The major variables of language, religion, ethnicity, and class are used not as topics in themselves but rather as the means for delimiting groups. The symbolic quality of landscape is considered. This chapter is the clearest indication of a combined cultural and social geography. Chapter 8, the final substantive chapter, tackles the ecological emphasis. This is considered last because it is perhaps the best indication of a cultural geography related to other disciplines, notably sociology, anthropology, and psychology. At the same time, it is a theme that has generated a relatively distinct research tradition, often tied to a particular systems framework—a framework emphasizing the relationships between variables in strong contradistinction to determinist views. The final chapter is a brief concluding statement primarily concerned with future research directions.

2

Views of Humans and Nature: Related Disciplines

The cultural geographer does not stand in isolation, detached from the wider academic world. Cultural geographers share methods and interests with other social sciences and humanities, most notably with anthropology (Ellen, 1988). The purpose of this chapter is to evaluate anthropological and other concepts with only incidental reference to cultural geography. The impact of this discussion is suggested in the conclusion to this chapter and is further detailed in chapter 4. The motivation behind this organization of material is the a priori suggestion that developments elsewhere have influenced cultural geography and, even where influences may not be evident, that these developments offer valuable insights. The interplay between anthropology and geography is an intriguing one with large areas of overlapping interests. Perhaps the greatest single area of overlap concerns human and environment relationships. "Anthroplogists and their associates in geography have been studying relationships between humans and the physical environment for a very long time" (Bennett, 1976, p. 1). The late nineteenth-century emphasis was on description and classification, and if explanations were sought then one of the two variables was designated as cause. More recently, the concept of environment has broadened to encompass social as well as physical factors, and the notion of system has assumed analytical importance. Therefore, the primary concern in this chapter is the theme of human and nature relationships. It is evident that an appreciation of this concern is useful to an understanding of the central theme of cultural geography, namely the evolution of the cultural landscape, which is one outcome of the relationship. Indeed, the ideas introduced in this chapter include most of those traditionally contained in a "theories of culture" discussion.

HUMANS AND NATURE: INTRODUCTORY COMMENTS

Relationships between human behavior and environment have been studied by scholars in a variety of disciplines, and a history of changing emphases is evident. Determinism, possibilism, cultural ecology, and views derived from biological and systems concepts have all been proposed. Detailed appraisals of these views have been offered by Douglas Feldman (1975) and Roy Ellen (1982). One general trend has been a gradual rejection of the traditional human and nature separation, and therefore, of the various dualistic concepts that led to either the extreme of human dependence on nature or human independence from nature. This trend is exemplified in cultural ecology in particular, although Richard Watson and Patty Watson (1969) opt for an approach that they define as human ecology, which details eight types of human and nature relationship. Three of these ways of life were seen as controlled by nature, one was seen as alteration of nature, and four were seen as control of nature. R. A. Watson and P. J. Watson (1969, p. 159) acknowledged that such a typology appeared to imply a deterministic stance and justified this by observing that "scientific knowledge of any sort is deterministic."

The organization of this chapter is essentially chronological. The ideas discussed are as follows: evolutionism and diffusionism in anthropology; the superorganic, a determinist stance that emerged in both sociology and anthropology in rather different guises; functionalism in anthropology; new evolutionism and the view of culture developed by Leslie White; human and cultural ecology in social science in general; structuralism and related approaches that view culture as systems of ideas; sociobiological ideas; and Marxist orientations.

EVOLUTIONISM AND DIFFUSIONISM

Two important developments in anthropology merit attention initially, namely the ideas of evolution and diffusion. Both of these ideas were early, perhaps premature, generalizations. The evolutionist view developed in the eighteenth century when a number of social thinkers argued that all cultures passed through a series of increasingly superior stages. Enlightenment philosophers such as Condorcet, Montesquieu, Adam Smith, and Voltaire used new data produced by European overseas expansion to argue this view of unilinear evolution. A second major inspiration for evolutionism was provided by Charles Darwin, and "once the idea of a close fit between linguistic and biological evolution was accepted, a fit between biological history and political and ethnic history was not far behind" (Leaf, 1979, p. 105). Explanations of assumed relationships between biological and cultural evolution were put forward notably by Herbert Spencer. But the evolutionist view was spurred also by Karl Marx in his independently derived materialist conception of history, which assumed that "nature and history fit together to comprise a totality" (Heyer, 1982, p. 27).

Each of these three sources contributed to the adoption of an evolutionist view by two nineteenth-century anthropologists who are generally considered to be the founders of modern anthropology. Lewis Morgan proposed seven stages of cultural evolution.

1. Lower savagery, characterized by wild-fruit gathering.
2. Middle savagery, characterized by the eating of fish, origins of speech, and use of fire.
3. Upper savagery, characterized by the use of bow and arrow.
4. Lower barbarism, characterized by the use of pottery.
5. Middle barbarism, characterized by agriculture.
6. Upper barbarism, characterized by the use of iron tools.
7. Civilization, characterized by writing.

It was assumed that all cultures would, by means of independent invention, pass through all stages.

A very similar proposal was made by Edward Tylor with three stages.

1. Savagery, characterized by hunting and gathering.
2. Barbarism, characterized by agriculture.
3. Civilization, characterized by writing.

Good discussions of evolutionist arguments are contained in several sources, for example, Ino Rossi and Edward O'Higgins (1980).

Morgan and Tylor established the comparative method of inquiry, which consisted of collecting ethnographic data from different cultures in order to demonstrate the increasing complexity of culture through time. The implicit assumption was that European civilization represented the apogee of evolution whereas primitive peoples were both biologically and culturally inferior. Tylor further proposed a theory of the evolution of civilization, based partly on the "doctrine of survivals," which argued that there are some elements in a culture that are actually remains of past conditions. This doctrine was borrowed from biology and archaeology, but is necessarily a circular argument.

Evolutionist thinking was soon challenged by the emergence of a diffusionist paradigm closely linked to the culture area concept and the idea of cultural borrowing. Influential diffusionists included Franz Boas, Clark Wissler, Alfred Kroeber, and Robert Lowie. This Boasian school, which emerged circa 1900, rejected evolutionism and in turn dominated American anthropology for perhaps the first half of the twentieth century. The basic premise was that the crucial cause of cultural change was culture contact, a factor largely disregarded by evolutionists. Boas further argued against environment as a cause of culture, proposing instead that culture results largely from itself.

Objections to the earlier evolutionist view were also based on its implicit racism and lack of objectivity. The Boasian school emphasized diffusion, culture areas, historical data collection, induction, and possibilism. Diffusion was seen as the key process. Culture areas were logical organizations, at least partly resultant from diffusion processes. The need for historical data and for inductive logic was paramount, because observed facts were seen as the only basis for law creation. A form of possibilism was advocated despite the concern with geographic areas, because of the importance placed on culture in the human and land relationship. The influence of Boas was such that evolutionism was "laid . . . to rest for more than half a century" (Friedl & Pfeiffer, 1977, p. 300). Pertti Pelto (1966, p. 24) described the Boasian view as seeing

> the history of man as a sort of "tree of culture," with fantastically complex branching, intertwining and budding off—each branch representing a uniquely different cultural complex, to be understood in terms of its own unique history rather than compared in cultural complexes in other world regions in some grand scheme of "stages of evolution."

Cultural relativism was favored over cultural evolution.

THE SUPERORGANIC AND RELATED IDEAS

The primary consequence of late nineteenth-century social science ideas about culture was the rise of the superorganic interpretation. The early sociological conceptions were both mechanistic and deterministic "portraying society as a totally integrated entity, analogous to a physical or biological system that entirely determined the behavior of the people within it" (Leaf, 1979, p. 60). Auguste Comte and H. Spencer were responsible for initiating and diffusing this view, which largely dominated nineteenth-century sociology. Two of Comte's themes carried over into anthropology, namely the conception of an organic society and, more generally, the positive philosophy. H. Spencer promoted both these concepts and, furthermore, was responsible for popularizing social Darwinism. To an important extent, all three of these themes were incorporated in the superorganic concept expressed by Spencer, wherein societies were seen as wholes "created either by growth from within or absorption of groups from without, precisely like Comte's organic state" (Leaf, 1979, p. 77). The influential sociologist Émile Durkheim argued for the separation of sociology from both biology and psychology and used the term *social organism* to refer to the social as a "phenomenon *sui generis* a process separate from the qualities of the individuals comprising it and one that is inexplicable by any reference to psychology and biology" (Heyer, 1982, p. 235). Both the social organism of Durkheim and the superorganic of Spencer see the social or cultural as a force constraining individual behavior.

These early ideas were more fully developed by first Kroeber and subsequently Leslie White in anthropology, and the work of Kroeber is usually also regarded as a reaction against environmentalism. The most prominent anthropological assault on environmentalism was one part of the Boasian rejection of evolutionism. Larry Grossman (1977, p. 127) saw this as a reflection of the "cautious, inductive approach" of Boas and of the "then current relativistic approach in American anthropology." Kroeber extended the rejection of nature as a controlling force by arguing for culture as the principle variable above both nature and the individual. For Kroeber, the length of time involved in culture precluded the possibility of a paramount role for individuals, rather culture itself was the cause of change.

As part of the antievolutionist Boasian school, Kroeber was against theory and opposed to the use of the scientific method and causal logic (M. Harris, 1968, p. 336). Given that Kroeber was part of an idiographic school, the superorganic concept requires careful evaluation. Kroeber (1917), in a seminal paper, protested the equating of race and culture and the tendency to apply Darwinian principles of evolution to cultural phenomena. In this sense, the superorganic of Kroeber is not the direct intellectual descendant of Comte and H. Spencer.

It is necessary to discuss the superorganic of Kroeber further, because of its undoubted importance in twentieth-century anthropology and its possible transmission into cultural geography (J. S. Duncan, 1980). Kroeber began with a key distinction between social processes and biological or organic processes and noted that, in contrast to biological evolution or changes in organic structure, human societies do not utilize the principle of heredity to transmit new adaptations to other members of the species. For Kroeber (1917, p. 169), "the distinction between animal and man which counts is not that of the physical and mental, which is one of relative degree, but that of the organic and social, which is one of kind . . . in civilization man has something that no animal has." Humans may be biological organisms but they are social animals and through language and social and cultural institutions they learn the values of the civilization in which they live. Thus the argument is that the acquistion of values and traditions is nonorganic and external to the individual.

> All civilization in a sense exists only in the mind. Gunpowder, textile arts, machinery, laws, telephones are not themselves transmitted from man to man or from generation to generation, at least not permanently. It is the perception, the knowledge and understanding of them, their *ideas* in the Platonic sense, that are passed along. Everything social can have existence only through mentality. Of course civilization is not mental action itself; it is carried by men, without being in them. (Kroeber, 1917, p. 189)

The term *superorganic* is used to refer to this nonorganic human product of human societies, to cultural institutions, modes of production, and levels of technology. The term is borrowed from Spencer, but is only similar to Spencer's in that the term refers to nonbiological aspects of human societies. Kroeber (1917) also argued that to understand the cultural world, analysis needed to commence in the culture because culture is the context in which decisions are made. None of this, however, means that Kroeber was a cultural determinist (Harris, 1968, p. 342). Kroeber (1917, p. 205) did note that to infer "that all the degree and quality of accomplishment by the individual is the result of his moulding by the society that encompasses him, is assumption, extreme at that, and at variance with observation." On another occasion, "no culture is wholly intelligible without reference to the non-cultural or so called environmental factors with which it is in relation and which condition it" (Kroeber, 1939, p. 205). This is essentially what Marvin Mikesell (1969, p. 231) called a "cautious philosophy roughly comparable to the geographic concept of possibilism."

Despite the typically strong commitment to culture as cause, then, there appears to have been an implicit environmentalism in much early sociology and anthropology, including the early racist and evolutionist phase. Comte was critical of environmentalism, but at the same time exaggerated physical causes; Spencer saw history as a steady move from warmer to colder areas; and Morgan explained cultural differences of people at similar levels environmentally. Environmental causes were attractive at a time when the subtlety of human and land relations was not appreciated.

Environmentalism in sociology and anthropology thus emerged separately from the major works of Friedrich Ratzel. His studies were responsible for the theory of systemically regarding environment as a cause of culture and were taken to extremes by Ellen Semple and Ellsworth Huntington (see chapter 3) in human geography, but were much less influential in other disciplines. As Grossman (1977, p. 127) detailed, "the response of the anthropologist to the deterministic viewpoint came in the early 1900's, twenty years earlier than the response from American geographers."

The related culture area concept had its origins in the work of Ratzel and was first explicitly used by Otis Mason (1895) to delimit twelve North American ethnic environments. Although there were environmentalist overtones in this and related work, Wissler (1917) argued for a close correspondence between natural and cultural areas with mode of subsistence as the key determinant. In a similar vein, Kroeber (1939) examined environment and culture relationships from a viewpoint that saw culture as cause of culture. Thus, the culture area concept was used by anthropologists in a variety of ways including environmentalist, superorganicist, and diffusionist. A detailed appraisal of the concept as used in anthropology and a comparison with geography is included in Marvin Mikesell (1967, pp. 621–624, 626–628). A more detailed account of the interest is contained in chapter 6 of this volume.

FUNCTIONALISM

Following evolutionism and the broad-based reactions to that approach, especially diffusionism and related concepts, the doctrine of functionalism developed in the 1920s as the next major interpretation of culture. Two names are associated with the emergence of this view, namely A. R. Radcliffe-Brown and Bronislaw Malinowski. Both objected to the prevailing particularist view, which tended to see cultures as pieces and traced the diffusion and distributions of these pieces. Thus functionalism was at least partly a direct reaction to diffusionist views. But it was also, for Radcliffe-Brown, a positive outgrowth of Durkheim's sociology adopting Durkheim's basic fourfold conception of society (Leaf, 1979, p. 178): "1) a theoretical entity that 2) contained individuals as its parts in some way and 3) determined their action, while 4) moving by its own law." Durkheim, the leading French sociologist at the turn of the century, employed functional explanations in conceiving society as a social organism comprising social phenomena that functioned or served societal needs. Radcliffe-Brown and Durkheim explained human behavior with reference to society, explicitly rejecting individual explanations. Malinowski, on the other hand, strongly emphasized the psychological basis of culture.

Functionalism rejected historical reconstruction, focused primarily on contemporary cultures, and stressed the functions of institutions. Radcliffe-Brown emphasized the internal dynamics of culture and related functions to structure whereas Malinowski explained cultural features by referring to human biological needs. Thus, there are two rather different concepts of culture contained within the general functionalist paradigm: culture as a dynamic functioning structure and culture as a response to biological needs. For Radcliffe-Brown, the function of social institutions was to maintain social structures. Thus, culture was not functioning for the individual, but rather for the larger society. This is essentially the Durkheimian view of society. For Malinowski, the function of social institutions was to serve the needs of humans; kinship, for example, is the response to the reproductive need. The Radcliffe-Brown approach has been the more enduring, partly because it allowed "a comparative anatomy of societies, in which social arrangements in different societies were compared systematically with one another" (Wolf, 1964, p. 5). Perhaps the appropriate interpretation of Malinowski is that his was one of various attempts to "put the pragmatic conceptions of behavior-as-adoption on a more 'scientific' footing" (Leaf, 1979, p. 188).

NEW EVOLUTIONISM AND WHITE'S VIEW OF CULTURE

The evolutionist view was revived in the 1930s by the anthropologist White in the development of a set of ideas that combined evolutionist and superorganicist arguments. The basis of these ideas was a form of technological determinism. "Culture advances as the amount of energy harnessed per capita per year increases, or as the efficiency or economy of the means of controlling energy is increased or both" (L. A. White, 1959, p. 56). The structure and functioning of culture was directly the result of the amount of energy produced and the manner in which that energy was used (L. A. White, 1949, p. 367). It was technology, in turn, that determined the energy available and the efficiency of its uses. Thus technology, through energy, was the cause of cultural characteristics and change.

Regarding evolution, L. A. White focused on universal culture and not on particular cultures. The ideas on cultural evolution have been tested and expanded. In a study of Polynesian societies, Marshall Sahlins (1958) considered the relationship between technology and social stratification and argued for White's ideas. But the most significant advances in this area were made by Julian Steward, who was a student of both Kroeber and the geographer Carl Sauer. Steward (1955) described White's ideas as being universal, not unilinear, evolution such that there are a series of stages through which culture as a whole has passed. Unhappy with both the nineteenth-century unilinear evolution and White's universal evolution, Steward (1955) advocated a multilinear version that recognized that different cultures typically proceeded through similar stages. Multilinear evolution aimed to discover the laws that determined cultural development.

White (1959) extended his evolutionist ideas to argue that the principle of minding is the basis for understanding culture. The argument is as follows. Minding is the reaction of a living organism to a thing as an event via interaction or relation. Four types of minding were distinguished. Type I minding is characteristic of inanimate objects and involves attraction, repulsion, and indifference; concepts determined by the inherent properties of the objects and their topological relations. Type II minding involves reactions characterized by the conditioned reflex of Pavlovian theory with the relation being between organism and stimulus and not being dependent on their intrinsic properties. Type III minding involves relations that result from the conscious intent of the organism with the organism playing the major role. Type IV minding implies symboling, defined as the free and arbitrary bestowing of meaning on things and events and the ability to grasp such meaning. Only humans are capable of this fourth type of minding and it is from this type, symboling, that culture becomes possible. Culture is thus a term applied to the particular symbols used by members of a community to relate together in society. Thus, culture is dependent on interaction, and symbols such as language are extrasomatic phenomena. Following this argument, the determinants of human behavior are not properties of the biological organism but are to be found in the culture, the extrasomatic tradition. White's view of culture was deterministic in that culture was seen as determining human behavior. Understanding culture required objective analyses rather than participant observation type analyses.

HUMAN AND CULTURAL ECOLOGY

The reemergence of evolutionary concepts contributed greatly to the rise of cultural ecology as one variant of the interest in human and land relations. The term cultural ecology was first used by Steward in 1937 but is perhaps most appropriately interpreted as one aspect of the wider field of human ecology (see

Bennett, 1976, p. 24). This section first reviews the concept of human ecology and second, narrows the discussion to a consideration of cultural ecology as used in anthropology.

Robert Park and Ernest Burgess (1921) are typically credited with introducing human ecology as an approach basing their ideas on earlier works by H. Spencer, Durkheim, and Talcott Parsons. The human ecology that has evolved since 1921 is contained within a variety of conventional social science disciplines, especially sociology, anthropology, geography, psychology, and economics. The following definition was developed by Gerald Young (1974, p. 8).

> Human ecology may be defined (1) from a bio-ecological standpoint as the study of man as the ecological dominant in plant and animal communities and systems; (2) from a bio-ecological standpoint as simply another animal affecting and being affected by his environment; and (3) as a human being, somehow different from animal life in general, interacting with physical and modified environments in a distinctive and creative way.

Sociological emphases see organization as a fundamental principle, often treat structure as a dependent variable, and emphasize the analysis of distributions. According to John Bruhn (1974, pp. 116–117), however, sociologists have made few attempts to work as interdisciplinarians in human ecology. Psychological emphases focus on the role of nonpsychological inputs into human behavior, these inputs are collectively called behavior settings. Relevant psychological work includes the "life space" concept of Kurt Lewin, which sees the individual and the environment as a single set of related factors; the use of space in everyday behavior, and the perception of space. Economic emphases are quite limited, although Kenneth Boulding (1950, 1968) sees both ecology and economics as being concerned with how humans make their livings. Geographic emphases began with Harlan H. Barrow's (1923) assertion that geography was human ecology and today include a variety of claims about the centrality of human ecology (see chapter 3).

Within anthropology, the notion of human ecology has been transformed into cultural ecology. Late nineteenth- and early twentieth-century anthropology was explictly concerned with relationships between humans and the land, but an explicit ecological thrust was not evident until the 1930s. "Steward (1955) used the term 'cultural ecology' to differentiate the anthropological concept from that of biology, geography and sociology and admitted that it was 'not generally understood' " (Young, 1974, p. 20). Three fundamental procedures are evident in this anthropological version; namely, analysis of technology and environment relations, analysis of behavior patterns affecting environment, and determination of relations between the behavior patterns and other aspects of culture. Thus, the ecological approach is typically functionalist. Expressed simply, cultural ecology is the analysis of human adjustments to environment by means of culture. For Steward, the environment did not only set limits on what adjustments could be made but also played a creative role.

Interestingly, cultural ecology still characteristically incorporated a distinctive view of culture. As proposed by Steward (1955), cultural ecology was to be focused on the superorganic factor of culture, which affects and is affected by the total web of life. In a similar fashion, much ecological work incorporated the concept of energy as developed by White (1959) and also White's superorganic version of culture. Criticisms of the superorganic content of cultural ecology were evident from John Bennett (1976, p. 48) and from Andrew Vayda and Roy Rappaport (1968, p. 492). For the latter writers, a desirable aim was to develop a single unified science of ecology.

Young (1974, p. 58) painted a realistic picture of human ecology as a whole: "It is a fragmented field, far from interdisciplinary, though many of the concepts are shared." A key feature of ecology is an emphasis on process, especially processes of interaction, such that "interaction has the potential to be a basic human ecological concept" (Young, 1974, p 68). At the same time, there is as yet little indication of the emergence of human ecology as a distinct field, and major advances may be expected to continue to be within established disciplines.

A theoretical development related to the work of Steward is the cultural materialism of Marvin Harris. This argues for the theory of sociocultural evolution based on the doctrine of natural selection and is labeled techno-environmental determinism. M. Harris (1968, p. 199) focused on the demographic, economic, technological, and environmental causes of cultural evolution.

STRUCTURALISM AND RELATED APPROACHES

Most of the approaches discussed above regarded culture as an adaptive system. Several views have emerged since the 1940s that regard culture as systems of ideas. The principal approach of this type is known as structuralism and is associated with the French anthropologist Claude Lévi-Strauss. In structuralism, culture is viewed as a system of shared symbols, the functioning of the human mind. For example, a structuralist interpretation of gift giving in primitive societies focuses on the act of giving rather than on what is given. This is an original interpretation because of the concern with relationships and not on the things that create and maintain the relationships. Again, a structuralist interpretation of marriage and kinship systems argues that these systems are only relationships.

A structuralist approach thus aims to remove the difficulties of cross-cultural comparisons by showing that elements of all cultures are the product of a common single mental process. This idea has proved attractive and many anthropologists have found the "reduction of seemingly complex structures to applications of the fundamentally abstract ideas of dichotomous characteristics both fascinating and stimulating" (Leaf, 1979, p. 256). Major influences in Lévi-Strauss include the Durkheimian idea that there are principles that apply to all types of social relation, and also methods from linguistics, which argue that an unconscious infrastructure underlies language. In the kinship example, there are only four basic terms, namely brother, sister, father, and son; and all marriage rules are specific instances of the principle of exchange. Despite the impact made by Lévi-Straus it is clear that many of the arguments are highly impressionistic.

In addition to structuralism, two other recent contributions also see culture as a system of ideas. The approach known as ethnoscience interprets culture as a system of shared cognitions. According to this view, culture results from mental processes. Stephen Tyler (1969, p. 3) stated that "the object of study is not the material phenomena themselves but the way they are organized in the minds of men. Cultures then are not material phenomena; they are organizations of material phenomena." An ethnoscientist attempts to understand how individuals see their cultural world. A third approach, typically labeled symbolic anthropology, is most closely related to Clifford Geertz, and sees culture as a system of shared symbols and meanings. Perhaps like many new developments this idea has its beginnings in earlier work, in this case in the work of V. Gordon Childe (1956), which acknowledged the need for symbolic content in cultural analyses. The primary focus for Geertz (1965, 1973) was on symbolic action, or the ways in which humans use symbolic systems.

THE SOCIOBIOLOGICAL DEBATE

One aspect of late nineteenth-century thought is emerging as a major issue in contemporary research into culture and culture change. The question is that of the relation between biological and cultural evolution. This revival of interest might be ascribed to the developments in cultural ecology, which began as either environmental or cultural determinism but which have successfully developed into a broader systems approach. This involved the inclusion of biological factors as possible causes of culture. Mark Flinn and Richard Alexander (1982) summarized this revival of interest as follows. First, the traditional superorganic view separated culture from biology but failed to specify the causes of culture change. Second, humans are biological organisms. Third, the abilities to acquire and retain culture are evolved abilities. A variety of interests are currently investigating the biological basis of behavior, especially ethology, physical anthropology, comparative psychology, and sociobiology.

Clearly, Darwin was the major initial researcher. "In *The Descent of Man* he applied the biological knowledge he derived from the empirical observation of animal and human behavior, together with evolutionary theory, to examine the phenomenon of social organization in a wide range of species" (Heyer, 1982, p. 138). Such nineteenth-century thinking was criticized especially from religious quarters while, today, a principal critic is social science. Contemporary sociobiology is unacceptable to many social scientists because of the implications of racism and social Darwinism.

Darwin effectively linked the social and the natural. This linking was criticized by Durkheim who argued for the autonomy of sociology and hence for the separation of the social and the natural. Once again, the superorganic concept emerges and the possibility of the social emerging from the biological is rejected by Durkheim. But some scholars today are suggesting that understanding culture requires a combined approach, a sociobiological approach. William Durham (1976) asserted that human behavior is a product of the coevolution of human biology and culture and was critical of both the human and natural sciences for their narrow perspectives.

> The rather chauvinistic adherence to traditional disciplinary biases has had a major role in preventing anthropologists and biologists from attaining a more thorough understanding of human cultural behavior. To date, there remains a tendency to debate biology vs. culture or instinct vs. learning, and this tendency has almost totally obscured the suggested complementarity of organic and cultural evolution ... the anthropologists' reluctance to consider basic principles of evolutionary biology *and* the biologists' failure to provide for cultural transmission in the evolution of adequate traits have prevented the formulation of a general theory of human evolution where natural selection and culture change really are complementary. (1976, pp. 90–91)

Given this argument, there is a perceived need for a theory of culture change to explain how social behaviors that help humans survive are culturally evolved. Durham (1976, p. 114) outlined tentative ideas aimed at such theory creations and suggested that a process of cultural selection influences cultural trait retention according to the same criterion as natural selection.

The proposed coevolutionary approach is not, however, without its critics. Flinn and Alexander (1982) viewed culture as one part of the environment and as being gradually developed by humans throughout history such that "the challenge now before students of culture is to understand the proximate mechanisms . . . that result in the acquisition and transmission of cultural traits" (p. 397). Perhaps the most compelling critic has been Stephen J. Gould (1981, p. 324) who wrote that "we are inextricably part of nature, but human uniqueness is not negated thereby." The distinction between cultural and biological evolution is that the former operates by the inheritance of acquired characteristics and is, therefore, both rapid and reversible, whereas the latter is slow and indirect. For S. J. Gould (1981, p. 327–329), there are two major insights from modern biology. First, even in situations where adaptive behaviors are nongenetic it may well be that biological analogies aid understanding; this does not mean that analogies reflect common causes. Second, it is true that, as animals, the behavior of humans is necessarily constrained by human biology—for example, by the very limited range of average adult size. Given the generally critical view of sociobiology from the human sciences and the inevitable internal disagreements, it seems unlikely that the approach is to make a major impact on the understanding of culture and culture change.

MARXIST ORIENTATIONS

It is interesting that, just as the work of Darwin was misused by H. Spencer to promote social Darwinism, the work of Marx was misused to support an environmentalist position. Although Marx viewed the environment and economy relationship as complex, Russian environmental Marxists have argued for nature as a determinant, however the logic of this view is not altogether clear. Indeed, Marx most characteristically saw nature as a passive landscape. A second misuse of Marx in this respect is Karl Wittfogel's (1968) argument, based partly on Marx, concerning the difference between European and Asiatic societies. Marx acknowledged the societal relevance of advanced irrigation systems and Wittfogel (1968) used this idea to see the Asiatic human and land relationship as an ongoing ecological dialectic. Distinct hydraulic societies emerged in this unfolding dialectic.

Marx has also been used by anthropologists to develop a cultural materialist view. Marx and the cultural materialists "are alike holistic in their approach to understanding human society; they agree there is more to the shaping of a society than meets the eye; they insist that history is made by people who are creatures of nature, through their work and their modes of production" (Worster, 1984, p. 15). Despite these shared interests there are in fact major differences between cultural materialism as detailed by Harris (1968) and the Marxist viewpoint (Ellen, 1982, pp. 59–61).

In the light of these various and varied interpretations it is necessary to briefly review Marx's views of human nature and the environment. Paul Heyer (1982, p. 73) emphasized that this view was strongly biological and psychological in orientation although "Marx ranged widely and was often ambiguous and contradictory." Three themes were evident to Heyer (1982, p. 76).

1. Continuity is established among man, nature and history. Man is viewed as part of nature to counter the rift opened up between the two realms by traditional theologies and the Western metaphysical tradition of Descartes, Kant and Hegel.

2. Man is seen as possessing a network of species characteristics distinguishing him from the rest of creation. Nevertheless these characteristics are said to have a naturalistic basis.

3. The natural capacities of the human species interact with external nature through labor to produce the constantly changing economic, social and ideological situations— culture in the modern sense—in which man defines himself and his nature.

Thus, Marx stressed the continuity between humans and nature in contradistinction both to earlier idealist thought and to the developing anthropological and sociological views, which stressed the dominant role of culture or society. Indeed there are interesting conceptual parallels between the idealist reification of history, the superorganic reification of culture by Kroeber, and the social organism reification of society by Durkheim. For Marx, humans were social beings and were not merely passive in the face of society. Thus the Marxist view of humans, human nature, and the environment is not one that favors either environmentalist or superoganicist views.

According to James Wessman (1981, p. 68), however, a major difficulty with Marxist discussion of culture is the very lack of discussion. Culture has been ignored by Marxists because it was seen as simply a reflection of material reality. It is this separation of Marxist thought and the culture concept that has permitted alternative views of culture to dominate twentieth-century thought. Thus, a major Marxist task is that of developing an adequate concept of culture, a task begun by Raymond Williams (1977).

What are the contemporary implications of the above for the culture concept in anthropology? Wessman (1981, p. 25) attempted a detailed answer. "My argument . . . is that anthropology can be reoriented as an historically sophisticated, dialectical tradition in science and the humanities, so that the concrete and specific concepts which are devised to deal with historical circumstances replace those of evolutionary analysis." Whether or not such is to be achieved remains to be seen. What does seem necessary to help achieve such objectives is a clearer understanding of the potential contributions of such new directions to the human and land relationship. To a certain extent, this has been achieved by some recent work under the headings of structural Marxism and political economy.

Structural Marxism is a diverse set of ideas but may be characterized as locating key determinants in neither the evironment nor technology but, as may be expected, in the structure of social relations. The culture concept was, accordingly, narrowed substantially to become largely ideology. The political economy approach is quite different, stemming as it does from sociological concepts of world systems and underdevelopment. A primary focus is that of analyzing the effects of capitalist penetration into communities, and thus, the focus of attention is that of regional systems in an historical context. A characteristic of both these approaches is the concern with practice or action, and for Sherry Ortner (1984, pp. 145–146) this characteristic is also evident in a number of other emerging emphases. Indeed, Ortner (1984, p. 158) takes "practice as the key symbol of eighties anthropology." The aims of such an anthropology are those of explaining the two-way relationships between human action and global entities or systems. Such explanations require an understanding of how society and culture are produced and reproduced through human action. It seems clear that a practice-centered anthropology is not a direct consequence of a Marxist orientation, but is in fact a form of merger between Marxist and Weberian frameworks.

CONCLUDING COMMENTS

The concepts of culture and society are key integrating ideas for the disciplines of anthropology and sociology respectively. Such is evident from the varied discussions presented in this chapter. It is equally clear that there is continuing uncertainty as to what these concepts imply, although the standard definition of culture remains that offered by Tylor: ''that complex whole which includes knowledge, belief, art, morals, law, customs and any other capabilities and habits acquired by man as a member of society'' (see Friedl & Pfeiffer, 1977, p. 288). It needs to be noted that Tylor was equating culture and civilization in this definition. For late nineteenth-century North American anthropology, culture became the intellectual tool that confirmed human uniqueness and combated the concept of instinct (Moore, 1974). Culture was also the means by which anthropology was differentiated from other disciplines under the leadership of Boas particularly. It seems likely that one reason for the emergence and acceptance of the superorganic concept was the need, conscious or otherwise, to establish anthropology as a legitimate discipline. This development was despite the very close links between geography and anthropology, especially in Germany where Carl Ritter had suggested that the Berlin Geographical Society have an ethnographic section and where that same society had Adolf Bastian, a distinguished ethnologist, as president from 1871 to 1873. Major twentieth-century statements are those of Kroeber, who advocated the superorganic; L. A.White, who added a technological determinant; M. Harris, who followed White and incorporated reproduction and population pressure; Geertz, a symbolic anthropologist who argued that culture is embodied in public symbols; Steward, who focused on subsistence activities and adaptation to evironment; and Lévi-Strauss, who argued that cultural phenomena could be understood by indicating the shared relationships of the phenomena to a few simple principles. In addition, sociologists argued for society as a key causal variable under the inspiration of Durkheim.

Given that the culture concept lies at the heart of anthropology, both the changes of meaning over time and the possibly bewildering array of contemporary meanings are necessarily of concern. A comparable uncertainty as to the relevance of theory prompted Murray Leaf (1979, p. 3) to assert that ''anthropology is in trouble.'' Trouble perhaps, but it also seems appropriate to suggest that times of intellectual diversity are healthy for academic disciplines. Anthropology and sociology appear to be advocating diverse approaches and tackling diverse problems. In this sense, a keen appreciation of current developments in the human sciences in general will necessarily contribute positively to the continuing evolution of a vital, stimulating, and relevant cultural geography. This chapter has not attempted to indicate the role that these various and varied ideas can and do play in cultural geography. Such a discussion is contained in chapter 4, where an attempt is made to clarify the relevance of some of these ideas to the stated central theme of cultural geography, namely landscape evolution. This chapter has been suggestive, not conclusive, concerning the need to consider society and culture not as separate issues, but rather as different yet closely related concepts. This argument will be extended to include the need to integrate social and cultural geography.

3

Development of Cultural Geography

The emergence of cultural geography as a distinct subdiscipline or as a distinct approach is necessarily bound up with the intellectual environment of the late nineteenth and early twentieth centuries, particularly with both the institutionalization of the discipline of geography and the experiences of related disciplines. The cultural geography that emerged has proved a substantive and long-lasting component of geography, especially in North America. Throughout the current century, the character of this tradition has changed and diversified and rather different interpretations have been evident in different countries. This chapter concentrates on the North American experience, which includes cultural geography as a major emphasis, but also considers the European experience, which has placed lesser emphasis on the tradition, and the British experience, which has not involved any clear identity of cultural geography. In a review, David Ley (1981, p. 249) noted the "enigma" of cultural geography in reference to the different countries. This consideration of origins and development has the dual aims of providing an account of the history of cultural geographic thought and research and of setting the scene for the discussion, in chapter 4, of the contemporary status of cultural geography. Some readily identifiable characteristics of the North American experience include the important role played by cultural geography in the development of the discipline of geography, the importance of Carl Sauer and the related landscape school, the traditionally close ties to historical geography, the implicit opposition to the regional concept as the core of geography, the dissociation with spatial analysis, and the recent humanistic rebirth.

This chapter traces the early development of geography, as it pertains to cultural geography, and the development of cultural geography. Close links with other social sciences are evident and the material introduced in chapter 2 is an invaluable basis for helping to place cultural geography in that essential wider context. A number of concepts and views are discussed, but there is little effort to include any substantive examples. Rather, the examples appear in chapters 5 to 8, with each chapter concentrating on a limited number of concepts.

ORIGINS AND THE PREINSTITUTIONAL PERIOD

It is conventional to trace the origins of geographic thought to the Greeks and their observations and descriptions of lands and peoples, to identify Bernard Varenius as the first (circa 1650) scholar to acknowledge the need for geographic knowledge to be formally structured, to credit Immanual Kant with providing a philosophic basis for the discipline (late eighteenth century), and to focus on Alexander Von Humboldt and Carl Ritter as major nineteenth-century scholars (both died in 1859) prior to the formal institutionalization of geography as a discipline in the late nineteenth century (Broek, 1965, pp. 10–16). With this institutionalization it became necessary for geographers to write about a discipline that had not previously existed, and the historiography of geography became "a progression from achievement to achievement towards an independent science with its own object of study" (Grano, 1981, p. 21). Necessarily, this is a misleading interpretation, for the development of geography is, as Olavi Grano (1981, p. 22) noted, first, a period characterized by the existence of geographic knowledge without the existence of a discipline and, second, a period from circa 1870 onward characterized by the existence of a discipline in appropriate institutions.

The preinstitutional phase is necessarily continually being rewritten as part of the search for a justification of contemporary concerns. Accordingly, this discussion pays attention to scholars traditionally regarded as geographers and to those whose interests have included cultural or human and land concepts often as part of much wider concerns. David Stoddart (1986, p. 4) employed such an approach in an attempt to radically rewrite aspects of nineteenth-century geography. This discussion is organized chronologically. There are several excellent accounts of the history of geography including Arild Holt-Jensen (1982) and Preston James and Geoffrey Martin (1981).

The first attempt to develop a schema for geography was the *Geographia Generalis* of Varenius published in 1650. This distinguished between *special geography*, the description of countries and regions, and *general geography*, the consideration of laws applicable to all countries and regions. In several respects, Varenius was far in advance of his time. There was an insistence on the practical importance of special geography, but also a realization that special geography required that the specific features be explained in scientific terms, by means of concepts or laws. A second major contribution to the development of geography was that of Kant who, in the second half of the eighteenth century, classified geography as *the* chorological science studying phenomena in space. History was similarly identified as *the* chronological science studying phenomena in time. Both were seen as essential companions to the other systematic sciences.

Thus, Kant provided geography with a central but different place among the sciences. Geographers have often used these views to justify the existence of the discipline and its special place in the range of sciences.

In addition to the major statements of Varenius and Kant there are numerous other developments that are pertinent to a history of geography including issues such as exploration, navigation, and mapmaking. But the focus of this section is on the antecedents of cultural geography and, accordingly, some additional developments merit consideration, the most significant of which relate to the work of Giambattista Vico, Johann Herder, and Karl Marx.

The Vichian conception of humans and their place in the world developed in direct opposition to the mechanistic world view emerging at much the same time (circa 1700). Thomas Berry (1949, p. 18) detailed the Vichian view as arising from a realization that positive science did not ''provide a basis for a reintegration of the sciences into a unified system of human knowledge though this was the very thing it professed to do.'' Vico was explicitly opposed to Cartesian rationalism and the assumption that humans could acquire full knowledge of both themselves and the world through mathematics (Norton & Pouliot, 1984). For Vico, humans could understand their own creations more profoundly than they could understand nature. This is the key insight: humans had been responsible for building the cultural world and thus this world could be better comprehended than the divinely created world of nature. Furthermore, humans were seen as members of groups, not as isolated individuals. Given these assumptions about the inadequacy of natural sciences to explain human phenomena and about humans themselves, Vico proceeded to argue for a *new science,* which incorporated a cyclical view of history and a clear statement about culture. Three stages were delimited: the prehistoric, primitive culture stage; the beginnings of a civil-political state; and a society structured according to reason and with justice for all. Each stage had its own structure and cultural climate. Thus Vico introduced the culture concept as a systematic whole. Furthermore, the third stage was not final because Vico saw an inevitable decline and a return to barbarism; thus a cultural cycle was established. This cyclical view was elaborated on by Montesquieu but was never popular in comparison to the progress of history view, which promised a state of permanent happiness. According to Robert Nisbet (1980, p. 4), ''no single idea has been more important than, perhaps as important as, the idea of progress in Western civilization for nearly three thousand years.'' Explicit discussions of progress are central to some work in historical geography (for example, Harris, Roulston, and De Frietas, 1975).

The ideas of Vico are of importance in this context because there was a clear distinction made between human and physical science, and it was recognized that any society is culturally and historically specific and thus, an emphasis on evolutionary analyses was required. Societal evolution is neither fortuitous nor governed by law, but is seen as the result of human goal-oriented activity. The culture concept was introduced and a cyclical history detailed. Overall, the Vichian view can be seen as ''positivism reversed'' (Mills, 1982, p. 3); but it is also different from idealism, being interested not in individual actions, but rather in cultural evolution as expressed in individual actions.

In the second half of the eighteenth century, Herder articulated the Volk concept as the key theme of history. "The Volk was not a man-made but an organic collective whole which united diverse individuals through a common language, shared institutions, the arts, and literature" (Breisach, 1983, p. 222). Thus the Volk concept was an organic whole with a cultural base. Like Vico, Herder saw the basic character of a culture being established early and deemphasized the role played by diffusion as a cause of cultural change. The Volk concept also implied criticism of the state, which Herder saw as an artificial imposition on the social mode of life.

Both the Vichian view and the criticisms of the state by Herder were utilized by Marx. Marx rejected the Hegelian view that the rationality of history is a result of the "spirit" working out its logical implications via the state. Rather, the "logical moments" were in fact the result of individuals aiming to satisfy basic needs. Thus, human activity in an environment was relevant because it altered material conditions. This latter statement is comparable to Vico. As Marx noted, "and would not such a history (the history of the productive capabilities of man) be easier to compile, since, as Vico says, human history differs from natural history on this, that we have made the former but not the latter" (cited in Quaini, 1982, p. 63). Thus, Vico asserted that humans are the authors and actors of their own history and Marx added that it was the need to satisfy basic material requirements that prompted the creation of culture.

So far in this section on the preinstitutional phase, two rather separate strands have been identified: first, the beginnings of a formal discipline under Varenius and Kant and second, the contributions of Vico, Herder, and, briefly, Marx to the culture concept. Although the second set of ideas are not characteristically regarded as part of the history of geography, it is suggested that they are directly relevant to the emergence of cultural geography in that they represent a part of the appropriate intellectual history. Given this argument, the remainder of this section proceeds to note the geographic contributions of Humboldt, Ritter, and others and notes pertinent developments in the evolution of the culture concept and particularly culture history.

Humboldt and Ritter were scholars in the first half of the nineteenth century, achieving important positions in science and society. "Never before or since have geographers enjoyed positions of such prestige, not only among scholars but also among educated people all around the world" (James & Martin, 1981, p. 112). Accordingly, it is perhaps surprising that geography was not successful in achieving disciplinary status at this time. Rather, a close relationship continued between geography and history, and on many occasions, geography was essentially an appendage of history. Indeed, Ritter was both historian and geographer. The primary geographic concern for Ritter was human geography, including human and nature relationships. In a similar vein, Humboldt emphasized the unity of nature and saw the aim of physical geography as being the clarification of this unity. "The earth and its inhabitants stand in the closest reciprocal relations, and one cannot be truly presented in all its relationships without the other. Hence history and geography must always remain inseparable. Land affects the inhabitants and the inhabitants the land" (Humboldt, cited in Tatham, 1951, p. 44). Physical geography was the prime theme in his writings. It is traditional to regard Ritter and Humboldt together as founders of contemporary geography, but this discussion of humans and nature needs to focus on several other geographers in this preinstitutional phase as well.

The Danish geographer Joachim F. Schouw saw humans as part of nature and yet capable of transforming nature. Thus, culture "has its intellectual soil in *history,* out of which it springs—it has its intellectual climate in *language,* in which it lives and moves" (cited in Olwig, 1980, pp. 32–33). The relationship is one of interaction with both nature and culture changing. Elisée Reclus, a French geographer, similarly emphasized the processes by which cultures used environments to satisfy their needs. A third geographer who focused attention on humans as agents of change was the American George Perkins Marsh who noted that "man is, in both kind and degree, a power of a higher order than any of the other forms of animated life, which, like him, are nourished at the table of bounteous nature" (cited in James & Martin, 1981, p. 150). Finally, the Russian geographer Peter Kropotkin "like Humboldt . . . regarded nature as a dynamic whole, subject to constant change and including mankind, social institutions and human reason" (Bowen, 1981, p. 261).

This brief account of the six nineteenth-century geographers and their view on the human and land relationship is instructive. A relatively clear picture is emerging of a sophisticated process-oriented approach emphasizing the interdependence of humans and nature, minimizing the influence of environment, and, indeed, bringing to the fore the role of humans as agents of change. Kenneth Olwig (1980) persuasively argued that the works of Schouw, Reclus, and Marsh exemplify this view of the relationship and also noted the comparable views of Marx and Sauer. Overall, however, this was not the direction the institutionalized discipline of geography was to follow.

The nineteenth century witnessed attempts to redefine history as a positivist science with the evolution of humanity as the focus. As noted in chapter 2, Auguste Comte saw positivism as explaining even social phenomena. The resultant view of the human and land relationship was exemplified by Henry T. Buckle, an English historian, who explained the onset of the scientific age in Europe in terms of climate, soil, and configuration. Clearly, these views were essentially a contribution to environmentalist thought and not in accord with the prevailing mid-nineteenth–century view already described, and yet it was views of this type that became dominant in the late nineteenth and early twentieth centuries as geography became a university discipline. It appears that the emerging university geography largely ignored earlier geographic and other thought that emphasized humans as part of nature, preferring instead to develop a more obviously cause-and-effect emphasis with environment as the cause.

THE INSTITUTIONALIZATION OF GEOGRAPHY

Since the time of Kant, geography was closely associated with history. Those ties, however, were disturbed by the rapid development of the natural sciences in the nineteenth century, which caused physical geography to be seen as a natural science with close ties to geology. At about the same time, geography was formally established as a university discipline, first in Germany in the 1870s, then in France, and in Britain and the United States at the turn of the century. Most of the "founders" of geography were physical geographers, and in 1887, the German geographer, Georg Gerland suggested "that the study of cultural phenomena should be separated from geography" (Holt-Jensen, 1982, p. 23). The basic rationale for this view was that physical geography was a science and that cultural phenomena could not be studied from a comparable viewpoint. Certainly this view was prevalent in early American geography.

The turn of the century saw three basic responses to the important question, what is geography? First, as noted, geography was seen as the science of physical geography. Second, an environmentalist hypothesis emerged as a major theme. Third, the regional or chorological approach was adopted. The view of geography as a physical science was short lived; the environmentalist view was quickly challenged, especially by French and later American geographers; and the regional view became the self-proclaimed core of geography, notably in the United States. There seems little doubt that the institutionalization of geography was accomplished prior to any clear perception of what the "new" discipline was to be. Indeed, the growth of geography and its increasing popularity in the late nineteenth century were more a response to the role geography was perceived to play in infusing a nationalistic spirit than they were to any of the three themes mentioned. Also, geography was seen as crucial to the process of acquiring and disseminating knowledge of new European colonies.

The new discipline of geography emerged at a time when two ideas were prevalent, namely a positivist view of science and Darwinian evolutionism, and these two ideas help explain the character of geography circa 1900. The relation of these ideas to the developing views of geography is considered.

The Environmentalist View

The assertion that physical environment was a cause of both culture and cultural landscape has a long and erratic history beginning with the Greeks and continuing with the French political philosophers Jean Bodin, in the sixteenth century, and Montesquieu, in the eighteenth century. It was, however, raised to its highest level of acceptance with the establishment of geography as a discipline. There are certainly correspondences between the need to provide geography with a clear, distinct, and valid identity; the dominance of physical geography; the perceived need to bridge natural and social sciences; and the concepts provided by Darwinian evolutionary theory and the prevailing positivism. Environmentalism offered geography an identity and a method, it was in accord with prevailing intellectual thought, and it asserted the primacy of geographic explanation over sociological and anthropological explanation. Unfortunately for the new discipline, the environmentalist approach was overly simple and overstated, and the consequence was a rapid rejection. However, the stigma of environmentalism remained with geography throughout much of the twentieth century precisely because the basic cause-and-effect logic was superficially attractive. The geographic environmentalism ignored much earlier work on the human and land relationship, particularly that which saw the relationship as a form of interrelationship, electing instead to focus on a unilinear cause-and-effect framework.

The relationship between Darwinian evolutionary theory, social Darwinism, and environmentalism is well documented by geographers (Stoddart, 1966). The post-Darwinian search for the laws of nature involved a search for the physical causes of human actions, and, as one part of this search, the geographer Friedrich Ratzel accepted Herbert Spencer's ideas concerning the similarities of human societies and animal organisms. The result was that Ratzel strongly emphasized that humans were subservient to nature and, consequently, he is often seen as the originator of modern environmentalism. However it is clear that Ratzel regarded this concept only as a generalization, not as a scientific law, and in his later writings he substantially modified the view. It was, however, the early Ratzel who appears to have been most influential. This is not surprising because it was the early Ratzel whose views mirrored the needs of geography at the time, specifically a subserviency of human to physical geography and an apparent scientific emphasis. The leading British geographer circa 1900, Halford Mackinder, was more interested in questions of world power than he was in human and land relations. Nevertheless, he accepted the view that human geography was derivative from physical geography (Mackinder, 1902). Although this was not a well-developed theme it can be interpreted as having deterministic overtones.

Examples of environmentalist work are well known and include the statements of Ellen Semple and Ellsworth Huntington as well as much anthropological and historical work. Huntington was "an imaginative interpreter of the effects of climate on human life" and he "developed the hypothesis that man's civilizations could only develop in regions of stimulating climate and that the monotonous heat of the tropics would forbid attainment of the higher levels of civilization" (James & Martin, 1981, pp. 301–302). Semple (1911, p. 1) asserted that "man is a product of the earth's surface." However, Semple did not consistently argue for environmental controls, only that human behavior is predictable under certain circumstances.

Careful appraisal of stereotype environmentalist work shows that such work may be more flexible than selected dramatic quotes might suggest. Nevertheless, it is fair to say that the geography of the twentieth century includes many examples of implicit environmental cause and human effect logic. Perhaps the most disturbing aspect of environmentalism is that, as a geographic approach, it quickly proved to be embarrassingly simplistic. Issues of cultural variation, technology, and economics were subservient to environment. The vast body of literature, including earlier geographic literature, that argued for the unity of humans and nature was ignored.

> May I remind you that much faulty thinking on the part of historians, philosophers and others is due to the fact that they always will set man against nature as if they were two distinct categories. Man *versus* Nature instead of man and his environment being regarded as a single complex. (Taylor, cited in Spate, 1952, p. 425)

At the same time Griffith Taylor (cited in Spate, 1952, p. 425) acknowledged that "as young people we were thrilled with the idea that there was a pattern anywhere, so we were enthusiasts for determinism." Therein lay much of the attraction. Environmental determinism purported to offer explanations, explanations in close accord with the prevailing mechanistic view of science and Darwinian theory. It was soon evident to geographers, however, that the explanations offered were inadequate, thus demonstrating the inadequacy of the starting hypothesis. Proving environmentalism required a nonscientific selection of cases.

One further reason why simplistic environmentalism continued to hold sway through the first half of the twentieth century was its implicit incorporation in the chorological approach. This approach was detailed by Alfred Hettner in the late nineteenth century, owed much to the earlier work of Ferdinand von Richthofen, and was at least partly dependent on Kant's classification of sciences. The approach was defined by Richard Hartshorne (1939, p. 13) as follows. "To know the character of regions and places through comprehension of the existence together and interrelations among the different realms of reality and their varied manifestations, and to comprehend the earth surface as a whole in its actual arrangement in continents, larger and smaller regions, and places."

In Germany, this chorological emphasis was important from circa 1900 onward, and in America and Britain, it began to achieve a dominant status in the 1920s. Involved in this emphasis was a clear acknowledgment that geography was defined by its method, not by subject matter or by concepts. Also, the emphasis was invariably implicitly determinist, and there was a continued focus on the theme of human relations to physical environment. Physical cause and human consequence were generally assumed.

Reactions, or more appropriately alternative emphases for geography, were evident concurrently with the emergence of environmentalism in France, in the form of possibilism, and in Germany, in the form of *landschaft*. These two concepts are now detailed along with the subsequent American emphases on landscape and human ecology.

REACTIONS TO ENVIRONMENTALISM

As a central theme for geographic research, the cause-and-effect approach of environmentalism was inadequate. Alternative views of humans and nature, and of geography, were readily available and tended to emphasize unity and also an associated focus on some version of the region such as the zone in Russia, landschaft in Germany, natural region in the British Empire, and *pays* in France. French possibilism and German landschaft concepts are now appraised.

Possibilism

In 1889, the eminent French geographer Paul Vidal de la Blache argued for the study of close relationships between humans and environment, forcibly refuted the idea of environmental determinism, and formulated the alternative concept of possibilism. Thus, is may be appropriate to regard possibilism as a reaction to environmentalism, but at the same time, it seems proper to recognize elements of earlier nineteenth-century thought in the possibilism concept. There are, for example, close links between the views of Alexander Humboldt concerning the inseparability of humans and nature and those of Vidal. Both felt that natural and cultural landscapes were one, such that the relationship between humans and nature became so entwined that distinguishing the influence of one on the other was not feasible. Vidal emphasized the concept of genre de vie, which is comparable to that of culture, asserting that the meaning, or indeed perception, that a given group has of a given environment varies according to the genre de vie of that group. A third aspect of Vidal's work was that of recognizing distinctive areas of human occupance—regions or *pays*—in which particular human and land relations had evolved. It was emphasized that this regional aspect was particularly meaningful in a rural context prior to the industrial revolution, which Vidal saw as a major disturbance.

The possibilist component of Vidal's work appears to suggest a separation of humans and nature, but this is not a correct interpretation. It is correct that possibilism rejects the notion of environmental necessity in favor of acknowledging various possibilities and that, superficially, this implies a human and land separation, but the paramount thrust evident from a consideration of all three of Vidal's concerns is one of unity between humans and land. This emphasis on unity is also evident in the work of those French geographers succeeding Vidal, especially Jean Brunhes. The homogeneity of an area was a response to human use of the land. "*Genres de vie* (styles of living), the products and reflections of a *civilisation*, represented the integrated result of physical, historical and socio-cultural influences surrounding the human relationship to milieu in particular places. . . . *Milieu* signified the organically integrated physical and biotic infrastructure of human life on the earth" (Buttimer 1978, pp. 60–61).

There is thus much more to possibilism than a mere rejection of environmentalism. Fundamentally, the Vidalian concern was the ongoing dialectic of milieu and civilization. Furthermore, possibilism developed in opposition to the Dur-kheimian concept that social phenomena are only explicable in terms of social phenomena. For Vidal, neither extreme, environmental or social determinism, was acceptable (Berdoulay, 1978).

Landschaft

In Germany, a disenchantment with both environmentalism and the chorol-ogical view led to adoption of the view of geography as *landschaftskunde*, landscape science. This view dates from 1906 and is associated with Otto Schlu-ter. The principal area of interest is seen as the visible landscape and the emerg-ence of that landscape from the natural state, *Urlandschaft*, to the cultural, *Kulturlandschaft*. This geography became the study of landscape evolution. Overall there are close similarities between possibilism and landschaft in terms of primary concerns and in terms of the attitude toward humans and land.

The Landscape School

The results of a questionnaire about the status of American geography in 1914 are illuminating. The most important task facing geography and geographers was judged to be "the exact determination of the influence of geographic en-vironment" (James & Martin, 1981, p. 315). Clearly, neither French possibilism nor German *landschaftskunde* had made inroads into American geography at this time. The second task was that of conducting regional studies. It was into this intellectual environment, favoring environmentalism and chorology, that the landscape school was thrust.

It is appropriate to regard the seminal statement by Carl Sauer (1925), "The Morphology of Landscape," as similar in genesis and purpose to both the French and German developments. All were opposed to the idea of environmental in-fluences, were concerned with areas of the earth's surfce, and were attempts to clearly define the subject matter and methods of the discipline. The views ex-pressed by Sauer, often seen as the landscape or Berkeley school, were thus out of accord with the prevailing American perceptions of geography and closer to some European views. Indeed, Sauer (1925) made several references to European geographers such as Hettner, Vidal, and Brunhes in the seminal statement. A second influence is possible. According to James Duncan (1980, p. 182), Sauer was also reflecting the view of anthropology, particularly the superorganicist arguments of Alfred Kroeber and Robert Lowie, both of whom were contem-poraries with Sauer at Berkeley in California. It is certainly the case that Sauer was intellectually close to Kroeber, as reported by others at Berkeley (Leighly, 1979, p. 6; Parsons, 1979, p. 13), but it is also clear that Sauer was impressed by the frontier historian Herbert E. Bolton, as noted by James and Martin (1981, pp. 325–326). Furthermore, the extent to which Sauer accepted superoganicist arguments is less clear. The 1925 paper included but one reference to Kroeber and no explicit acknowledgment of the superorganic concept. The intellectual antecedents for the 1925 paper were primarily European cultural geography and not American anthropology. What Sauer (1925, p. 46) achieved was a statement of geography as the study of "cultural landscape . . . fashioned from a natural landscape by a culture group." The landscape school was not a carbon copy of Kroeber's and Lowie's methods, but rather an original contribution to the analysis of landscape. Interestingly, although it was the 1925 paper that attracted interest, Sauer (1924) had in fact detailed much of the argument in an earlier paper.

It appears that the content of the landscape school, although subject to change, remained faithful to the European antecedents. A later statement by Sauer (1931) again referred to numerous European geographers and neglected any mention of anthropology. John Leighly (1976, pp. 339–340), however, emphasized the very close ties betwen Sauer and the Berkeley anthropologists Kroeber and Lowie: "Basic to Sauer's course in world regional geography was the concept of "cultures,' now used in the ethnological sense, which he learned from the anthropologists at Berkeley." Whatever the detailed origins, the landscape focus initiated by Sauer in the 1920s has proven to be the most enduring aspect of North American cultural geography incorporating definitions of culture and of cultural geography. This emphasis is now detailed.

A basic thrust of the landscape school was a forceful rejection of environmentalism, which Sauer, (1924, p. 18) regarded as "facile, alluring and plausible." A key point was that "the protagonist of a particular viewpoint ordinarily arrives at results that are inferior in value to the conclusions formed without predisposition in favor of a particular answer" (Sauer, 1924, p. 18). An environmentalist hypothesis thus meant a loss of objectivity. For Sauer (1924), geography was unfavorably compared to history, a discipline that avoided needless generalization. A second thrust was the related emphasis on fact as the basic object of analysis to be followed by interpretation "without either priority or disregard of physical factors" (Sauer, 1924, p. 24). A regional emphasis was implicit in geographic analyses but the term *landscape* was thought to be a clearer alternative concept. Three factors were regarded as basic to landscape, namely the physical environment, the character of the people, and time. Working from European sources, Sauer (1924, p. 24) thus defined geography as "the derivation of the cultural area from the natural area." This definition allows for three basic geographic questions. First, what is the relevance of environment? Second, how are human groups different in their potential for progress? Third, how have humans modified environment? It is clear that Sauer was neither an environmental nor a cultural determinist, and that the influence of European cultural geography was considerable and that of American anthropology less evident (see Sauer & Leighly, 1924).

It is in the seminal 1925 paper, however, that the landscape school is especially detailed. This paper reaffirmed the position stated in 1924 concerning environmentalism, the need for facts, the replacement of "area" or "region" by landscape, and the unity of physical and cultural components of landscape. The 1925 paper extended and developed these ideas (see also, Sauer, 1927). Culture, for the geographer, was seen as "the impress of the works of man upon the area" (Sauer, 1925, p. 30). The importance of a temporal approach was continually emphasized and the possibility of "a succession of these landscapes with a succession of cultures" was noted (Sauer, 1925, p. 37). This was comparable to the sequent occupance concept, a term coined in 1929 by Derwent Whittlesey. Sequent occupance involved relating changing landscapes to changing cultural occupances and, as such, was explicitly opposed to environmentalism. In a pioneering sequent occupance study, James (1929, p. 85) referred to the 1925 statement by Sauer. Despite this early association and the shared emphases on human occupance and time, the two are not usually grouped together. The seminal sequent occupance statement was a brief footnoteless example (Whittlesey, 1929) that made little if any impact on the landscape school.

Sauer (1925) detailed the evolution of both natural and cultural landscapes with the latter being summarized as follows. Humans, through culture, transform the natural landscape; the object of study is the cultural landscape not culture. In a classic statement, Sauer (1925, p. 46) noted that "culture is the agent, the natural area is the medium, the cultural landscape the result." Although culture is thus the "shaping force," Sauer (1925, p. 46) affirmed that the physical landscape "is of course of fundamental importance, for it supplies the materials out of which the cultural landscape is formed." It is not difficult to understand how Sauer might be construed as a cultural determinist given the labeling of culture as the "factor," the "agent," and the "shaping force." A full reading of the methodological writings, however, seems to preclude this possible inter-pretation.

This emerging landscape school was regarded by Sauer (1931, p. 623) as cultural geography with the aim being to explain the "facts of the culture area, by whatever causes have contributed thereto." The approach is explictly opposed to both cultural and environmental determinism, because there is a "persistent curiosity as to the significance of the environment" and there is not a "com-pulsion to dress up the importance of the environment" (Sauer, 1931, p. 623). Geographic and anthropologic culture areas were distinguished, with the former being simpler and restricted essentially to the expressions of human occupation.

There is some suggestion that what Sauer (1924, 1925, 1927, 1931) wrote and what he practiced were rather different. The influence of Kroeber and Lowie referred to by Leighly (1976) is not evident in the writings. A recent detailed study by Michael Williams (1983, p. 6) noted that

> once Sauer left the rarified babble of methodology and concentrated on an actual case study of man and landscape the history of what had happened to make the landscape became his paramount concern, and the formal structure of morphology was abandoned for the intuitive feel for behavior and object through time.

This assertion is confirmed by appraisals of the many empirical works produced by Sauer following the early methodological statements; a theme that is further pursued in chapter 6.

In a retrospective comment, Sauer (1974, p. 191) wrote that "the morphology of landscape was an early attempt to say what the common enterprise was in the European tradition." Thus the landscape school of the 1920s was an American version of established European thought, first, and a use of American anthropology, second, although Sauer (1974, p. 192) also commented that "anthropologists were our tutors in understanding cultural diversity and change. Robert Lowie in particular introduced us to the work of such geographers as Edward Hahn and Ratzel as founders of an anthropogeography that I had not known."

Human Ecology

The origins of human ecology as an approach in American geography also date from the 1920s, specifically from the work of Harlan H. Barrows (1923) who defined geography as human ecology. The precise intent of Barrows's emphasis is unclear as he is conventionally regarded as an environmentalist but can also be seen in a different light (Clarkson, 1970, p. 704; James & Martin, 1981, p. 319). Barrows (1923) essentially aimed to delimit clearly the discipline of geography by arguing for human adjustment to physical environment as the one unifying theme. Despite the attraction of this concept for the emerging landscape school, it was not easily embraced, although Sauer (1981, p. 259) wrote in 1967 that environmentalism "was a mode of explanation that Barrows tried to keep within proper limits by making the distinction between 'geographic' and 'non-geographic' factors"; the nongeographic factor being humans. James Clarkson (1970, p. 705) suggested that the failure to integrate the two approaches was partly a result of Sauer objecting to the exclusion of physical geography by Barrows. Whatever the explanation, it is the case that intellectual contact between the ecological and landscape views has been limited such that two different themes remain evident today (Taafe, 1974, p. 4).

For other early human ecologists, especially the sociologist Robert E. Park, the role of geography was that of supplying facts that the human ecologist could then explain (Entrikin, 1980, p. 55). Ecological emphases also developed in anthropology and the general confusion as to the identity of the ecological thrust in all three disciplines of geography, sociology, and anthropology was related to the presence of several and varied attempts to identify the method for different purposes. Overall, the Barrows conception was unfavorably received within geography and it was not until the 1950s that an ecological focus really emerged in cultural geography. This is despite a close similarity between the Vidalian emphasis on *pays* and the Park social world emphasis.

CULTURAL GEOGRAPHY TO CIRCA 1970

The period from the 1920s to the 1950s was one dominated by the atemporal regional geography of Hartshorne with the various human and land themes being of much lesser importance quantitatively speaking. For cultural geography, this period was characterized by continuous growth of the landscape school, an increasing emphasis on time, and some revisions to the human and land concept. The period ended with the rather rapid demise of regional geography and the associated emergence of spatial analysis. The latter dominated geography briefly, perhaps until 1970, since that time the discipline has been characterized by a multiparadigm state. Throughout the hegemony of spatial analysis, cultural geography again continued to be largely unaffected by developments elsewhere in the discipline, except for the analytically oriented perception research of the later 1960s. One reason for the failure of the landscape school, or of cultural geography in general, to establish a dominance in geography was the general unwillingness to participate in epistemological questions. This comment applies to the major traditions of Vidal and Sauer. The resultant lack of a sound philosophy also permitted the rise of spatial analysis and the incorporation of perception within spatial analysis. This section reviews developments in cultural geography between the important early stages already detailed and the contemporary scene that is the focus of the succeeding chapter.

Mainstream American Cultural Geography:
The Landscape School

The landscape school has survived from the 1920s to the present, but it has always been a secondary concern. The lack of a strong philosophical basis in both the landscape school and related European cultural geography can be unfavorably compared with both other social sciences and other geographic emphases. Nevertheless, cultural geography persisted.

The landscape school thesis has been modified in three important ways. First, the suggestion that it was possible or necessary to analyze the evolution of cultural landscapes from natural landscapes was dropped. Second, the early links with a chorological focus were gradually weakened as an increasing emphasis was placed on the appearance and quality of areas. The logical integration of the landscape and sequent occupance schools did not occur as the latter lost vigor in the 1930s because, as a regional approach, it was unsuited to the Hartshornian mold. Third, the concern with evolution became dominant in empirical work, and the cultural and historical traditions drew closer. Work in this tradition stressed form over process, despite the concern with time, and generally eschewed cause-and-effect logic. A similar comment is appropriate to the continuing Vidalian tradition with its anti-Durkheimian, and related antipositivistic, focus. For Sauer, this was possibly a continuing rejection of environmentalism and its unproven assumptions and also, possibly, an implicit rejection of the superorganic and its unproven assumptions. Paul English and Robert Mayfield (1972, p. 6) mourned the "intense preoccupation with the visible material landscape," which "led to an unfortunate neglect of the less obvious, invisible forces which in some cases form cornerstones in the explanation of spatial patterns of human behavior." Somewhat similarly, the landscape school had been criticized for ignoring values, beliefs, and institutions (see Brookfield, 1964).

The increasing importance of time for Sauer and the landscape school may have been related to the influence of anthropology. Rather than cross sections through time, anthropologists saw time as continuous, a view to which Sauer had fully subscribed by 1941 (Sauer, 1941, pp. 5–6). Indeed, the 1941 paper produced some strong assertions. "Human geography, then, unlike psychology and history, is a science that has nothing to do with individuals but only with human institutions, or cultures" (Sauer, 1941, p. 7). Further: "An environmental response, therefore, is nothing more than a specific cultural option with regard to the habitat at a particular time" (Sauer, 1941, p. 7). Again: "The whole task of human geography, therefore, is nothing less than comparative study of areally localized cultures" (Sauer, 1941, p. 8). Finally: "Culture is the learned and conventionalized activity of a group that occupies an area" (Sauer, 1941, p. 8). Combined, these statements provide a program for cultural historical geography that is clearly tied to developments in anthropology and that retains the European flavor of the Vidalian school but that does not imply cultural determinism. Cultural processes are seen as a base, but the concern is with culture *not* Culture. More than the seminal 1925 paper, it is the 1941 paper that more truly reflected the empirical work being accomplished by Sauer and colleagues.

View of Humans and Land

The landscape, the Vidalian, and even the ecological viewpoints allowed for broad-minded interpretations of the human and land relationship. In anthropology and sociology, the major concern was with cultural or social causes, but in geography both culture and society per se were neglected in favor of visible material landscapes. Despite the claims by J. S. Duncan (1980) to the contrary, there is little evidence that cultural geographers embraced superorganic concepts or Durkheimian views, preferring instead the less rigid geographic traditions of Sauer and Vidal. One major textbook exception to this was the work by George Carter (1964, p. 477). "It is human will that is decisive, not the physical environment. The human will is channeled in its action by a fabric of social customs, attitudes and laws that is tough, resistant to change and persistent through time."

Despite a general status quo on this issue, several geographers did contribute originally to human and land concepts, most notably Griffith Taylor and Oscar Spate. The former argued for "stop-and-go" determinism, which recognized that some areas allowed a host of possibilities whereas other areas were too extreme to allow such a variety of options (Taylor, 1951). This theme was a limitation imposed by nature. Spate (1952), in a penetrating discussion of Arnold

Toynbee and Huntington, coined the term probabilism as an appropriate middle road between the perceived extremes of determinism and possibilism and also noted that it was probabilism that was really implied by the Vidalian school. This term allows the "possibilities" to have varying "probabilities" of occurrence. Indeed, this concept of probabilism is very close to both Sauer and Vidal, because it deemphasizes environment, recognizes that culture is not a sole determinant, and confirms that individual behavior is modified when the individual is a member of a cultural group.

In addition to the above two ideas, a major elaboration of the human and land theme was provided by an increased interest during the 1960s in environmental perception. Larry Grossman (1977, pp. 139–143) identified origins and made useful comparisons with related anthropological perspectives. The fundamental foci are acknowledgment of differences between real and perceived environments; establishment of the determinants of perceptions, and the relation between perception, decision making, and behavior. For many geographers, such an emphasis was a welcome relief to the economic man concept of spatial analysis. A perception emphasis was quickly evident not only in cultural geography, where it was always implicit, but also in economic geography and hazards analysis. Much of this work continued to have limited philosophical underpinning, at least until the 1970s.

A final thrust in human and land relations was an increasing concern with an old theme, that of humans as agents of landscape change. Intellectual origins can be traced to George Perkins Marsh, Elisée Reclus, and William Morris Davis, but reemergence of the theme was a phenomenon of the 1950s. Sauer was a prime mover in this instance and a seminal volume of readings appeared in 1956 (Thomas, Sauer, Bates, and Mumford, 1956). The motivation for this thrust was explicitly stated by Thomas et al. (1956, p. xxxvi).

> Every human group has had to evaluate the potential of the area it inhabits and to organize its life about the environment in terms of available techniques and the values accepted as desirable. The identification, use and care of resources is in the end a problem of human values and behavior.

It is clear that the focus is comparable to those of Vidal and Sauer as regards emphasis, although the subject matter is somewhat different being close to much of human ecology.

CONCLUDING COMMENTS

This discussion of the development of cultural geography as one component part of the larger discipline of geography has particularly emphasized the minority status of the cultural interest, at least partly a result of the Hartshornian rejection of time. The failure of cultural geography to assume a dominant position is despite the well-articulated statements from the landscape school and the explicit association with French and German geography. It is also despite a number of other statements that might have been expected to contribute positively to the arguments of cultural geographers. The statement on human ecology by Barrows (1923) and the parallel drawn between the landscape school and sequent occupance by James (1929, p. 85) might have been expected, in retrospect, to enhance the status of Sauer and his students. Similarly, a 1928 presidential address to the Association of American Geographers (D. Johnson, 1929) argued forcibly for dynamic analyses and praised Vidal and his followers. The long-run impact appears to have been slight.

Twentieth-century American cultural geography remained, until the 1970s, a minority focus in the discipline. Despite the Vidalian and landscape schools, it was the regional concept and implicit environmentalism that dominated geography until the 1950s and a positivistic spatial analysis that assumed prominence from perhaps 1955 to 1970. A roundtable discussion on cultural geography in 1936 (Dodge, 1937) provides a useful benchmark. The focus was on American regions from a cultural perspective. Several issues were raised including the false separation of cultural and natural landscapes, the need for studies of the past, the classification of various cultural elements, and the focus on visible and not nonmaterial culture. An emphasis on chance was detailed by Leighly (1937, p. 139), with cultural features being "the result of a choice among several possibilities." A dominant concern with environmentalism versus possibilism was evident, and a strong argument for possibilism was that by George Tatham (1951) who recognized the similarity of the Vidal and Sauer positions and, indeed, the possibilistic implications both of stop-and-go determinism and of probabilism.

The relationship with other disciplines was limited prior to the 1970s. Several of Sauer's students worked closely with Berkeley anthropologists and published various anthropology journals. However, the impact on geography as a whole appears slight. The geographic relevance of some anthropology was recognized, by Carter (1948), for example, in an obituary for Clark Wissler. Generally, however, the intellectual links between geography and anthropology were limited. A similar conclusion is valid with reference to geography and sociology despite the statement by J. Wreford Watson (1951, p. 466) that argued for a social geography: "it is . . . the social constituent that distinguishes one place from another and gives character to a region." J. W. Watson (1951, p. 468) referred favorably to Patrick Bryan who used cultural landscape as the basis for regional divisions but proceeded further and argued for a human factor including ideologies as well as technologies. Such a position was quite different from the typical view of both the Vidalian and landscape schools and argued for a sociological content in cultural geography.

By the 1960s cultural geography was a secondary but persistent aspect of geography, which survived the regional to spatial analytic transfer almost without affect. Despite this continuance, a sound basis was still lacking. One substantive attempt to correct this omission was that of Charles Gritzner (1966, p. 7) who defined cultural geography as "the application of the idea, or concept, of culture to geographic problems" and defined culture as "that which differentiates man from all other forms of life." A close tie with anthropology was noted, with the geographer focusing on human and land relations and the anthropologist focusing on cultural determinants of human behavior. Culture was acknowledged as the means by which humans use land, and a primary focus was placed on the human ability to symbolize and thus to transmit culture through time. Cultural processes were identified as invention, discovery, innovation, diffusion, borrowing, adaptation, evolution, acculturation, and education. This typology remains valuable today. Gritzner (1966, p. 10) wrote that

> cultural geography begins with the anthropological concept of culture, considers culture traits and cultural groups in terms of their historical development, weights the interactions between culture and the physical landscape, interprets cultural landscapes and, in the final analysis, through the mapping of traits and trait complexes as they appear on the earth, provides a sound basis for the division of the globe into culture regions and subregions.

The above statement provides a fitting conclusion to this chapter: there is a link with anthropology, a concern with process, an emphasis on time, an acknowledgment of the role of land, a clear meaning to culture, and a recognition of the presence of culture regions. In general, there are close ties to the earlier French and landscape schools. What was not anticipated, necessarily, was the massive impact in the 1970s of a variety of "new" humanistic and materialistic emphases. The status of contemporary cultural geography as a result of the traditional links and as a result of recent contributions remains to be considered.

4

Contemporary Cultural Geography

The concern with human and land relations outside of geography and the rise of cultural geography have been detailed in the previous two chapters. Accordingly, a sound basis should now be available to facilitate evaluation of contemporary cultural geography. This evaluation is, however, complicated by the rapid emergence to prominence of a variety of emphases since circa 1970. These include humanistic approaches such as idealism, phenomenology, and existentialism as well as radical approaches such as Marxism and structuralism. This plethora of recent contributions to the available methodologies reflects a disenchantment with positivism, which dominated human geography in the 1960s, and with the characteristic restriction of interest to the visible and material landscape. It also reflects a growing appreciation of the contents of the Vidal school and of a wide range of social science methodologies. This chapter attempts to embrace this diverse scenario and includes both cultural and social geography as they are usually identified in North America and Britain respectively. The following organization is employed: (1) an evaluation of the model of humans used by geographers, (2) a consideration of the distinction between cultural and social geography, (3) an appraisal of radical emphases, (4) an appraisal of humanistic emphases, (5) an evaluation of recent themes and directions, and (6) a concluding section.

THE MODEL OF HUMANS IN GEOGRAPHY

The greatest single distinction between the pre–1970 and post–1970 periods is the preoccupation of the later period with questions of methodology. A recent abundance of questions about culture, society, and landscape appears to be leading to a transformation of the traditional subdiscipline. The extent to which this might prove to be a departure from Sauerian and Vidalian traditions is uncertain because, despite the newness of many concepts, authors are often at pains to demonstrate the links between old and new. This is partly because the elucidation of the new has not characteristically been in opposition to the old but rather in opposition to the positivistic spatial analysis of the 1960s. This point is now pursued with particular reference to the model of humans used in geographical work.

The recent articulation of explicitly humanistic concerns has characteristically been antipositivistic in thrust. Opposition to the positivistic view of humans as being economic men was clearly stated by David Ley (1977, p. 501) who saw "implicit economic determinism, with a pale spectre of man." Critics of positivism also argued that to treat humans objectively was to treat them as objects and thus to reify them or, following Ley and Marwyn Samuels (1978, p. 7), to consider humans as an "image of nature." These humanistic criticisms are, then, criticisms of the model of humans that became central to the spatial analytic paradigm. There is a close conceptual similarity between the earlier critics of environmentalism and the later critics of positivism. For both sets of critics, a major concern was the dehumanization of the discipline. It is not surprising that the recent body of criticism sought support from the earlier schools as well as from relevant earlier nongeographic schools such as the idealism of Wilhelm Dilthey, which objected to seeing human phenomena as an analogue to physical phenomena. Overall, humanistic geography attempts to concern itself with complete human beings, a concern that Lambert van der Laan and Andries Piersma (1982, p. 418) saw as comparable to the Vidalian interest in genre de vie: "Humanistic geography has a similar objective, namely, by means of an interpretive analysis of the mental climate, to attempt to identify what ideas direct and stimulate the acts of the human beings . . . the mental climate can provide meaning for human activities." The images of humans adopted in positivism and humanism are fundamentally different, with the former seeing humans as passive and the latter seeing humans as active. This is comparable to the distinction between behaviorism and cognitive psychology. But it is not only the humanistic movement that objected to the mechanistic view. Recent work in social theory has aimed to reconcile individual action and social structure.

Certainly, a major stimulus for the growth of humanistic geography has especially been to reinstate human intentionality, humans, and culture into geography. This reinstatement promises better explanations and increased understanding but has not been accomplished without considerable growing pains as the succeeding sections demonstrate.

CULTURAL AND SOCIAL EMPHASIS

The confused identity of contemporary work is perhaps more easily identified by considering the identifying labels "cultural" and "social." The Sauerian type of cultural work never dominated the British or European scenes where the

Vidalian emphasis on social analysis and historical reconstructions proved more attractive. Consequently, rather similar work has typically been labeled differently. Of the Vidalian school it was Jean Brunhes whose work emphasized landscape in the Sauerian sense (Claval, 1984, p. 234). One indication of the rather confused identity of contemporary work is contained in recent issues of the journal, *Progress in Human Geography*. This journal has progress reports on cultural, cultural-humanistic and social issues. Although the cultural label is essentially North American, and the social label essentially British, it is now clear that such a division is misleading as the contents of the various progress reports are similar. Reports on cultural geography (see Ley, 1981, 1983a) focused on the Sauerian tradition and humanistic interests whereas comparable reports on social geography (see P. Jackson, 1984) emphasized a wider range of methodological initiatives but included a similar concern with humans, culture, and humanism. Thus a long-standing apparent division appears to be finally disappearing as both the cultural and social emphases share a desire to learn from and contribute to current social science. The basic stimulus for this development is undoubtedly the increasing appreciation of the unsatisfactory concept of humans, society, and of culture that characterized earlier work. Thus, recent work in the cultural and social traditions is showing conceptual upheaval, such as the recognition of the role of institutions, and the two can be profitably viewed as one. Perhaps one of the clearest indications of the convergence of cultural and social geography is the increasingly shared interest in such variables as language, religion, and ethnicity. These are traditional variables in cultural geography, often used for region delimitation, and are now being used by social geographers primarily for group delimitation.

RADICAL METHODOLOGIES

This section and the one that follows tackle the difficult task of identifying and evaluating the major methodological advances in contemporary work. Radical methodologies are the first concern. James Blaut (1980, pp. 25–26) offered the following guideline for radical cultural geography.

> Now I can define what I mean by "radical." The belief-systems which make up the body of lore in our science are culture-bound, that is bound to an ethno-class community. A radical approach is one which would be bound to a different ethnic culture, that is ethnic group, or a different class. . . . Today I think there are two important sources from which a radical critique of social science in general emerges. The older one, going back a century or more, represents a working-class critique, mostly a socialist critique of elitist European social science; it is embodied in marxism, anarchism and other working-class philosophies. . . . The other source is a matter of culture, instead of (or in addition to) class, and emerges mainly from modern Third World writers, most of whom are also socialists.

S. S. Duncan (1979, p. 1) argued that a more appropriate term for the so called radical geography was, in fact, *social geography*, "if this had not already been appropriated and so imbued with connotations of the isolation of the 'social' from the 'economic.' " This is because a primary concern of radical work is with social structure and social change and with humans as active social agents. Furthermore, reintroducing active humans also means that explanation requires an historical perspective. "Society, including space as part of society, is created by people and therefore, presumably, changed by them" (S. S. Duncan, 1979, p. 1).

Combined, these two sets of ideas provide a useful basis for discussing radical cultural geography; the origins and the basic conceptual stimuli are emphasized. For both authors, it is clear that human geography can and ought to progress beyond positivism to become a critical social science, that is, one that allows for appraisal of present circumstances and evaluation of alternatives. It needs to be stressed that a wide range of philosophies may be considered in this context. Ronald Johnston (1983b, p. 87–121) included several philosophies under the general heading of structuralism: Claude Lévi-Strauss and Jean Piaget were discussed with structure as construct; Marxism was discussed with structure as process; and realism, structuralism, and critical theory were also dicussed. Although such a classification is necessarily somewhat arbitrary, it is a valuable framework in the present context as it provides reasonably fixed limits to the content of the section. Relevant empirical work has focused on issues of development, residential segregation, and historical analysis.

Humans and Land: The Marxist View

One major contribution relates to the concept of humans in the world. A major task for Karl Marx was to highlight the importance of economic structure, but this was not achieved at the expense of implying social dependence on economic factors. This argument is now commonplace in cultural geography. Rod Burgess (1978, p. 1) wrote that

> the Marxist concept is then at once the concept of human reality not as in the classical view . . . that man is a part of nature, but rather that he shapes it. At the same time this act shapes him and his fellow man, a constant total interaction of subject and object in the historical process.

In a similar vein, Neil Smith and Phil O'Keefe (1980, p. 32) noted that, for Marx, nature is necessarily linked to societal activity. Andrew Sayer (1979, pp. 21–22) broadened this discussion considerably and argued that there has been "a distortion or wholesale omission of the nature and implications of labour as the most active and fundamental interaction between people and nature."

Recognizing that humans and nature are not separate, prompted Sayer (1979, p. 22) to refer to inner actions within nature rather than to interactions between humans and nature. Despite the complexity of Marx's writings, it is evident that many radical geographers choose to interpret the unity of humans and nature as one major contribution. As such, Marxist-oriented cultural geography opposes all determinisms. In a useful account of environmental relations in radical studies, Ben Wisner (1978, pp. 91–92) chose to argue for a socialist human ecology as the best means of *practice*. Such a human ecology might focus on environmental histories, human adjustments, system stability, and the fate of folk ecologies in cooperative structures.

These assertions by radical geographers have not met with general acceptance. Humanistic authors have typically contended, for example, that structural Marxism has necessarily to adopt a passive view of humans because it is a holistic school of thought (J. S. Duncan & Ley, 1982). Such critiques see "man as object" in the structuralist and Marxist approaches. These need to be tempered with the recognition that Marxist thought is open to a variety of interpretation ranging from humanist to structuralist, "from an active view of people as the makers of their own history, to a passive conception of human development as the determined product of relatively autonomous structures" (P. Jackson & S. J. Smith, 1984, p. 17).

Accepting that Marxist work is capable, in principle, of viewing humans and nature as one, what type of radical cultural geography emerges? For Blaut (1980), several deficiencies will be removed such as the failure to recognize that cultures have a political component and the failure to recognize that cultures are divided into classes. A radical view also avoids the humanistic tendency to oppose individuals and culture and the tendency to neglect external constraints from society at large. One attempt to achieve a synthesis of cultural geography and Marxism was that of Cosgrove (1983, p. 1). "Marxism and cultural geography share important basic presumptions concerning the significance of culture, but in different ways and for different reasons both have failed to sustain those presuppositions in their practice and have not developed a dialogue with each other." The attempt to correct this failing acknowledged the shared focus on the historical aspect of human and land relations and emphasized conceptual similarities such as the shared Marxian and Vidalian view of the relationship. Such shared views were not acknowledged by cultural geographers and have not typically been made explicit. For Cosgrove (1983, p. 7), the resolution lay in advancing and utilizing a symbolic interpretation of culture because "this allows for a synthesis of some of the traditional aims of cultural geography with historical materialism . . . " The radical cultural geography that emerges reveals the symbolic contributions of humans as creators of landscape and, furthermore, reveals the means by which the created landscapes maintain symbolic production. Available examples in the geographic literature include those of David Harvey (1979) on the Basilica of Sacre-Coeur in Paris as a political symbol and Barbara Rubin (1979) on ideology and urban design in America.

Despite the varied interpretations of Marxist and other radical work, there is a shared opposition to the perceived extremes of both positivism, with its de-humanization of geography and its emphasis on individuals, and humanism, with its emphasis on individuals. It is not unusual to draw parallels between Marxist and other nineteenth-century views, such as those of Peter Kropotkin and Elisée Reclus on the one hand, and Vidalian and landscape views on the other hand, because of the common concerns with social and historical processes.

Societies and Individuals: The Marxist View

A second major contribution of radical work concerns the scale of analysis—the individual or the group. It is possible to argue that radical approaches alone, not positivist or humanist interests, are in accord with a needed focus on groups. "The view that individuals are the moving forces in history is deeply embedded in positivist thought" (S. W. Williams, 1981, p. 34) whereas the behavioral approach eliminates the "historical and social elements from the study of man's relationship to the environment" (Burgess, 1978, p. 9). The basic thrust was well stated by Sayer (1979, p. 21) as an "inadequate recognition of the nature and role of intersubjectivity in social life—a failure shared by both positivists and, ironically, by those humanist geographers who have championed the study of subjectivity in geography." The question is one of who actually does something, is it an individual or is it a class, an institution or a culture? The radical answer is that individuals do not actually do anything because individuals have to be defined within the wider cultural context. When we appear to talk about individuals we are really talking about their beliefs or ideas, which need to be culturally defined. Sayer (1979, p. 25) contended that

> ironically, despite their avowed hostility to naturalistic approaches which ob-jectify human experience, phenomenological approaches which interpret the subjectivity of this experience in abstraction from intersubjective meanings and social norms invite similar regresses towards either psychologistic explanations of this experience, which situate its origin in our "inner Nature," or behavior-ist explanations which characterize it as a purely physical response to stimuli in "outer Nature."

Other radical critiques arrive at similar conclusions about the merits of analyses of groups somewhat differently. B. T. Asheim (1979, pp. 11–12) noted that the emphasis on individuals allows social inequalities to be interpreted as accidental and, furthermore, criticized individual-level analyses for not recognizing that the results of actions are often not those intended; "the consequences are a result of actions, and interactions, not of intentions."

Arguments of this type are part of a substantive set of ideas in social science regarding cultures and individuals. The specific argument noted above and linked to radical concerns is part of the wider concerns of Emile Durkheim and Alfred Kroeber who reify society and culture respectively. A different view is the voluntarist view of Max Weber, which sees society resulting from the intentional actions of individuals. A more recent and more complex concept is that of structuration, associated with Jurgen Habermas and Anthony Giddens especially, which sees societies as both mediums and outcomes of the practices that constitute them. For Jackson and Smith (1984, p. 63) this theory "suggests one way in which the fragile bridge between humanism and structural Marxism may be strengthened." All of these differing ideas are further evaluated in chapter 7, in association with particular empirical discussions. At this stage, it is adequate to note that structuration, particularly the version developed by Giddens (1984), is viewed most favorably by some social geographers (Gregory, 1982; Pred, 1984, 1986).

The Prospects for Radical Cultural Geography

Conceptual questions aside, it is abundantly clear that radical cultural geography does offer new perspectives, new ideas, and new problems. Certainly, for Blaut (1980) and Wisner (1978), it is these practical contributions rather than the conceptual issues that are of prime importance today. The recognition that traditional interests necessarily contribute to an ideology of domination, ignore classes, and frequently exclude culture highlights the value of a radical input.

One of the areas in which contributions are already numerous is that of development. Dependency theory argues that countries are underdeveloped because of their dependence on developed countries. Such dependency typically commenced in the colonial era but remains the norm today such that wealthy core countries and poor peripheral countries are evident. A further contention of dependency theory is that the developed countries are dependent by design such that development and underdevelopment are dialectically related (Browett, 1981). An interesting example of a dependency concern in geography is that by David Drakakis-Smith (1981) concerned with Australian economic development and the effects on the aboriginal group; an interdependence of those of European origin and aboriginal origin is clear to the detriment of the latter.

A second area that is already well developed relates to the world-systems perspective. Following Immanuel Wallerstein (see 1974) it can be argued that historical analyses of regions need to be at "the level of the overarching totality; the capitalist world economy" (Crush, 1980, p. 343).

Other major areas of concern in radical cultural and social geography include studies of urban segregation and of deprivation. As a result of, or perhaps in spite of, the diverse conceptual background, this is an area of research that shows every indication of growing. To date the impacts are principally in historical and social analyses, but the interests of traditional North American cultural geography are also being affected.

HUMANISTIC METHODOLOGIES

The conceptual advances evident in recent years that are most intimately tied to cultural geography are those with a humanistic thrust. For some North American geographers, the cultural and humanistic fields are one whereas social geography in Britain also includes much humanistic content. Indeed, just as some radical geographers feel comfortable turning to Paul Vidal de la Blache and Carl Sauer so too do those with a humanistic bent, albeit for rather different reasons. The humanistic concern incorporates a variety of philosophies and is as conceptually complex as is the radical concern. This section makes no attempt to provide a full discussion of humanism. Rather, the aim is to identify key concepts and to argue for a symbolic and interactionist view of culture.

A useful overview of the evolution of humanistic thought is provided by Ley and Samuels (1978) and the twentieth-century impacts on social science and social theory noted. For human geography the crucial first stage is that of Vidal but later contributions are limited and are identified with specific individuals rather than with distinct schools of thought. Only in the 1970s has humanism emerged as a set of philosophies with both conceptual and empirical contributions (Mackenzie, 1986; Rowntree, 1986). Overall, the period between the 1920s and 1970s was one characterized by a general lack of humanistic concerns, partly because of the overemphasis on, first, regional geography and, later, spatial analysis and partly because of the failure of both Vidal and Sauer to develop sound philosophical bases for their respective schools.

One "principal aim of modern humanism in geography is the reconciliation of social science and man, to accommodate understanding and wisdom, objectivity and subjectivity, and materialism and idealism" (Ley & Samuels, 1978, p. 9). This broad and ambitious aim has not, of course, been achieved, but it does serve to identify the varied emphases that humanism might assume. Regardless of specific emphases, humanism provides the characteristics of anthropocentrism and holism. The former recognizes that intents are present in all actions and all facts. The latter stresses the active ongoing human and land relations. Humanist approaches also exemplify a growing concern for individuals and a focus on unique events rather than the general. The varied humanist positions in contemporary geography may conveniently, without too much generalization, be grouped into the three categories of idealism, phenomenology, and existentialism, and these are now briefly noted prior to a more general discussion.

Idealism

Arguments favoring an idealist philosophy in geography are associated especially with Leonard Guelke whose forceful advocacy culminated in a book-length study (Guelke, 1982). Historically, idealism has frequently been seen as in direct opposition to positivism because of the insistence that phenomena are only significant when they are part of human consciousness. To understand the world, it becomes necessary to rethink the thoughts behind actions, to discover what decision makers believed rather than why they believed it. As such, idealism is a philosophy emphasizing the subjective, "knowledge is ordered by individuals according to their own theoretical systems, which are modified in the light of new knowledge but whose criterion of truth is internal to the theory" (Johnston, 1983b, p. 54). Guelke's advocacy of idealism was based principally on work by the historian Robin George Collingwood and did not turn to the long tradition of idealist thinking. Perhaps because of this there is as yet little indication that this particular humanistic philosophy is to make a real mark on cultural geography. Rather, the major humanistic thrust has been toward phenomenology.

Phenomenology

> When we talk about the realms of nature and of man we often take these realms to refer to the domains of objects investigated by the two main groups of empirical sciences, natural and human science.... What if it were the case that, in separating man from nature, the empirical sciences are unable to comprehend an original and undivided context of subject matter, which consequently remains hidden? Because these sciences necessarily reduce nature and man to the domain of objects, this hidden subject matter cannot be brought out by attempts to unify the domains of objective physical and human science.... Something else is needed. Phenomenology seeks precisely to disclose the world as it shows itself *before* scientific inquiry, as that which is pregiven and presupposed by the sciences. (Pickles, 1985, p. 3)

According to John Pickles (1985, p. 6), the seminal papers introducing phenomenology into geography have distorted phenomenology, and hence, criticisms of the geographic phenomenology are not criticisms of phenomenology proper. These arguments are not pursued in detail here but they generate concern. The geographic interpretation, for example, sees phenomenology as individualistic and subjective whereas Pickles (1985, p. 72) argued that it can deal with phenomena at aggregate levels. A few brief comments on conventional geographic phenomenology follow.

Unlike idealism, phenomenology argues that there is not an objective world independent of human experience. The central concerns are with the individual-lived world of experience and with the understanding of meaning and value. Although developed as a study of individuals, phenomenology has been adapted to the social scale by Alfred Schutz (see Johnston, 1983b, pp. 61–62). The implications for cultural geography are varied. For Y. F. Tuan (1971), geography is the mirror of man and knowledge of the world is knowledge of oneself. Thus a major task becomes that of reconstructing individual worlds. At the social scale, the geographer can study landscape and thus be studying the society that created the landscape; the two are as one. This research theme is pursued in more detail in chapter 7.

Existentialism

''The boundary between existentialists and phenomenologists cannot be drawn precisely . . . existentialists concern themselves with the question of the nature of 'being' and understanding human existence'' (Entrikin, 1976, p. 621). The focus is on individuals and their relationship both with the world of things and the world of others. Thus, existentialism is opposed to positivism and idealism because of their separation of thoughts and actions. Indeed there is a shared interest with Marxism in the recognition that humans are estranged from the world. Samuels (1978, p. 35) saw existentialism as encompassing both humanistic and abstract geographic concerns. Like idealism, however, there is as yet limited evidence to suggest that this philosophy is emerging as central to geography.

Humanistic Cultural Geography

Necessarily, a discussion of humanistic concerns as though there were but one is misleading, but a discussion of any one philosophy as though there were one clear and accepted interpretation would also be misleading. Humanistic philosophies are now evaluated together because of their common concerns of subjectivity and individuals and their shared antipositivism.

Much of the stimulus behind the humanistic movement has been the antipositivist element. For the humanist, nature can be explained, but humans, social life, and individual behavior need to be understood. The scientific method of positivism is seen as inappropriate for human research because humans have intentions; this is the key principle of subjectivity. Any investigation in social science needs to allow for the fact that social phenomena are not entirely external to the researcher. Thus a *hermeneutic* tradition has developed, a tradition that aims to reveal expressions of the inner life of man by *verstehen*. Verstehen, or empathetic understanding, is associated with both Dilthey and Weber and is thus a key concept in idealism as well as in critical science.

Overall, most humanist approaches are focused on individuals, although some have argued for analyses of society within a phenomenological framework, such that ''man is the determining factor, and society, in all its complexity, is the dependent product of human interaction'' (P. Jackson & S. J. Smith, 1984, p. 9). One example of the reliance on individual analyses is the notion that people are able to exercise individual preferences within a choice framework, there being an implicit assumption that the level of the individual can permit understanding (Leonard, 1982). This view is no longer widespread in social geography with the recognition that individual actions are suject to many constraints, hence the emphasis on such factors as social gatekeepers and urban managers. The early characteristic emphasis on individuals can be criticized because of the danger that society be explained in terms of individual mental processes, a route known as psychological reductionism. Thus a central problem of humanistic philosophies is that of "building an effective bridge between individual cognition, perception, and behavior, on the one hand, and on appreciation of man's place in society, on the other" (P. Jackson & S. J. Smith, 1984, p. 21).

Early humanistic work in geography includes that of William Kirk (1951) and David Lowenthal (1961), but the explicit philosophical arguments emerged in the 1970s. These philosophical arguments envisaged a cultural and social geography centered on an intersubjective world of lived experience and shared meanings, and it is these goals that are evident in the major humanistic works. Ley (1977), for example, wrote of the "taken-for-granted" world of everyday experience; Tuan (1980) focused on worlds of experience; David Seamon (1979) advocated the concepts of place-ballets and time-space routines, which apply to repetitious situations; and Edward Relph (1976) distinguished place and placelessness, the former being an emotionally attractive location and the latter being a location where one feels alienated. For many critics, the major difficulty of most humanistic approaches is the explicit concern with individuals. A variety of solutions has been advocated.

Cosgrove (1978, p. 70) advocated dialectical reasoning: "Since it is society which creates places and landscapes, and it is through individual consciousness, itself in interaction with society, that we experience these places and landscapes, it is social experience and change in relationship to these phenomena with which we are mainly concerned." An alternative solution involved a combination of phenomenology and relativity concepts: cultural geographers should proceed by "determining the composition of the living agents' common understanding of the situation within which they act" (Hufferd, 1980, p. 20). By such means cultural landscapes could be understood. But the most substantive solutions proposed so far have involved a focus on the interaction of individuals.

An interactionist perspective is evident in much social theory and some social geography. The basic argument was well stated by J. S. Duncan (1978) and has proved to be a useful perspective for Ley (1983b) and P. Jackson and S. J. Smith (1984) in their empirical analyses. Developed within sociology, symbolic interactionism centers on the social construction of individual selves. "The self is largely a product of the opinions and actions of others as these are expressed in interaction with the developing self" (J. S. Duncan, 1978, p. 269). Thus, individuals are socialized but are not merely expressions of their society. Communication is the means by which individuals maintain a common life. It is interactions with others that make up social life and these interactions pass through a continuum from face-to-face contacts to fleeting contacts. Both social and spatial organizations are negotiated via communication; both are dynamic, responding to individual choices.

> Culture, in the sense of a system of shared meanings, is dynamic and negotiable, not fixed or immutable. Moreover the emergent qualities of culture often have a spatial character, not merely because proximity can encourage communication and

the sharing of individual life worlds, but also because, from an interactionist perspective, social groups may actively create a sense of place, investing the material environment with symbolic qualities such that the very fabric of landscape is permeated by, and caught up in, the active social world. (P. Jackson & Smith, 1984, p. 205)

Thus symbolic interactionism offers not only to resolve the possible problems of a bias on societies or individuals but also provide a clearer concept of culture than do the more explicitly humanistic perspectives previously discussed. One key distinction between this approach and more general sociological views is the rejection of behavior as being caused by society, rather behavior results from individuals as group members. Thus the approach can be interpreted as correcting both the Durkheimian overemphasis on society and the humanistic overemphasis on individuals. Whether or not it will prove to be a viable approach to a variety of cultural geographic research remains to be seen. One immediate concern for the cultural geographer is that research in this area typically involves taking the role of others; that is, being socialized into the groups being analyzed. This is problematic, especially where past situations or different cultures are of interest. There is a second and more important concern. There continues to be confusion about the nature of social theory, confusion centering on the distinction between social activity and social relationships (Ellen, 1988, p. 247). Geographers are increasingly turning to social theory, especially structuralism, as they seek to clarify this issue.

Humanistic interests in cultural geography are not easily evaluated, partly because of their internal diversity and partly because of the proliferation of program statements and the relative paucity of actual research. One major criticism, of variable application necessarily, is noted above and concerns skepticism as to the ability to see into the minds of others. It is quite possible to argue that any attempt of this sort is doomed to failure and that the interpretations made by the researcher are primarily determined by the research methodology. Potentially, this is a devastating criticism. For the positivist, a key failing is the related lack of any verification procedure. More generally, geographic processes are not really understood even by the participants (Renfrew, 1981, p. 273). These three related comments touch on a major possible downfall of explicitly subjective research.

This discussion of humanism has attempted to highlight the central ideas of the better-known philosophies and it is clear that, currently, no one approach is dominant. Indeed, much of the present debate centers on attempts to link what are essentially different philosophies, such as Marxism and humanism. The way ahead is unclear, but likely to be full of excitement and new ideas.

CULTURAL GEOGRAPHY TODAY: RESEARCH THEMES AND DIRECTIONS

This discussion of contemporary cultural geography has left much unsaid. Perhaps surprisingly, a number of important issues are not easily incorporated into the discussions centered on philosophies. Much current cultural geography remains aphilosophical, or at least idiosyncratic. Furthermore, recent advances in anthropology and human ecology impinge directly on cultural geography and have not yet been discussed. It is the purpose of this section to accommodate these various and varied advances and to provide an evaluation of contemporary cultural geography.

Culture

The discussion so far has not excluded the culture concept but has relegated it to a secondary role. Only two of the approaches identified have contributed directly to an understanding of culture, namely Marxism in its focus on groups not individuals and symbolic interactionism with its focus on changing culture and society. When this general failing is placed in the context of a pre–1970 cultural geography, which is already uncertain as to the meaning of culture, the confusion of today is evident. Unquestionably, there is not an "agreed-upon published text of the contemporary geographical concept of culture"; one suggested concept incorporates both discrete societies and systems and classes and is acknowledged to be dynamic (J. E. Spencer, 1978, p. 81). There are, however, two major developments in anthropology that are of relevance. The first relates to the already noted symbolic focus; the second returns to the concept of minding noted in chapter 2. The first rejects the notion of culture as an independent variable whereas the second emphasizes that notion, and yet the two correspond on a number of key issues.

One interpretive theorist in anthropology has attempted to achieve a redefinition of culture because of dissatisfaction with the initial Tylor and later anthropological usage. Clifford Geertz (1965, p. 103) argued that the culture concept developed in reaction to the earlier Enlightenment view of human nature as regularly organized and criticized the search for cultural universals evident in the work of Clark Wissler, Bronislaw Malinowski, and others as being "crystallized responses . . . institutionalized ways of coming to terms" with reality. For Geertz, culture was most correctly interpreted not as complexes of concrete behavior patterns but rather as some set of control mechanisms for the governing of behavior. The view of culture elaborated by Geertz (1973) is in close accord with the symbolic interactionist view in sociology. For both views, human thought is taken to be social and public while thinking itself consists of significant symbols. Culture thus becomes the accumulated totality of organized systems of significant symbols. In geography, this view of culture was explicitly advocated by Miles Richardson (1981) and termed intersubjective reality. The key concerns are on the process of symboling and communication because all human interaction is via symboling. Objects do not have a fixed meaning, rather their meaning develops out of people's response to them. Thus, culture is dynamic and human behavior results from communication. Similar beliefs and similar patterns of behavior result from the fact that people share similar orientations to environment. To understand human behavior, it becomes essential to know the group with which an individual is identifying in the context of the particular behavior. The identity of each human is rooted in other people, situations, and places and thus, is liable to frequent modifications.

At first sight, the views of Leslie White (1959, 1975) are not closely related to those of Geertz, and the symbolic interactionists, such as White, are often regarded as proponents of culture as a determinant, while Geertz and the symbolic interactionists are seen as arguing against culture as an independent variable. But, "White begins at a point not far from Geertz"(Richardson, 1981, p. 285) in that culture, which is dependent on symboling, exists within social interaction processes. It is appropriate, then, to return to the work of White for further clarification. The superorganic concept, with which White has been closely associated, began with Herbert Spencer and was especially detailed by Kroeber. Spencer (Hudson, 1908) argued that all social development is toward a state of moving equilibrium; thus, society is dynamic, involving a gradual shaping of individuals. Kroeber (1917) modified the superorganic to be essentially a view opposing racism and environmentalism. Subsequently, White (1959) argued for minding as the route to understanding culture with minding being the reaction to a thing via interaction. Type IV minding is symboling, that is the giving of meanings to things, and culture arises from this minding. In these terms, it can be seen that culture changes and is based on interaction and symboling. Clearly, White and Geertz are not too far removed for there are basic similarities in their formulations that are not lost by the greater emphasis that White placed on culture as a causal variable. Indeed, the essential similarities between White and Geertz are sufficiently evident to allow the suggestion that herein lies a useful concept of culture for the cultural geographer, the anthropologist, and the sociologist. Richardson (1981, p. 287) is correct to assert that culture can be seen as "intersubjective, symbolic communication" and need not necessarily lead to culture becoming a causal variable.

The terminology developed by White (1975, pp. 3–4) merits emphasis here. The class of things and events that are dependent on symboling are called symbolates; symbolates considered in terms of their relationship to the human organism are behavior and are the realm of psychology; symbolates considered in terms of their relationship to one another are called culture and are the realm of culturology. Referring to Kroeber, Lowie, and Durkheim, White (1975, p. 6) reasserted the autonomy of culture and thus "its logical independence of its human carriers." Clearly, the insistence on culture as cause is at variance with other concepts, but general similarities are apparent regarding the relevance of symboling and the dynamic quality of culture.

Cultural and Environmental Determinism

Views that argue for particular cause-and-effect relationships remain attractive to many scholars (Earman, 1986). The discussion of White in the preceding section is influential in some cultural geography (Gritzner, 1966; Zelinksy, 1973). Even environmental causes, which were generally discredited some years ago, remain a potent argument. Several well-accepted studies have focused on the role played by environmental change. Martin Parry (1978) related climatic change and agriculture in historical times and Reid Bryson and Thomas Murray (1977) argued that drought caused major human abandonments in areas as diverse as Mycenae in 1200 B.C. and the American Midwest between A.D. 1200 and 1400. In a stimulating review of such work Michael Chisholm (1978) asserted that climatic change can be a factor in explaining some aspects of both historical and contemporary events. The conclusion is that geographers cannot avoid consideration of the physical environment. "Processes, of whatever kind, have an impact on the surface of the earth and the disposition of human activities" (Chisholm, 1978, p. 121). Interestingly, Clifford Darby (1983, p. 427) noted that much of the works of the Vidal school revolved around the facts of physical geography.

Both culture and the physical environment have a role to play in contemporary geography, with the specifics of a problem being likely to suggest the appropriate research direction. Neither White nor most cultural geographers are determinists, and similarly, environmental emphases do not imply monocausal explanations. Overall, most current human geography downplays physical factors, and the discipline continues to be characterized by an increasing divergence of physical and human analyses. The focus on humans as agents of change and on economic rather than environmental constraints leads to human and land relationships being viewed "not as interdependent or as complementary, but rather as economic confrontations" (Marchand, 1982, p. 72). In current cultural and social geography, three concepts are possible: first, the view that the land is unimportant or irrelevant, as in the works of Marx and John Maynard Keynes; second, the view that the land is a frame, following Vidal; third, the view that there is an interaction between land and socioeconomic space. This third concept distinguishes between static and dynamic environments and is comparable to the views expressed by John Chappell (1980) concerning the overemphasis placed on cultural determinism and the corresponding downplaying of land. One area that continues to stress human and land concerns is that of human ecology, although even here one current trend is toward increased social input.

Human Ecology

A recurring theme in these first four chapters has been the question of humans and nature, are humans a part of nature or apart from it? The ecological consensus for some time has been one of individuals in society as one part of a complex ecological system. Such a focus is clearly out of accord with current social theory, which relegates the environment to a minor role or even eliminates it altogether. Geographers have moved toward group analyses and consideration of decision-making institutions. Richard Chorley (1973, p. 167) wrote that "social man is, for better or worse, seizing control of his terrestrial environment and any geographical methodology which does not acknowledge this fact is doomed to inbuilt obsolescence.''

Perhaps the most ambitious attempt to move human ecology in such a direction is the work of Gordon Ericksen (1980), which argued that the central concern of human ecology quite simply misrepresents what is taking place in society. For Ericksen (1980), it was not appropriate to merely employ the ecological process of plant and animal communities to the human scenario, because of the necessary implications of humans as passive beings. Conventional human ecology does not allow for a correct interpretation of group life, because it is the ecological process itself that is allowed to be dominant rather than the ideas and feelings of the humans. Humans influence the ecological process; they lead rather than follow. An appropriate human ecology needs to view the ecological process via the social life of the group and not to view social life of the group as following from the ecological process. The preferred emphasis for Ericksen (1980) is that of symbolic interactionism whereby, as already noted, humans engage in interaction such that locations and institutions result from people defining and giving meaning to places. It follows, then, that humans react to places according to their assigned meanings. This proposed human ecology requires that research focus on the processes by which locations are defined, that is on the interactions themselves. This view certainly goes a long way toward satisfying Chorley's (1973) requirement that human ecology became explicitly social and is also in close conceptual accord with the definition of culture emanating from Geertz and White. It is interesting to note that many of the examples employed by Ericksen (1980), a sociologist, are of geographic work, such as that by Harvey (1975).

Such views, which demand a transformation of human ecology, represent a distinctive but still a minority viewpoint. For Arild Holt-Jensen (1982, p. 126) traditional views continue to have a key role to play although ''an understanding of the research methods of psychology and sociology'' was deemed desirable. In a similar vein, James Clarkson (1970) detailed the ecological perspective in both anthropology and geography largely from a conventional perspective, and Philip Porter (1978) saw human ecology as one way of bringing together natural science geography and social science geography.

A process-oriented ecology has been advocated by William Denevan (1983, p. 401), with cultural adaptation being ''the *process of change* in response to a change in the physical environment or a change in internal stimuli, such as demography, economics and organizations.'' Rather differently, Linda Newson (1976) focused on evolution, not adaptation, and argued for applications of the Law of Cultural Dominance, which states ''that the cultural system which most effectively exploits the energy resources of a given environment will tend to spread in that environment at the expense of less effective systems'' (cited in Newson, 1976, p. 251).

CONCLUDING COMMENTS

It is hardly necessary to state that, despite its persistence, cultural geography remains difficult to define and delimit. A principal reason for this state of affairs relates to the generally inadequate conceptions of culture and a secondary reason relates to an overly broad view of cultural geography (Norton, 1984b). Only recently have attempts been made to define culture more carefully and, hence, to restrict the range of interest. Conventional definitions have focused on way of life, or genre de vie. This is at once too broad and too narrow—too broad in that it allows discussion of all human geography and too narrow in that it appears to have restricted interest in material culture. This concept originated in anthropology and sociology but has received a strong regional interpretation by geographers. In their introductory textbook, Joseph Spencer and William Thomas (1973, p. 6) offered the following statement regarding culture. "Culture is the sum total of human learned behavior and ways of doing things. Culture is invented, carried on, and slowly modified by people living and working in groups as each group occupies a particular region of the earth and develops its own special and distinctive system of culture." Terry Jordan and Lester Rowntree (1986, p. 4) offered a shorter definition: culture is "a total way of life held in common by a group of people." These are only two definitions among many available but both are close to Tylor's original definition of culture.

Relevant research themes were detailed in the introduction to a pioneering book of readings edited by Philip Wagner and Marvin Mikesell (1962) as culture, culture area, culture history, cultural landscape, and cultural ecology. These five themes were revised by Wagner (1975, p. 11) in a brief, but forceful, manner: "The fact is that culture has to be seen as carried in specific, located, purposeful, rule-following, and rule-making groupings of people communicating and interacting with one another." This statement about culture anticipates the interactionist definition with the focus on the individual as a group member and on behavior as meaningful activity. Wagner (1975, p. 12) also extended his earlier work with a new emphasis on institutions, a logical corollary to the above statement about culture: "Most of the human behavior of interest to geography is institutionally motivated and managed. Much of the meaning we attach to human activity derives its significance as behavior from its institutional context." These ideas also summarize a provocative book by Wagner (1972), of which the twofold message is "an assertion of the importance of communication in the creation and maintenance of culture areas and the value of symbolic as well as functional interpretations of cultural artifacts" (Mikesell, 1977, p. 461).

As part of their definition of culture, Jordan and Rowntree (1986) suggested five themes as follows: cultural region, cultural diffusion, cultural ecology, cultural integration, and cultural landscape. These five were used as a generally successful framework for the diverse contents of their book. A quite different approach was taken by J. E. Spencer and Thomas (1973, pp. 21–22) who preferred not to identify themes, but rather to recognize four conceptual entities and six operative interrelationships. The conceptual entities were population, physical biotic environment, social organizations, and technologies. The operative interrelationships were those involving population and environment, population and social organization, population and technology, organization and technology, environment and organization, and environment and technology. These ideas are much more process-oriented than most work in cultural geography. In a later piece, J. E. Spencer (1978) placed much emphasis on process and the role of organizations in a manner comparable to that of Wagner (1972, 1975). Mikesell (1978) appraised cultural geography somewhat differently, emphasizing perception, cultural ecology, and a renewed focus on North America (see Noble, 1982). Detailed differences aside, it is evident that mainstream cultural geography is moving toward more rigorous definitions of culture and toward closer links with sociology and social anthropology.

It is this research orientation that in a variety of different ways, is coming to the fore in contemporary work. This chapter has drawn attention to the work of symbolic interactionism in sociology, to the work of such anthropologists as Geertz and White, to the pioneering statements by Wagner (1972, 1975), to the contributions of Duncan (1980) and Richardson (1981), and to the social geography of Ley (1983b) and P. Jackson and S. J. Smith (1984). Taken together, these offer a combination of ideas emphasizing the relevance of communication, symbolism, and individuals as group members. One major effort to transfer these ideas to an explicit empirical issue was an analysis of the preservation movement in Salzburg, Austria, since 1860. ''The cultural landscape in part functions as a narrative, a symbolic legacy conveying, if not realizing, information from one generation to another, information about subsistence ways, cosmology, territory or historical position'' (Rowntree & Conkey, 1980, p. 461). With this idea, it was possible to emphasize that social identity is realized by the landscape; in particular that symbolization in response to stress leads to cultural landscape transformation. It is also interesting to note that the concern here is once again the material landscape.

The concern with human and land relations needs to be summarized at this stage and this is attempted in Tables 1 and 2. These two tables actually serve as partial summaries of much of the content of chapters 2, 3, and 4. Table 1 focuses on the evolution of concepts relating to humans and land and, although necessarily simplified, includes the basic themes of cultural determinism, social determinism, environmental determinism, humans and land in close harmony, and the concern with individuals in groups. Cultural determinism is noted as the key anthropological concept, but it is stressed that much of the content of this loosely knit school was much more flexible than the cultural determinist label might suggest. A similar reservation is in order for social determinism. The environmentalist theme was proposed circa 1900 as the basis for the discipline of geography but quickly lost credibility, and it might be argued that the delay in introducing positivism to geography was a direct result of the early extremes

Table 1

Humans and Land: Evolution of Concepts

	Basic comments	Nineteenth century	1900 to 1980	Contemporary status
A. Culture as causal variable	Dualistic. Culture seen as above nature and above individual. Basic concept in anthropology. Reification of culture.	Culture formally defined by Tylor. Key concept in diffusionist emphasis initiated by Boas. Close links with B.	Superorganic concept becomes dominant in anthropology. Kroeber, Lowie, Wissler and White. Cultural ecology essentially superorganic. This view often modified in practice to be comparable to possibilism (D).	Remains key concept in anthropology. Type IV minding of White sees culture as dependent on interaction (focus also on symbols - as in E).
B. Society as causal variable	Dualistic. Social phenomena seen as explicable in terms of other social phenomena. Basic concept in sociology of Durkheim. Reification of society.	This view initiated and diffused by Comte and Spencer. Social Darwinism. Close links with A.	Social organism concept of Durkheim becomes dominant in sociology. Functionalism of Radcliffe-Brown.	Remains a key concept in sociology.
C. Land as causal variable	Dualistic. Physical environment seen as cause of culture and of cultural landscape. Basic to geography circa 1900. Long history; Greeks, Bodin, Montesquieu.	Implicit in much early anthropology and sociology, especially racist and evolutionist phases. Became basis for geography with Ratzel vol. 1. Prompted by positivism and Darwinian thought.	Semple and Huntington best known advocates. Also implicit in much regional geography. Did not prove to be a basis for a viable discipline, unlike A and B. Stop and go determinism and probabilism seen as variants but closer to possibilism (D).	Largely irrelevant in contemporary work. But renewed interest in climatic change and human history.
D. Humans and land in close relationship	Emphasis on unity of humans and land. Basis for cultural geography but never dominant in discipline of geography.	Darwin linked social and natural. Marxian view - therefore opposed to most anthropology and sociology (A and B). Key geographic emphasis of Humboldt, Ritter, Marsh, Réclus, Schouw, Kropotkin.	Possibilism of Vidal, Febvre. Landschaft of Schlüter. Landscape school of Sauer. Human ecology of Barrows. Possibly sequent occupance of Whittlesey.	Sociobiology. Human ecology. Contemporary humanistic focus in geography emphasizes individuals. Traditional cultural geography.
E. Focus on individuals in groups (cultures or societies)	Opposing sociological emphasis to B. Emphasis on individuals as members of groups not on group itself.		Symbolic interactionism of Mead. Geertz view of culture. Weberian sociology.	Basis for new human ecology of Ericksen. Basis for much current social geography. Focus on communication. Wagner in cultural geography.

involved in environmentalist cause-and-effect logic. Cultural geography itself developed largely within the fourth theme, which has been traced back particularly to late nineteenth-century European geography and which includes the landscape school associated with Sauer. The final theme noted introduces some current concerns, in both cultural and social geography, on interaction and symbolism.

Table 2 focuses on geographic emphases identifying four stages. In the nineteenth century, there was a clear, but by no means unanimous, interest in unity and evolution. Unfortunately for geography, this interest became one of many as geography was institutionalized, and Stage II, circa 1900, was characterized by divergent views. The period from 1920 to 1970 was dominated by, first, regional geography that continued the environmentalist concern and second, a spatial analysis that largely excluded humans as members of society. The final stage, from 1970 onward, is optimistically labeled "reconciliation?" and includes a renewed concern with unity, the emergence of radical and humanistic interests, and an increasing focus on groups.

It is appropriate now to refer back to the views of Humboldt, Vidal, and Sauer in order to stress that current work is, not surprisingly, best seen as a continuation of well-established traditions rather than as a set of revolutionary ideas. Humboldt stressed the intimate links between humans and land and the inseparability of history and geography, Vidal argued for analyses of relationships, and Sauer stressed the evolution of cultural landscapes. These interests remain central to cultural and social geography. Contemporary concerns remain with landscape and evolution but with the addition of more explicitly process-oriented themes. The variables affecting landscape are those related to interactions between group members and to the process of symbolizing. Hence, the reference in chapter 1 to both landscape and variables. Contemporary work flows from a sound, if occasionally neglected, geographic tradition and benefits from new ideas in sociology and social anthropology. Benefits are also derived from the realization that differing methodologies can each contribute to research positively rather than in an opposing manner. Both radical and humanistic interests, for example, have emphasized their links to traditional schools, and the differences in approach tend to be those of emphasis, not kind. Because of the current tendency to promote many different methodologies, it can appear that there are real differences of opinion, but this is not entirely correct for the diversity of views is unable to disguise the centrality of interest in processes and landscapes. There is a continued interest in landscapes and a growing recognition that individuals as members of groups are the appropriate scale of analysis.

The remainder of this book attempts a synthesis of selected cultural geographic research within the context already detailed. Chapters 5, 6, 7, and 8 are concerned with understanding landscape. Chapter 5 is centered on the realization that there is a basic distinction between real and perceived environments and that it is the latter that are of concern. It is not argued that human behavior results from environmental perception, rather that perception is one factor and not the sole

Table 2
Humans and Land: Geographic Emphases

Stage I - c19th	Stage II - circa 1900	Stage III - 1920 to 1970	Stage IV - 1970 to present
Emphasis on unity of humans and nature.	Divergent views.	Appraisal of views.	Reconciliation?
Humboldt Ritter Marsh Réclus Schouw Kropotkin	Ratzel (Vol. 1) - environmentalism. Vidal, Schlüter, Sauer - versions of possibilism, focus on unity and time. Barrows - human ecology.	Chorological view dominant. Decline of environmentalism. Continued focus on unity. Stop and go determinism and probabilism. Annales school.	Unity emphasised. Rejection of various determinisms. Emergence of humanistic views (idealism, phenomenology, existentialism).
Includes focus on time.	Sequent occupance - Whittlesey. Physical geography as basis of geography.	Rise of spatial analysis avoided focus on humans and land; perception largely within spatial analytic paradigm; general omission of time.	Radical thrusts. Increasing focus on individuals in groups; Wagner. Time emphasized.

cause. Psychological arguments and substantive geographic examples are included. Chapter 6 considers the evolution of landscape including such topics as innovation diffusion, visible landscape creation, contact, and transfer. Chapter 7 considers symbolism and social processes, and a principal focus is on work in urban social geography. Chapter 8 considers ecological processes and related cultural universals, cultural traits, and the value of case studies. The final discussion in chapter 9 is both retrospect and prospect.

5

Understanding Landscape: Behavioral Approaches

The preceding four chapters introduced a diverse body of materials with the major concern being the elucidation of methodological issues. This chapter and the three that follow serve the rather different purpose of introducing material that is representative of that produced by twentieth-century cultural and social geographers. Chapters 5–8 are both conceptual and empirical in character and, where appropriate, material from other disciplines is detailed. An understanding of the geographic literature is clearly enhanced by such interdisciplinary excursions, as the earlier chapters have strongly argued. Two overriding themes are evident throughout chapters 5–8, although they are rarely clearly distinguished; these are the overlapping and interrelated themes of human and land relations and of landscape evolution. No formal attempt is made to define these terms for, as previously argued, such definitions are difficult, necessarily questionable, serve the effect of limiting content, and are of dubious value. This chapter and the three that follow are concerned with an understanding of landscape, and the chapter differentiation is based on a particular methodological thrust. In this chapter, the focus is on behavioral approaches that, despite a long history in the geographic tradition, have only come to the fore since circa 1960 and remain in a state of conceptual turmoil. The discussion relies heavily, at times, on literature from psychology. The specific aims are those of indicating past and current research activities, identifying inadequacies, and erecting signposts to future work.

Writing in the late 1970s, Marvin Mikesell (1978, p. 6) noted that, for cultural geographers, the "recent development of greatest potential interest has been the proliferation of work on environmental perception." The essential logic of behavioral work is certainly most attractive to the cultural geographer with emphasis on subjectivity and cultural appraisals.

CONCEPTUAL BACKGROUND IN GEOGRAPHY
BEFORE 1960

Throughout the extended period from mid-nineteenth century to circa 1960 geographers occasionally acknowleged the importance of behavior and related issues but achieved few theoretical or empirical advances. It is perhaps surprising that more substantial work was not accomplished prior to the 1960s given the assertion by Alexander von Humboldt in 1850 that "in order to comprehend nature in all its vast sublimity, it would be necessary to present it under a twofold aspect, first objectively, as an actual phenomenon, and next subjectively, as it is reflected in the feelings of mankind" (cited in Saarinen, 1974, pp. 255–256). But, like so many of the nineteenth-century conceptual advances, the basic statement was not further developed. Rather, as already detailed, geographers focused their attention on environmentalism and regions. The suggestion that there were both objective and subjective worlds was not to be incorporated into mainstream geographic thought although it was certainly implicit in the works of, for example, both Sauer and Vidal. Indeed, Humboldt himself went much further than merely advocating such an approach. Humboldt effectively stimulated an aesthetic tradition in geography and, furthermore, was responsible for the emergence of a distinct American form of landscape painting. These emerged from the ability of Humboldt to combine "artistic intuition with scientific observations" (Bunkse, 1981, p. 133). For example,

> in the uniform plain bounded only by a distant horizon, where the lowly heather, the cistus, or waving grasses, deck the soil; on the ocean shore, where the waves, softly rippling over the beach, leave a track, green with the weeds of the sea; everywhere, the mind is penetrated by the same sense of the grandeur and vast expanse of nature, revealing to the soul, by a mysterious inspiration, the existence of laws that regulate the forces of the universe. (Humboldt, cited in Bunkse, 1981, p. 138).

Both Sauer and Vidal also demonstrated the ability to incorporate a strong visual emphasis in their observations and descriptions. A quote from Sauer suffices here.

> Looking back from the ease of the present, these older days may seem to have been a time of lonely and hard isolation. It was only toward the end of the period that the telephone and rural delivery were added. The prairie lacked wet-weather roads. In the hill sections, ridge roads might be passable at most times; on the plains, winter was likely to be the season of easiest travel, spring that of immobilization by mud. The country doctor was expected to, and did, rise above any emergency of weather. Life was so arranged that one did not need to go to town at any particular time. When the weather was bad the activities of the family took place indoors or about the farmyard. (Sauer, 1962, p. 6).

The possibilist school in general argued that the environment offered many alternative activities. Nevertheless the subjective-objective dichotomy did not become a focal point of substantive research. Prior to the 1960s there were two further contributions in this area but neither created a real impact. The first, by John K. Wright (1947), was not successfully related to other geographic literature and did not adequately signpost future research directions. The second, by William Kirk (1951), was published in a relatively inaccessible journal and was not generally known until the 1960s.

Wright (1947, p. 5) included a distinction between the subjective and the objective:

> Objectivity . . . is a mental disposition to conceive of things realistically. . . . The opposite of objectivity would, then, be a predisposition to conceive of things unrealistically; but, clearly, this is not an adequate definition of subjectivity. As generally understood, subjectivity implies, rather, a mental disposition to conceive of things with reference to oneself. . . . While such a disposition often does, in fact, lead to error, illusion, or deliberate deception, it is entirely possible to conceive of things not only with reference to oneself but also realistically.

In this sense, a subjective view of the world may range anywhere along a continuum from complete error to complete accord with reality. This idea was further developed and proposed as ''geosophy,'' a discipline centering on both true and false geographical ideas. Unfortunately, Wright (1947) did not relate these ideas to other disciplines, such as psychology, and did not himself pursue the concepts with substantive empirical works. Seeds were sown but not harvested.

A more explicit attempt to incorporate behavior into geographic analyses was that by Kirk (1951, 1963). A distinction was made between the world of facts, physical and human, and the environment in which these facts were culturally structured and acquired cultural values. The former was named the phenomenal environment and the latter the behavioral environment. This distinction is essentially equivalent to that made by Gestalt psychologists, but Kirk (1963) also included the notion that human behavior in the behavioral environment was rational. Neither of these two characteristics was to become central to later perception research.

The conceptual background discussed so far has noted three quite separate contributions: that by a variety of cultural geographers, from Humboldt onward and including both Vidal and Sauer; that by Wright; and that by Kirk. These three do not indicate a continuous development of ideas and did not generate explicit behavior-oriented research. They are essentially three separate contributions. The cultural tradition is part of a much larger conceptual scheme and behavior was not brought to the fore, while the other two focused on behavior but failed to generate either schools of thought or empirical work. This failure by geographers was despite some major developments in other disciplines, no-

tably psychology, but is perhaps quite understandable given the academic isolation of the discipline prior to the 1960s. The discipline to which cultural
geography was undoubtedly closest, anthropology, did not succeed in developing
a set of concepts that could be exploited by others. Developments in psychology
are now discussed followed by an account of geographic developments from the
1960s to the present.

RELATED DEVELOPMENTS IN PSYCHOLOGY

This discussion is important for two reasons, one being the need to appreciate
the sophisticated, albeit varied, psychological emphases per se, and the other
being the need to understand later geographic interests in the light of relevant
psychological underpinnings. Necessarily it is not possible to do full justice to
the diversity of psychological research if only because, in a broad sense, psychology is the study of behavior. Fortunately, the major schools are readily
identifiable and those to which geographers have turned for inspiration are rather
few. What follows, then, is a discussion of views rooted in positivism, a philosophy that appealed to geographers in the 1960s, and in humanistic traditions,
traditions more appealing to geographers in the 1970s. Indeed, it is somewhat
ironic that the first flowering of geographic behavioral research was positivist-
ically oriented given the pre–1960s statements and given the availability of
nonpositivistic ideas. The fact that perception work emerged as a part of the
spatial analytic tradition says much for the strength of that tradition and for the
research ideas promulgated.

The discipline of psychology comprises a great many general theories of
behavior and other, more specific, theories concerned with such issues as perception, rote memory, and discrimination. This discussion is essentially limited
to the general theories, theories that usually have to tackle a series of difficult
issues as follows.

Is it appropriate to regard human behavior as possessing purposive or teleological qualities? Some theories view goal striving and purpose as integral components of individual behavior; other theories see these factors as of marginal
relevance and argue they accompany behavior but are not the causes. Another
debate refers to the relative importance of conscious determinants of which the
individual is aware and unconscious determinants of which the individual is
unaware. Theorists also debate the importance of reward and pleasure as causes
with some arguing for cause and effect, others for association. Other issues
include the importance of learning to behavior, the question of individual uniqueness, the relatedness of acts of behavior, and the degree of relationship between
behavioral acts and environmental contexts. All of these are complex, unresolved
issues that have been largely ignored by behavioral geographers who have been
most attracted to those physchological concepts that are centered on the importance of the psychological environment, the subjective frame of reference. The
value of such concepts for the geographer is clear given the available geographic

Figure 2
The Lewin Field Concept

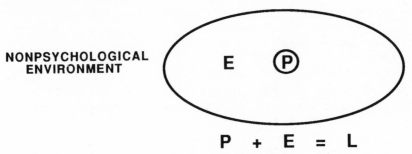

NONPSYCHOLOGICAL
ENVIRONMENT

E Ⓟ

P + E = L

ideas. Focusing on subjective environments involves emphasizing that the physical world can only affect individuals in so far as it is perceived or experienced. Objective reality is thus not a cause of behavior, rather it is objective reality as perceived by or assigned meaning by the individual. A contrary emphasis largely ignores individual differences arguing that sound theory cannot be based on subjective reports and inferential logic. Interestingly, the focus in the subjective environment did not result in geographers associating themselves with one particular theory, rather a number of very different theories were available as stimuli.

The psychological theory to which behaviorally oriented geographers were first attracted was the general movement known as Gestalt psychology. This movement has strong positivistic overtones, which proved of interest to 1960s geography. The first explicit use of Gestalt ideas was by Kirk (1963, p. 365) who asserted that the environment has "shape, cohesiveness and meaning added to it by the act of human perception." Implicit in this idea was the existence of both individually perceived worlds and group views. Subsequent behavioral work favored one particular Gestalt view, the field theory of Kurt Lewin. This theory is an application of field concepts evolved in physics, or more correctly an application of the methods rather than the physical concepts and facts. The theory possesses three crucial characteristics that rendered it of interest to behavioral geographers, in addition to the positivistic emphasis. These are the high emphases placed on the subjective environment and on group membership determinants and the recognition of a nonpsychological environment.

For Lewin (1951), behavior is a function of the field that exists at the time the behavior occurs. This field may be diagrammed as seen in Figure 2. As Figure 2 indicates the person *(P)* is within a psychological environment *(E)* and the sum of the person and the psychological environment is defined as the life space *(L)*. Beyond *E* is the nonpsychological environment comprising both physical and social facts. The importance of *L* is that it contains all facts that directly influence individual behavior, thus behavior is a function of the life space. But Lewin proceeds further. Facts that lie outside of *E* can also influence behavior in that such facts influence *E*, that is, physical and social facts are able to indirectly influence psychological facts. Lewin (1951) argued for "psychological ecology" as the study of the physical and social facts that influence psychological facts. In addition, Lewin (1951) saw the psychological world as influencing the social and physical world. Thus, a two-way interaction is proposed. A similar two-way interaction applies between *P* and *E*. Thus both boundaries in Figure 2 are permeable.

It is from this work that "ecological psychology" developed (Barker, 1968) or, more typically, "environmental psychology" (Ittelson et al., 1974). This interest emphasizes the physical environment external to the individual as a cause of behavior.

1. The environment is experienced as a unitary field.

2. Man is an integral part of the environment rather than an object in it.

3. All physical environments are inescapably linked to social systems.

4. The influence of the environment on individuals varies with the behavior in question.

5. The environment often operates below the level of awareness.

6. There may be significant differences between the "observed" and "real" environments.

7. Environments can be cognized as a set of mental images.

8. Environments have symbolic value.

The appeal of such ideas to geographers is evident with the focus on human and land unity, the relevance of society, the perceived environment, and the symbolism attached to environments. There is little doubt that these characteristics are relevant to geographic analyses regardless of scale, although work in environmental psychology would typically qualify as microgeography. Although environmental psychology and behavioral geography share research interests and techniques, there is little evidence of genuine integration (Gold & Goodey, 1983). It is possible that this lack of integration results particularly from the presence of distinctly different parent disciplines (C. Spencer & M. Blades, 1986).

This discussion of relevant ideas in psychology began with the assertion that geographers were attracted first to ideas with positivistic overtones and second to ideas with humanistic content. The initial flowering of behavioral geography occurred during the heyday of spatial analysis and, not surprisingly, borrowed from Gestalt ideas, especially those of field theory. These have since evolved into environmental psychology, which similarly proves most attractive to geographers. The humanistic interest in psychology that permeated geography largely during the 1970s was of interest for essentially the same reason that made field theory and its outgrowths of interest, namely the emphasis placed on the subjective environment. Major differences are that humanistic interests were little concerned with group membership causes and focused on understanding rather than cause-and-effect explanation.

Perhaps the most effective way of introducing this second input from psychology is to comment on existential psychology. Although the existentialist movement has nineteenth-century philosophical and literary origins, the movement flowered in the mid-twentieth century. The philosopher Martin Heidegger is typically seen as a key link between the original philosophy and later social science developments. Heidegger is also labeled a phenomenologist. An important tenet of existential philosophy is that each individual is a being-in-the-world whereas phenomenology centers on descriptions of the data of immediate experience. Interestingly, both Gestalt and existential psychology have employed the phenomenological method.

What are the basic ideas of an existential psychology and why have these ideas proved attractive to behavioral geographers of the 1970s? For the existentialist, attention is on motivation as the means of understanding behavior; causality is not considered. Furthermore, the existentialist "stands for the unity of the individual-in-the-world" (Hall & Lindzey, 1978, p. 318). Necessarily, the existentialist opposes any dehumanization of humans, a view that makes the approach consistent with humanistic ideas in general.

Thus the basic idea of an existentialist emphasis is that being-in-the-world is in itself human existence. This idea emphasizes the unity of humans and the world. Three regions are proposed (Hall & Lindzey, 1978, p. 321).

1. The biological or physical surroundings on landscape (*Umwelt*).

2. The human environment (*Mitwelt*).

3. The person him or her self including the body (*Eigenwelt*).

The appeal of such ideas for 1970s' geographers is apparent given the disillusionment with positivism and the perceived need to focus on place and not space. These ideas are discussed by Walmsley and G. J. Lewis (1984, pp. 157–158) under the three philosophical headings of phenomenology, existentialism, and idealism. In the present context, the first two are not really separated, with existentialism using the phenomenological method, and idealism is not seen as sufficiently influential to be considered.

This section has centered on two areas of psychological work that have permeated behavioral geography. Despite some similarity, the two are almost diametrically opposed in their basic philosophical orientation. The next section discusses the geographic concepts that evolved in response to these inputs from psychology as well as to developments in geography.

PERCEPTION, BEHAVIOR, AND LANDSCAPE

The emergence of a behavioral geography was initially focused on the centrality of perception. Basic distinctions were made between real and perceived environments and the notion of "images" emerged. Geographers were frequently encouraged to turn to Kenneth Boulding (1956) for conceptual content and to Kevin Lynch (1960) for empirical examples. Increasing awareness of the psychological literature introduced the more general idea of cognition, a term that groups together a variety of mental processes such as perceiving, recognizing, conceiving, judging, and reasoning. Cognition refers to how experiences are structured, how people make sense of experiences, and how environmental stimuli are transformed into usable information. The cognitive psychologist sees humans as aware and actively interpreting. John Gold (1980, p. 20) observed that "cognition is regarded as a wider term that *intera alia,* includes perception." This is an important distinction emphasizing that the two ought not to be used interchangeably. Awareness of the psychological literature also encouraged the development of "often mutually antagonistic" positivist and humanist foci (Goodey & Gold, 1985, p. 585). The presence of two such opposed views has, perhaps, been a contributing cause of the failure of behavioral geography to fulfill ambitious initial aims and the partial failure to respond to critics.

Several geographers writing in the 1960s anticipated that a behavioral approach would prove to be a panacea for the ills of the discipline (Burton, 1963; Brookfield, 1969). This has clearly not been the case, and one reason cited is a too close correspondence between spatial analysis and behavioralist work (Cullen, 1976; Bunting & Guelke, 1979). A second reason relates to the characteristic neglect of evolutionary content, despite some notable work on images by historical geographers. Most persuasively, a third reason refers to the failure of behavioral work to acknowledge that all behavior occurs in some given social context. Walmsley and G. J. Lewis (1984, p. 13) suggested that

> what geographers need is a geographical imagination paralleling sociological imagination . . . to enable them to take account of the individual's recognition of the role of space and place in his own biography and of the way in which transactions between individuals and between organizations are affected by the space that separates them.

This general theme is contained within the current chapter but is more fully exploited in chapter 7 where the focus is on social processes and symbolic landscapes.

Given the diverse geographic and other background to behavioral work, it is understandable that behaviorally oriented analyses cover a wide range of topics and utilize varying conceptual frameworks and methods of analysis. Much behavioral work does not qualify as cultural in character, and the remainder of this section selects a sample of behavioral work that is either clearly cultural in character or appears to have potential for cultural geographic applications.

Images and Mental Maps

The basic implication here is that "people do not respond directly to the environment but to their mental image of the environment, and, as a result, the location of human activities is very much influenced by geographical images and mental maps'' (Haynes, 1980, p. 2). In a similar fashion, Roger Downs and David Stea (1973, p. xiv) noted that ''cognitive mapping is a construct which encompasses those cognitive processes which enable people to acquire, code, store, recall, and manipulate information about the nature of their spatial environment.'' Much research in the 1960s and 1970s centered on these basic assertions following the pioneering work of Lynch (1960). As a result of querying residents about landmarks, routes, and areas in Boston, Jersey City, and Los Angeles, Lynch (1960) succeeded in creating city images. The resulting maps appear to represent an abstraction that describes how cities are viewed. In a related fashion, David Ley (1974) mapped a perceived environmental stress surface in Philadelphia. Valuable as such work is, it does nevertheless raise serious issues. Is it really the case that people represent their environments as maps? However plausible this may sound, the answer is far from clear. Evidence from psychology is contradictory, with descriptions of human spatial memory as both propositional and analogical in form. The former implies that place knowledge is stored in lists and the latter implies that the storing is directly comparable to the depicted objects. A review of these ideas is presented by John Darley and Daniel Gilbert (1985, pp. 966–969) and a synthesis appears unlikely at this time.

In general, the principal concerns of geographic mental map research are the origin and organization of the map and the impact of the map on behavior (Gould & White, 1986). The typical geographic approach to the first concern is to argue that the mental map results from experience and learning and to uncritically accept ''the traditional explanation of the development of the cognitive map in an individual'' (Spencer & Blades, 1986, p. 240). Regarding the impact of a mental map on behavior, it is appropriate to acknowledge the inadequacy of information. More generally, a series of fundamental questions have been posed by Reginald Golledge (see 1981). What is reality? What is the relationship between an objective reality and the perception of that reality? What are mental maps? These heady questions remain unanswered but serve as a caution to future behavioral research.

It is generally acknowledged that mental maps err in certain consistent ways. Local areas are known in relative details, more distant areas are less known. By ''more distant'' is meant any one of several measures of distance, such as physical or social. Downs and Stea (1973) noted that there is a tendency to straighten curves and to generally simplify reality. One example of detailed research in this direction was that by William Chase and Micheline Chi (1981) focusing on the varying abilities of people to get around in environments. Following an account of literature on visual-spatial skills, especially chess-playing skills, Chase and Chi (1981) reported the results of a study that asked students to draw a campus map. A consistent error, mapping an intersection at 90 degrees rather than 45 degrees emerged, and it was argued that this resulted from ''a grid structure that people impose on their memory locations'' (Chase & Chi, 1981, p. 123). It was also noted that architecture students were less likely to make this error than were nonarchitecture students. It would be interesting to conduct similar research to ascertain the spatial skills of geography students.

For Chase and Chi (1981), mental maps were not psychologically real although they were useful abstractions. This is an important point but one that does not, in a practical sense, invalidate the wealth of geographical research on images and mental maps, which is most typically concerned with large areas such as regions or countries. Some of this geographical work is considered shortly.

The cultural geographer is also interested in the development and relevance of international images that have largely been researched by historians such as Daniel Boorstin (1960, 1962) on images of Europe and America and Philip Curtin (1964) on the image of Africa. More recently, Craufurd Goodwin (1974) analyzed the changing middle-class British image of Australia. Initially Australia was classed under the general heading of colony and judged largely in economic terms. As such, it was favorably viewed, because it caused little trouble and required little expense, unlike Canada, which was adjacent to a powerful neighbor. A useful contrast can be drawn to the work of Jürgen Tampke (1982), which considered the images of Australia held by Germans between 1850 and 1914. Needless to say, the images of some colonial masters and those of a minority ethnic group were based on radically different criteria and were radically different as a consequence.

Historical Concerns

> Every day, all over the world, men are making decisions which lead to transformations of the earth environment. Although the impact of an individual decision may be small, the cumulative effect of all such decisions is enormous, for both the number of people and the technological power at the command of each is greater than ever before and is growing rapidly (Saarinen, 1974, p. 252).

If we add a time dimension to the above quote, the situation becomes even more complex. A cultural landscape can be seen as the end product or, more correctly, the dynamic product of many individual decisions made at different times within differing social and physical environments. Landscape creation is complex. In principle, some insights can be gained by considering the causes of behavior with the assumption that behavior and decision making are at least partly dependent on individual or group perceptions of the real world, often called images. Operationalizing this procedure is difficult. Are we to structure our research around the logic that images cause behavior or should we infer images on the basis of actual behavior? Both approaches create difficulties. Using images to explain behavior is difficult in that it can be argued that, first, images cannot even be objectively measured and, second, a close correspondence between image and behavior has not been demonstrated (Bunting & Guelke 1979). Inferring images from behavior also poses logical problems as it is one example of the inference problem, that is, assuming "causes" on the basis of an analysis of "effects." It is fair to say that inference is an uncertain form of discovery for there are no guarantees that the inferred cause is indeed a true cause. Consider the simplified situation where farmer A perceives that either crop x or crop y will produce a satisfactory income; farmer B perceives that either crop y or crop z will produce a satisfactory income; both choose y and therefore the landscape decisions are identical, but are based on different images.

It is not satisfactory to approach an understanding of the cultural landscape solely from the overly naive proposition that perception causes behavior causes landscape. Factors other than perception influence behavior, and the factors other than behavior influence landscape. Nevertheless, much useful and innovative work has centered on a perception or behavioral theme. Some of this is now considered.

Geographers have devoted much attention to the question of settlement in new lands and the extent to which such activity has been affected by prior experience. Walter Kollmorgen (1969), for example, examined "geographic conditions colored by eastern conditions, which led to misguided efforts to project westward certain basic man-land relations that proved inoperative in the drier grasslands." There were possibly three specific errors of perception concerning rainmaking, irrigation, and dry farming. What is happening here is that a general consensus is arrived at concerning the potential of an area prior to actual settlement. For whatever reasons, that consensus is wrong and the process of amending and correcting may be both time consuming and costly in terms of individual effort.

A view may be actively fostered by authorities or by promoters who have a vested interest in the settlement of the area, but little, if any, knowledge. For the Great Plains, Kollmorgen (1969) demonstrated that both government scientists and real estate promoters overestimated the irrigation potential of the high plains and the feasibility of dry farming and that the government policy of enlarged homesteads implied that such larger holdings were adequate to resolve any difficulties. The fact that often radically different images are held by different groups is well established. Roy Merrens (1969) discussed the descriptive literature of colonial South Carolina and asserted that the image described was largely a function of the source of the account rather than the date when it was produced. The five basic sources identified were promoters, officials, settlers, travelers, and natural historians. The general applicability of this classification is suggested by the fact that it is also appropriate for southern Africa. A. J. Christopher (1973, p. 20) wrote that

> the value of the study of environmental perception in southern Africa lies in the manner in which people were influenced by propaganda, erroneous writings and hearsay. To a large extent men believed what they wanted to believe or that which they were given to believe, rather than the truth; and there can be little doubt that large tracts of southern Africa would never have been settled by Europeans or

would have been settled in different circumstances had the true state of affairs been appreciated.

What these ideas demonstrate is not atypical. Much human activity takes place in a learning situation. In general, humans know little of the consequence of actions that are not repetitive. It is appropriate to distinguish, as Chase and Chi (1981) have done, between the perceived environment, immediately accessible and known, and the inferred environment, which is a larger area where knowledge not explicitly stored in memory is inferred. The logical, and quite elementary, conclusion is that "people who have spent more time in a region, and who are familiar with the area, should perform better (Chase & Chi, 1981, p. 131). This theme is also pursued by Christopher Spencer and Mark Blades (1986, p. 241) in a distinction between familiar areas, where individuals can rely on "cognitive representation," and unfamiliar areas, where "external information" is necessary.

Perhaps the clearest examples of inferred environments are those nurtured by armchair geographers and explorers. The supposed existence of a navigable Northwest Passage played an important role in the exploratory history of northern North America. British armchair geographers have a lot to account for, in terms of wasted effort and loss of human life.

> This channel did not exist where men reasoned it must be—or, at least did not exist, in any form which could be of practical use to seamen, in any age down to our own. The whole enterprise was founded on a misapprehension, a geographical fiction, a fairy tale, springing out of the kind of stories sailors tell to amaze landsmen or to delude other sailors, to which were soon added the inferences, speculations and downright inventions that scholars manufactured to amaze themselves. (Thomson, 1976, p. 1)

One of the best researched examples of the creation of an incorrect image relates to the Swan River colony of Western Australia in the early nineteenth century. The first basic information source was an 1827 exploration conducted by Stirling and Fraser that was both "cursory and surrounded by fortunate circumstances" (Jim Cameron, 1974, p. 58). The report of this exploration was available to the public in the form of an article published in the journal *Quaterly Review*, and this article was then the basis for later journal articles in the *Mirror*, *New Monthly Magazine*, and *Westminister Review*. All of these appeared in 1829 or 1830. Cameron (1974) described the resultant distortion in detail. Two examples of factual distortion suffice here. The perceived cultivable area increased from 100 to 22,000 square miles and an 1830 publication included 84.9 percent conjecture in the description of climate. Cameron (1974, p. 73) acknowledged that conditions favored distortion in this case but asserted that "the sequence by which the information was disseminated differed only marginally from that pertaining to other colonies and other colony types." There is every reason to accept this assertion. Two further examples of distortion are now noted.

John Allen (1975, p. 103) offered a detailed discussion of the early nineteenth-century

> idea of the Missouri River as the key to the riddle of the Northwest Passage. . . . Foremost among those men who dreamed of a passage to India was Thomas Jefferson, owner of America's greatest collection of literature on the passage and the area through which it must run and the conceiver/sponsor of the Lewis and Clark expedition.

A rigorous research of available materials led Thomas Jefferson to infer the presence of a passage and to propose the Lewis and Clark expedition. It is evident that the Jefferson image was, unlike some governmental and most promotional image creations, based essentially on the known "facts"; unfortunately, these facts were not all correct. Jefferson imagined the source region of the southern Missouri as a plateau, not mountains, essentially creating a hypothetical geography. Subsequent explorations gradually amended the known geography to a closer accord with reality.

Another example of the creation of hypothetical geographies concerns western Canada. This area was largely known to Europeans in the mid-eighteenth century, and the processes of mapping and exploration abounded with uncertainty. Richard Ruggles (1971, p. 235) detailed the emergence of the area as a geographic region emphasizing that the "unfolding of the knowledge of the Canadian West was part of the larger search for the Western Ocean." Known, or perceived, areas were mapped correctly whereas the relatively unknown, or inferred, areas were mapped incorrectly. Errors reflected the aspirations of map-makers and explorers, namely minimizing east to west distance and maximizing access via water.

What lessons for cultural geography are to be learned from the above? It is clear that much human behavior is occurring in uncertain environments, and hence, what happens in an environment may be more closely related to views developed from legend than to the realities of the local scene. Although the exploratory examples above are extreme in their divergence from reality, such extremes may affect the basic evolution of landscape. For example, the size of landholding in the high plains was institutionally determined outside the region and was inappropriate. Furthermore, key location decisions, such as town sites and transport routes, were often made outside of regions and prior to the availability of relevant local knowledge. The following section looks explicitly at landscape and evaluates the impact of images on landscape change.

The Behavior of Colonizers

> The very art of colonization invariably resulted in the confrontation of imported cultural systems with new, strange and often inhospitable environments. Rarely were the particulars of these environments consistent with colonists' perceptions

of them, and even more rarely were they totally amenable to the resolution of colonists' aims. Perceptions and aims had therefore to be modified and this initiated a process of active, conscious adjustment of learning which continued until such time as perceptions were consistent and aims became realistic and attainable. (Cameron, 1977, p. 1)

The thrust of the above quote can be applied to a wide variety of situations. Cameron (1977) utilized a model of adaptive learning, based on William Found (1971), to provide the framework for an analysis of settlement in pre–1850 Western Australia. Briefly, the model is as follows. Entry to a new environment prompts a search for actions that will satisfy goals. Preferably, such actions will be evident from the actions of other colonizers; if not, actions will be determined subjectively. Once the consequences of actions are known, then a process of evaluation takes place. Actions that were successful in achieving desired goals will be repeated and those that were unsuccessful will be rejected and a new search procedure initiated. The sequence of search, operate, evaluate will take place as many times as necessary until the desired goals are achieved. The essential outcome is that the colonizer learns a set of actions, which then become repeated on a regular basis. Cameron (1977, p. 4) noted that this proposed procedure is in close accord with Gestalt ideas.

The model detailed is useful for many colonization situations, but it does neglect several complications including the prior experience of the colonizer, interactions with the new environment, the effect of such personality traits as attitude, and the role of group learning.

Factors Determining Behavior

It is now appropriate to consider the variety of factors influencing behavior in landscape. As noted, these things are varied, complex, and interrelated. They include

1. Prior experience,
2. Individual characteristics,
3. Group membership,
4. Institutional considerations,
5. Goals,
6. Environment,
7. Links with other groups,
8. The image held of the new environment, and
9. Attitudes.

It is commonplace to acknowledge that behavior in landscape is affected by behaviors practiced in earlier and in some way comparable situations. This is the notion of "cultural baggage," and a clear example is that of the Irish in nineteenth-century eastern Canada. Focusing specifically on aspects of the material folk culture and settlement morphology, John Mannion (1974) concluded that the movement of the Irish to Canada meant a rapid loss of cultural traits. The rate of loss varied notably among the three locations analyzed. The extent of transfer and the durability of transferred traits was greatest in the Avalon Peninsula of Newfoundland; thus, it was here that prior behavior played the greatest role in affecting later behavior. In the Peterborough area of Ontario both transfer and durability were less evident; thus, prior behavior was less critical. The third study area, the Miramichi River area of New Brunswick, represented a middle ground. Why the difference in transfer and durability? The Avalon Peninsula possessed two characteristics facilitating a repeat of previous behavior, namely an environment similar to that in the Irish source area and lack of contact with other cultural groups (numbers 6 and 7 above). It is useful to take this example one step further.

Question 1. What Factors Influenced the Behavior of Irish Settlers in the Avalon Peninsula?

Answer. Important factors were: prior experience repeated unless shown to be unacceptable; group membership important for a cohesive close knit group; the environment, being similar to that previously experienced, encouraged a continuation of past behavior.

Question 2. What Factors Influenced the Behavior of Irish Settlers in the Peterborough region?

Answer. Important factors were: the goal of rapidly achieving commercial status, an environment that offered opportunities for more diverse agriculture than previously practiced, the presence of and links with other cultural groups, institutional controls such as the land survey and holding system. The importance of the above factors rendered group membership and prior experience of lesser importance, although both played a role initially.

What is being demonstrated here is that any colonization process involves the establishment of behavior patterns in a new environment and that these behavior patterns, themselves dynamic, are a consequence of a complex interplay of factors. The complex interplay of factors can be demonstrated by considering the circumstances under which a given factor may assume particular importance. For example, in what situations might prior experience, group membership, or individual characteristics be important?

Prior experience is likely to be an important determinant if the goals established in the new area are similar to those pursued previously, if the new environment is similar to the old, if there are limited links with other groups, if the image held of the new environment is such that repetition of prior behavior is judged appropriate, if institutional considerations do not play a major role, and if group membership is more important than are individual characteristics. The characteristics of each individual are likely to be an important determinant if group membership patterns are weak, if institutional considerations are lacking, if goals are unclear, and if the environment is relatively benign. Group membership will be important if individual characteristics are invariable, if institutions do not dominate, if links with other groups are limited, and if there is a shared environmental image.

William Norton (1988) used the suggested nine factors to discuss four colonization scenarios, typical behaviors, and related landscapes. Marwyn Samuels (1979) proposed that a focus on "landscape biography" facilitated explanations of landscape evolution. This approach is especially relevant when boosterism is evident and requires a focus on the beliefs and attitudes of the boosters. Meredith (1985) analyzed the landscape impact of one booster that was important in the Upper Columbia Valley of western Canada between 1900 and 1920. He concluded that a complete explanation involved environmental, social, and individual considerations.

Considered in this way, it becomes clear that any attempts by cultural geographers to explain behavior are complex. Certainly, there is much more to behavior in landscape than "mere" perception. Detailed explanations will vary according to the particularities of the example. This section concludes with two brief studies that highlight this variety of explanatory factors.

The attitude of early European settlers to the vast North American forests was one of dislike. In southern Ontario, for example, civilization and progress were not compatible with forest. The result was an onslaught "with a savagery greater than that justified by the need to clear the land for cultivation" (Kelly, 1974, p. 64). The agricultural value of retaining some forest was well publicized but largely ignored. Lack of prior experience clearly played a role here, because most incoming settlers were ill prepared for the vastness of North American forested areas. In a similar fashion the image, essentially "incorrect," of a threatening and antagonistic forest was a cause of the attack. The goal of establishing commercial wheat farming required some land clearing. Individual characteristics were of little import here as most settlers responded in a similar fashion, at least at the regional scale being considered. The sameness of behavior suggests that group considerations were a cause. In this example, the behavior of settlers largely resulted from their lack of prior experience with the type of environment that they encountered as well as from the behavior of others, the perception of the forest as some sort of threat to advancement, and related attitudes. The notion that attitudes can affect landscape is evident in much behavioral literature beginning with the works of David Lowenthal and Hugh Prince (1964, 1965), which emphasized that landscapes are created, in some instances, by tastes.

A second example highlights a different set of explanatory factors. Nineteenth-century European settlers in Florida strongly favored viticulture such that a distinctive land-use pattern emerged. Carolyn Lewis (1979, p. 634) noted that settler behavior in this instance could be characterized as cultural conservatism. This situation arose because of a close similarity between old and new environments, close links with groups in the origin areas, a similar prior experience, and a close correspondence between image and reality. These two examples demonstrate that consistent patterns of behavior can emerge in a given region for very different reasons. Most important, the image held of environment is one, but only one, cause of behavior.

LANDSCAPE EVALUATION

A rather separate component of the behavioral interest relates to questions of landscape evaluation approached from a humanistic perspective. The central theme here is that of impressions of nature and landscape and of the social and cultural forces that influence perception. This theme has been most fully exploited by Clarence Glacken (1967) for the period up to 1800, with three ideas being emphasized, namely the teleological view of nature, environment as cause, and humans as modifiers of nature. In a preliminary consideration of the period after 1800, Glacken (1985) identified the four themes of interrelationships in nature. The first three are environment as cause, humans as modifiers of nature, and subjective attitudes to nature. In regard to the fourth theme, Glacken (1985, p. 54) wrote that

> I believe the period, roughly from the middle of the 18th to the latter part of the 19th centuries was one of a real efflorescence of writings on the subjective, emotional and esthetic attitudes toward nature. Most of the ideas were old. It was the depth and extent to which they were explained that mattered.

The idea of landscape has recently been investigated in detail by Denis Cosgrove (1984, p. 13) for whom landscape "is not merely the world we see, it is a construction, a composition of that world." Furthermore, landscape is a social product, the consequence of a collective human transformation of nature" (Cosgrove, 1984, p. 14). Thus, a dual ambiguity is identified between subject and object and between personal and social. These ideas are central to contemporary cultural geography and further reinforce the integration of cultural and social themes. This view of landscape as an ideological concept can teach us about the way groups view themselves, nature, and their relationship with nature. Most important in the present context, it is inappropriate to assume that landscape evaluation can be assessed via analyses of individual perspectives and analyses of particular scenes. A full appreciation of landscape evaluation can only result from analyses of the social level. This argument leads to recognition of the value of a humanistic focus and the merits of viewing landscapes as *places* occupied by social groups.

The humanistic perspective is not without difficulties. The rapid growth of the perspective in North America is, at least partially, a reaction to the extremes of positivism, and a clear unified set of ideas is not yet evident. Indeed much landscape evaluation research retains strong positivistic overtones (Hamill,

1984). Overall, this theme is marginal to most contemporary cultural and social geography despite the emphasis on both human and land relations and on landscape. For Cosgrove (1984), this state of affairs can be, at least partially, attributed to the difficulties that geographers have with the term *landscape*. As suggested in chapter 4, there is much to be gained from viewing landscape as produced by and habitated by social groups or communities, although the conceptual frameworks on which to structure detailed empirical analyses remain wanting. It appears likely that, despite the often compelling arguments of humanistic geographers, landscape will remain an integral but uncertain term. In this respect, it is surprising that Cosgrove (1984) did not refer to Neil Evernden (1981) because the latter focused explicitly on a phenomonological approach to landscape. Posing the problem of landscape as resource, Evernden (1981, p. 147) asked "how can something that has no adequate definition be measured? Is it realistic to treat landscape beauty in the same way as timber or minerals?" There are various possible responses to these questions: landscapes may be described, assigned essentially arbitrary values, or differentiated quantitatively (Evernden, 1985). Attitudes to landscape, including the evaluation of landscape as a resource, do change, and Evernden (1981, p. 154) contended that "landscape is simply a different type of phenomenon from timber or iron and is too amorphous to be easily regarded as an object."

There is a voluminous literature developing in the areas of landscape perspective and evaluation. Much of this literature focuses on literary, poetic, and artistic impressions—for example, John Barrell (1972) on the poetic landscapes of John Clare; Barrell (1982) on the landscapes of Hardy's Wessex; and Ronald Rees (1984) on the artistic landscapes of western Canada. One of the more penetrating studies was concerned with the influence exerted by Humboldt on a new type of American landscape painting exemplified by Frederick E. Church. According to Edmunds Bunske (1981, p. 140),

> Humboldt was remarkably modern in his interpretations of the aesthetic pleasures that humans derived from landscapes. He went beyond many modern studies in which perception and cognition are the principal objectives and placed the matter squarely where it ought to be: in the human imagination as it interacts with its surroundings.

A different conclusion is evident from an appraisal of the writings of John B. Jackson (Meinig, 1979a). Five key features of landscape emerged: landscapes are places to be lived in, not viewed from outside; landscape actually is a consequence of human and land unity; landscape evaluation is based on practical usefulness; landscapes are symbolic; and landscapes change along with society. J. B. Jackson (1970) contains a good sample of the author's writings. Overall, these themes are not very different from those evident in environmental psychology.

CONCLUDING COMMENTS

Behavioral geography has made great strides since the 1960s and the initial association with spatial analysis. From a somewhat uncompromising view of perception causes behavior causes landscape there has been increasing acknowledgment that behavior is more complex in origin. In addition to a closer association with humanistic philosophies, there is developing an ever increasing appreciation of the relevance of psychological, largely social psychological, concepts and methods. Although the early links with the work of Lewin were valuable, it is clear that social psychology has a wealth of varied and often contradictory ideas and that environmental psychology is a closely related field of interest. The environmental psychologist considers a wide range of research material including natural, built, and social environments whereas the social psychologist emphasizes that "action is not necessarily predicated upon cognition," that is to say, attitudes are not a sole cause of behavior (Darley & Gilbert, 1985, p. 966). Interesting as such material may be, it is actually difficult to anticipate the impact on cultural geography. This is essentially because the scales of analysis differ. Most of the psychological research remains at the level of the individual, which is not typically the focus of the cultural geographer.

This chapter has centered on work usually labeled behavioral geography as one part of cultural geography. Given the cultural geographers' concern with the evolution of landscape and with human and land relations, it is clear that increased awareness of behavioral interests and related disciplines will be of value in developing coherent explanations.

6

Understanding Landscape: Evolutionary Emphases

"I believe that the primary concern of cultural geography is with the nature, genesis, and distribution of observable phenomena of the landscape directly or indirectly ascribable to man, and of course including man himself" (Kniffen, 1937, p. 163). In a similar vein, the NAS–NRC (1965, p. 23) report identified cultural geography as "differences from place to place in the ways of life of human communities and their creation of man-made or modified features." These two statements are representative of the prevailing pre–1970s view of cultural geography, a view that acknowledged the close relations between historical and cultural themes and that largely rejected the notion of geography as environmentalism, as a chorological science, or as spatial analysis. According to Ronald Johnston (1983a, p. 90) cultural geographers were even less concerned than were historical geographers with "their apparent drift away from the mainstream of geographical activity." The result of this lack of concern was a distinctive cultural geography with a strong evolutionary content, which was missing from much geography. Regional geography was explicitly atemporal and spatial analysis similarly focused on static issues until the emergence of process to form approaches in the late 1970s (Norton, 1984a, pp. 23–26). Only cultural geography, along with historical geography, offered a view of geography as explictly time oriented. Thus, the material presented in this chapter includes much of that which is classed as cultural. Indeed, time is not an ideal organizing concept for this very reason. Much of the content of the other chapters has a time dimension, but the key distinction is that in this chapter time is usually the integral characteristic, not just an incidental one.

The close association between cultural and historical geography stems from the clear emphasis placed on time by both Paul Vidal de la Blache and Carl Sauer and their respective schools. Sauer (1941, p. 1) argued forcefully for genetic forms of explanation and, indeed, was critical of Richard Hartshorne for not following "Hettner into his main methodologic position, namely, that geography, in any of its branches, must be a genetic science; that is, must account for origins and processes." David Harvey (1969, pp. 408–410) noted that several cultural and historical geographers had gone so far as to commit the genetic fallacy, that is, they assumed a genetic approach to be the only acceptable mode of explanation. Such assertions have not been characteristic, and the general tendency has been to incorporate time, but not necessarily to argue for time, as the ever-present overriding interest. In the current chapter, the first concern is with the methodology of landscape and region evolution, especially as articulated by Sauer, and with links between cultural and historical interests. A second concern is with examples of region and regional landscape evolution. Questions of culture contact and transfer and the effect on landscape constitute a third concern, which is followed by an evaluation of the innovation diffusion literature as a body of ideas facilitating landscape comprehension. The fifth concern is with questions of cultural evolution.

EVOLUTION OF LANDSCAPE AND CULTURAL REGIONS: THE ARGUMENT

Landscape

"The current viewpoints in cultural geography began to take shape in the mid–1920's" (J. E. Spencer, 1978, p. 79). Principal among these viewpoints was the need to take a long-term perspective. This need was paralleled by an appreciation of the great variety of human cultures and the resultant recognition that different cultures typically generated different landscapes. Questions of environmentalism, possibilism, and so forth were considered in chapter 3; here it is assumed that natural landscapes are modified by humans to create cultural landscapes. This is, of course, little more than a reiteration of frameworks developed in Germany and France before 1910 and in the United States in the 1920s. The idea that evolution was important to an understanding of landscape was incorporated in the work of Friedrich Ratzel. In a spirited defence of Ratzel, against those critics who saw him as a naive environmentalist, Robert Lowie (1937, p. 120), wrote that "Ratzel did not exaggerate the potency of the physical environment. . . . What saves him from such naïveté is the recognition of the time factor. . . . No one could emphasize more than Ratzel the force of past history." Ferdinand von Richthofen similarly advocated a genetic approach and the culmination of these ideas appeared in the work of Otto Schluter. As noted in chapter 3, Schluter regarded geography as the study of the visible landscape as it changed through time; his writings circa 1900 effectively founded German cultural geography. "Schluter was the first to raise the landscape forming activity of man to a methodological principle" (Waibel, cited in Dickinson, 1969, p. 132). Similar ideas, at least partially aimed at creating a distinct discipline, were evident in the writings of Vidal and his pupils. Vidal is generally credited with the introduction of the term *personality* into the geographic literature. Gary Dunbar (1974, p. 28) reviewed the uses and meanings of this term and emphasized that "geographic personality is something that grows through time" creating a distinct regional landscape. The North American contribution was, of course, that of Sauer and it closely parallels that of Schluter, in particular.

Each of these contributions, although different in detail, emphasizes evolution and visible landscape. In the United States, a principal example was Jan Broek's (1932) analysis of the Santa Clara Valley. The purpose of this study was to understand landscape change as a result of a succession of different cultural and economic occupances within a relatively short period (less than 200 years). The technique used was to describe process first and landscape second for each of the occupances. Many more studies of this type emerged in Germany and France where "landscape" schools were more influential. The relative paucity of U.S. studies was a reflection of the minority status of Sauer and his pupils; a status that resulted, in part, from the opposition of Alfred Hettner, and subsequently Hartshorne, to visible landscape analyses. Perhaps more surprisingly, the landscape concept failed to emerge as a central concern in Britain. Robert Dickinson (1969, p. 133) cited the work of the historical geographer Clifford Darby as clearly lacking visible landscape or evolutionary content. A major exception in British work was Dickinson's (1939) introduction of landscape and society, seen as equivalent to the habitat and habit of Sauer.

These comments help to explain subsequent developments. A concern with landscape evolution persisted in France and Germany, building on a rich intellectual heritage and often close associations with history and anthropology. Cultural geography continued to thrive in the United States as a secondary, but persistent, concern with close links to historical geography. In Britain, the historical interest was more focused on past landscapes and provided little incentive for cultural landscape studies. A rather separate emergence of an interest labeled social geography, often concerned with visible landscape, emerged (see Evans, 1939). Alan Ogilvie (1952, p. 15), a committed British regional geographer who characteristically argued for a substantive physical content in regional analyses, also recognized that "due weight . . . be given to the influences of the geographic past."

Recent appraisals tend to interpret these developments as follows. Cultural geography aimed to "understand the present landscape as a result of long-time processes involving the changing relations between man and land" (Broek & Webb, 1978, p. 34). This goal of understanding landscape was accomplished by looking at major components of culture, such as technology, race, language, and religion, in both time and space. Joseph Spencer and William Thomas (1973, p. 6) favored a focus "on the slow growth of systems of culture and on the development of separate systems in different regions of the earth"; this was achieved by focusing on the humanization of the earth. Terry Jordan and Lester Rowntree (1986, p. 27) similarly acknowledged the centrality of evolution, despite their employment of the five themes: "The spatial distribution of cultural features is the result of changes through time, and cultural geographers have traditionally been concerned with areal patterns as they evolved through time." The consensus is clear: landscapes are the product of human action over time.

Cultural Regions

Anthropologists employed the concepts of culture area or region initially as a means of establishing some semblance of order on cultural phenomena. Thus, the regional concept was a means of classifying and was used by Alfred Kroeber (1904) in early work, refined as a concept in 1917 by Clark Wissler, and culminated in 1939 with the publication of a major work on the cultural and natural areas of North America (Kroeber, 1939). In most of this work, the culture area concept was a tool to assist in the recognition of culture wholes. Cultural cores were seen as emerging in the most favorable parts of an area, and this was followed by a spread of the area to the limits (Wissler, 1926). These anthropological contributions "attracted considerable geographic attention" (Carter, 1948, p. 145).

The two terms, *landscape* and *region,* are not typically interchangeable although they are closely related and defy definitional concensus. For the current purposes, a cultural region may be simply regarded as an area that possesses a similar landscape. It is conventional to distinguish three types of region as follows. *Formal* regions are those characterized by uniformity of a given trait or traits. Thus, the Canadian wheat belt is a single-factor formal region whereas the area of Inuit occupance may be regarded as a multifactor formal region. Discussions of cultural regions normally imply formal regions. *Functional* regions are those, ranging in scale from a home to a given group of countries, that in some way operate as a unit. Such functional regions are of limited utility in cultural analysis. The third type of region is labeled *vernacular,* which refers to a locally perceived regional identity and name. An example might be the "Canadian West" although the term is more typically applied to local, often tourist, areas. The present concern is essentially with the formal region.

Although the terms *landscape* and *region* may be seen as representing two different views of human geography, namely the Sauer school and the Hartshorne school, they were not typically treated as different by European geographers. The "conflict" between the two terms was more apparent than real. In 1928, Albrecht Penck noted that "the visible content of the landscape determines the content of modern geography" and advocated landscape study in regions (cited in Dickinson, 1969, p. 130). In a similar fashion, Schluter saw regions as distinctive parts of the earth's surface. No conflict is evident between landschaft and region in this German tradition. Nor so in North America where Sauer and landscape have frequently been portrayed as different from Hartshorne and region. This difference is valid to the extent that the Hartshornian regional method excluded time. It is invalid, however, in that cultural geographers following

Sauer felt comfortable with both landscape and region. This is hardly surprising given that Sauer (1925, pp. 25–26) wrote that "the term 'landscape' is proposed to denote the unit concept of geography, to characterize the peculiarly geographic association of facts. Equivalent terms in a sense are 'area' and 'region.' . . . It may be defined, therefore, as an area made up of a distinct association of forms, both physical and cultural." Similarly, Sauer (1931, p. 622) wrote that "the culture area is then an assemblage of such forms that have interdependence and is functionally differentiated from other areas." From the very beginning of North American cultural geography, as in Europe, landscape and region have been related terms. Landscape is the more general, typically referring to the visible landscape, whereas region is the more specific, referring to an area of similar landscape. For both, the cultural geographic tradition has emphasized their change through time. It is therefore logical to now consider examples of landscape and region evolution.

EVOLUTION OF LANDSCAPES AND CULTURAL REGIONS: EXAMPLES

Landscapes, cultural regions, or geographic personalities emerge in response to cultural occupance through time, becoming "as it were, a medal struck in the likeness of a people" (Vidal, cited in Broek & Webb, 1978, p. 32). The processes by which distinctive areas emerge are complex and have been approached in diverse ways as the following discussion indicates.

World Regions

It is correct to assert that the landscape and cultural region concepts have not typically been employed at a world scale and were not devised, methodologically speaking, with such a scale in mind. Nevertheless, they can serve as a valuable descriptive device for heuristic purposes. Divisions of the world into regions are essentially classifications aimed at facilitating general world comprehension. Fred Kniffen is properly regarded as the father of the culture region concept as used in this fashion (Gritzner, 1981). In a pioneering textbook, aimed at first-year students, Richard Russell and Kniffen (1951) grouped people according to culture, related culture to area to derive culture worlds, and showed that such worlds had become differentiated over a long time period. They presented the basic characteristics of cultural geography, namely a focus on cultures, resultant landscapes, and cultural and landscape change. This pioneering work acknowledged, for example, the problems of regional classification and the existence of subregions. The broad divisions recognized are labeled European World, Oriental World, Dry World, African World, Polar World, American World, and Pacific World. A transitional area is located between the European and Polar worlds and large areas outside of Europe are seen as affected by a New World Revolution, notably the American, African, and Pacific worlds. Each of the regions is discussed in detail; physical, historical, and cultural aspects are considered. This pioneering use of the cultural region concept at the world scale is a major development within the Berkeley tradition. Other textbook authors have developed different schemes for world regionalization.

Such regionalizations serve as heuristic devices within the specific contents of the textbooks of which they are a part. Unfortunately, such maps are open to criticism as attempts at delimiting cultural regions, partly because the larger the area to be divided into regions, the more superficial, or more numerous, the regions become (see de Blij, 1978, pp. 45–55; Zimolzak & Stansfield, 1979, pp. 24–25). Harvey (1969, pp. 235–237) noted that world region classifications typically result from a process of logical division of a large area, in this case the world. Such a process is a difficult procedure presupposing a thorough background knowledge. Harvey (1969, p. 236) wrote that "classification by logical division in the absence of adequate theory amounts to stating an *a priori* model and the consequent methodological difficulties require clear recognition."

World cultural regionalizations are highly suggestive of the value of regionalization as a device for obtaining a clearer understanding of the world. They are also highly suggestive of the difficulties, indeed dangers, of oversimplification. If the area being considered is large, then the ability to derive meaningful generalizations is limited. The examples that follow for the New World and the Old World are more convincing and appropriate uses of regional concepts, and thus, permit a more elaborate consideration of processes and consequences.

A Comment on Cultural Processes

These regional examples can be most usefully prefaced by reference to a pioneering analysis of agricultural region evolution that viewed change as a result of essentially cultural, not environmental or economic, processes. The American Corn Belt can be viewed as the "landscape expression of . . . the totality of the beliefs of the farmers over a region regarding the most suitable use of land in an area" (J. E. Spencer & Horvath, 1963, p. 81). A specific development contributing to the emergence of the Corn Belt was the decline of sheep, which resulted from the general lack of interest in sheep rather than from any crucial environmental or economic factors. The relevant cultural process was essentially that of innovation diffusion whereby once a process of change is initiated, the mechanics of local communication networks ensure that such change becomes widespread; this is particularly effective in an area experiencing settlement, where the change is that from an essentially natural landscape. In a related fashion, the coconut landscape of the Philippines resulted from a particular farming mentality.

> Coconut planting occupies a prominent place in the minds of most farmers in the southern Philippines. This psychological mind-set is a strong force in the evolution of the coconut landscape. It is a culturally habituated predisposition toward a

particular crop providing a stable return which helped to start an agricultural regionalism. (Spencer & Horvath, 1963, p. 84)

This origin is similar, but different in detail, to that of the Corn Belt. Because the coconut had long been known, all farmers were cognizant of the crop and the appropriate techniques. The specific stimulus for the emergence of a commercial landscape was a change in demand, and the farmers were able to respond accordingly. The third example of cultural causation offered by J. E. Spencer and Ronald Horvath (1963, pp. 86–87) is that of the Malayan rubber landscape, which similarly emerged as a result of "the psychological change among the Malays themselves." Malays originally viewed rubber as an alien system of agriculture, and it was not until their cultural "conversion" that the rubber landscape began to expand.

On the basis of the three examples, it was argued that agricultural region evolution involves processes with cultural content (Spencer & Horvath, 1963, p. 96). Included in the term cultural are psychological, political, historical, technological, economic, and agronomic factors. Although this use of the term cultural is necessarily broad, the examples and argument are a convincing statement. The relevance of innovation diffusion, identified specifically for the Corn Belt, had earlier been introduced to American geographers by Leighly (1954) in a brief commentary on early work by Hagerstrand. It is a little surprising that neither of these two works created major research activity.

Delimiting Cultural Regions

A discussion of cultural regions in the New World is especially useful in that the topic is well researched, most areas are of relatively recent cultural origin in terms of dominant characteristics, and the scale is appropriate for a discussion of region and landscape evolution. There is not the wealth of studies dating back to circa 1900 that there is for, say, France but there has been a series of conceptually interesting and empirically detailed studies since circa 1960. These studies together comprise a set of alternative explanations for region development and a fairly comprehensive set of factual statements. This discussion begins with the now classic analysis of the emergence of the Mormon cultural region by Meinig (1965). The evolution of the region was described in detail, and a generic model proposed as a basis for both delimiting the region and identifying internal variations. The model proposes a *core,* which is likely to be the hearth area and is the zone of most intense activity. Surrounding the core is a *domain,* the area in which the culture is dominant, but without the intensity of occupance and complexity of development evident in the core. Surrounding the domain is the *sphere,* which is an area only partially belonging to the culture region in question. The model thus depicts a decreasing cultural identity with increasing distance from the core. Meinig (1965) acknowledged the distinctive character of the Mormon region in terms of the initial isolation of the area occupied and in terms of the especially distinctive character of the Mormon group. These two would appear to be necessary prerequisites for this type of evolution to occur.

In North America, a good argument might be made for a French-Canadian cultural region of this type, with a Montreal–Quebec City core and a southern Quebec domain. More general applications of this proposal would appear to be limited, however, largely because most groups occupy areas in close contact with other groups in adjacent areas, and most groups do not actively seek to emphasize their differences from the wider society. Nevertheless, for some regions the Meinig model is likely to prove a valuable device, because of the explicit focus on evolution. An example for Wales is referred to later in this section.

The settlement of the Mormons was an example of what Wilbur Zelinsky (1973, p.13) called *first effective settlement*.

> Whenever an empty territory undergoes settlement, or an earlier population is dislodged by invaders, the specific characteristics of the first group able to effect a viable, self-perpetuating society are of crucial significance for the later social and cultural geography of the area, no matter how tiny the initial band of settlers may have been.

An earlier proposal was made by Kniffen (1965, p. 551) under the guise of "initial occupance." These provocative suggestions might not be easily applied to areas of Old World culture where such settlement is difficult to determine, and they might not be easily applied to New World areas where contemporary cultural identity is a composite product of a series of contributions.

This latter point is evident from a consideration of the regionalization that Zelinsky proposed. Five first-order regions were demarcated for the United States; namely the West, Middle West, South, Midland, and New England. For each, the date of first effective settlement and of cultural formation were indicated as were the major sources of culture. Each of the five regions was further subdivided into secondary regions, and three areas that were difficult to categorize were noted. Only one of the primary regions has a single major source of culture, namely New England has England. The other four primary regions do not have stated dates of origin or sources. Rather, it was appropriate to indicate dates and sources for each of the secondary, and in three instances, tertiary, regions. In most cases, more than one source was identified. This regionalization is thus an acknowledgment of the complexity of cultural regionalization, despite the apparent simplicity of the rationale for the regionalization. The unequal size of regions is essentially a reflection of the different natural landscapes and the different settlement processes, but it does appear to suggest that the criteria for delimitation are not uniformly appropriate. One additional interesting issue raised concerns the possibility of extending the regionalization into Canada with the noteworthy addition of a French-Canadian culture region. Two other researchers have utilized approaches comparable to that of Zelinsky. The migration of cultural traits was basic to analyses by Daniel Elazar (1984), which identified sets of attitudes derived from areas further east. The first effective settlement concept was employed by Raymond Gastil (1975) to define areas of cultural homogeneity.

For the United States, there have been several further attempts at regionalization using variants of the Meinig model and of the doctrine of first effective settlement. Much of this work was accomplished by Meinig in a series of innovative regional analyses. In the case of Texas, Meinig (1969) delimited a culture region that evolved through four stages: implantation, which reflected both Spanish and Mexican influences; assertion, which included the periods of republic and early statehood; expansion, which followed the Civil War; and elaboration, which involved more recent developments. In a more general discussion, Meinig (1972) identified a set of six regions in the American West by means of an approach that was developmental, synthetic, and generic. The six regions did not cover the entire West in 1900, but each was recognizably a distinct region. A detailed analysis of the Hispanic region has been provided by Richard Nostrand (1970), again with a major evolutionary component, and a review of Great Plains regional concepts by Frederick Luebke (1984) explained most developments in terms of distinct incoming cultures. The prospect of viewing American development from a series of initial units has been advocated by Meinig (1978, p. 1191) as follows.

> The most important task in the historical geographic study of colonial America is to define as clearly as possible this sequence of territorial formation from points to nuclei to regions on the North American seaboard and to describe the changing geography of each in terms of spatial systems, cultural landscape, and social geography.

An alternative approach to American culture regions is the frontier thesis of Frederick Jackson Turner. This thesis argued that American culture returned to primitive conditions on the ever-moving frontier. Much detailed historical research has been prompted by these ideas, notably work by Ray Billington (1966). There are, however, major problems with a simple frontier argument, and Robert Mitchell (1978) noted three of these. First, the frontier thesis assumes an initial subsistance phase of economic activity that was not typically the case (Norton, 1976). A second problem is the related assumption of initial regional isolation. Most areas were, in fact, closely linked to other areas from the outset of settlement. The third deficiency of frontier logic in this context is the resultant need to seek origins of American culture west of the Appalachians. Mitchell (1978) argued that the cores of colonial culture acted as dynamic culture regions, creating intermediate regions and, in due course, trans-Appalachian regions. There were three possible mechanisms responsible for this regional creation: *duplication* of a previous set of traits, *deviation* from a previous set of traits, or *fusion* of two or more sets of traits. Thus, Mitchell (1978) proposed an explanation of early American regionalization using a variant of the first effective settlement concept that allowed for a variety of formative processes. These ideas are similar to much of the work in cultural geography that focuses on the diffusion of culture traits or innovations.

An alternative approach proposed by Cole Harris (1978, p. 120) argued for an "underlying sameness about North American life," an interpretation that "downplays local differences in physical environment, immigrant background, and economic organization." Superimposed on this sameness were, however, some very real regional variations, albeit at a much larger scale than had previously been the case in Europe. The pervading pattern is, then, one of cultural convergence with some notable exceptions. This interpretation by R. C. Harris (1978) reflected a distinctive argument about the experiences of Europeans in the North American environment, which emphasized the significance of society in the New World.

This focus on American regions is clearly beginning to incorporate a complex set of ideas and alternative explanations. The various works by Meinig (1965, 1972, 1978) center on region creation in the West and on the dynamic character of regions. Zelinsky (1973) proposed a basic process, which is valuable for its simplicity. Mitchell (1978) acknowledged the complexity of region creation and proposed specific mechanisms by which regions were created. Finally, Harris (1978) argued for regional cultural differentiation superimposed on an essential American sameness. Overall, comparable ideas have not been generated in other New World areas and these ideas have not been significantly applied. This section concludes with a discussion of cultural regions in the non-American areas of European overseas expansion.

Although several of the American studies already noted are, in principle, readily applicable to other regions, there has in fact been little comparable work elsewhere. Many of the studies of other regions are more conventionally historical and descriptive and less analytical in approach. Australia, for example, has been well researched in terms of historical and geographic regional analyses, but with little explicit cultural content. A preliminary analysis by Dennis Jeans (1981) suggested that Australia offered fewer opportunities for culture region delimitation than did the American West but suggested a number of appropriate regional indicators. For Australia, one especially interesting issue seems to be the question of state-cultural region concordance. It may be that many cultural regions cross state boundaries and that most states are not culturally homogenous. A similar situation is apparent throughout much of Africa, where the notion of state-nation discordance as a consequence of colonial policies is a common one. Perhaps the most dramatic example of a changing political and cultural landscape today is in South Africa, where technically independent African states are in the process of being created. Elsewhere in Africa, the colonial process destroyed many preexisting societies and "new European societies were formed which were able to impress their ideas upon the landscape and create an image of France or England overseas" (Christopher, 1984, p. 193). For the area of East Africa, John Kesby (1977) employed a quite different approach to the cultural regionalization problem, closely relating natural vegetation regions to cultural regions. Again, however, a strong evolutionary focus prevailed. "By 1890 there were in existence in East Africa two cultural regions and parts of three others. They owed their distinctiveness, not only to the habitats which the people occupied, but also to the contacts between the peoples, to their relative prestige and to specific cultural innovations and borrowings" (Kesby, 1977, p. 269).

The current paucity of New World analyses, other than for the United States, is not a reflection of research potential but rather one of a preferred focus. The various alternative explanations developed in the North American context can be usefully amended and applied elsewhere.

One of the attractions of analyzing cultural region evolution in areas of European overseas expansion is its relative simplicity. The problem of delimiting regions in areas of the Old World is far greater and the problem of determining causal processes might often be insurmountable. Nevertheless, these problems have been tackled and they do indeed have a venerable tradition in some countries, notably France with its distinctive *pays* landscapes. A regional textbook of Europe with an especially significant cultural content did not, however, seriously attempt a subdivision of the continent although maps were produced of, for example, language regions (Jordan, 1973). One detailed analysis of region creation utilizing the Mormon-derived model of Meinig (1965) was of an area of northeast Wales (Pryce, 1975). In this study, language was the key cultural variable, and the relative strengths of the English and Welsh delimited two major cultural regions. The bilingual zone was equated with the Meinig domain in the sense that it was the contact area with other cultures.

The relative paucity of both conceptual and empirical analyses for Old World areas is hardly surprising and results from the greater complexity evident in researching Old World regions and the differing aspirations of research. For the United States in particular, there is a definite preoccupation with understanding both national and regional character and landscape. The preoccupation is reflected in the number, type, and variety of studies.

Landscape Studies: The Berkeley School

In addition to a concern with regional evolution there is also a significant cultural geographic concern with landscape evolution. This is quite logical given that the initial impetus for cultural geography generally, and in North American specifically, was one of cultural landscape creation from natural landscape. Necessarily, the content of this section is closely related to the regional discussions, but here the focus is on landscape per se and not on region.

Interestingly, much of the work by Sauer is not in close accord with his methodological assertions whereas the work of many of his students is. Sauer and Donald Brand (1932), for example, detailed the prehistoric occupance of Sonora, Mexico, and Sauer (1948) focused essentially on the aboriginal geography of Colima, Mexico. Neither of these studies displayed a specific concern with the arguments in "Morphology of Landscape" (Sauer, 1925). Kniffen (1932), however, considered the natural and later cultural landscape of the Colorado River delta area, recognizing three stages of occupance and Peveril Meigs (1935) analyzed the Dominican mission frontier of lower California, similarly identifying natural and cultural landscapes and the processes of change. Some of the better examples of landscape evolution analyses are concerned with areas outside of North America. An historical geography of the Netherlands by Audrey Lambert (1985) is in close accord with the Berkeley school, the focus being cultural landscape evolution. The initial concern is with the physical background, the approach is chronological, and the material landscape is the focus. Despite this content, there is actually little concern with culture; economics is the central concern. Even more closely associated with the Berkeley school is an historical geography of a small group of islands off Honduras, the Bay Islands (Davidson, 1974). This study reconstructed past landscapes, viewing culture as cause, again commencing with the physical landscape. A sequence of eight cultural occupances occurred, each affecting the form of the landscape, although the principal cause of change was the long-term conflict between the English and the Spanish.

For North American studies, the influence of Sauer has been especially noteworthy. Two major studies by Peter Wacker (1968, 1975) are centered on the concepts of landscape creation and provide detailed examples of this approach. The particular relevance of first effective settlement was noted for the Musconetcong Valley of New Jersey. "The cultural landscape reflects a continuity from the eighteenth-century pioneer period to the present. Houses and barns, as well as many auxiliary structures, still reflect types established in the area during the eighteenth century. This is true despite the recent arrival of many present owners of rural property" (Wacker, 1968, p. 151). Wacker (1968) also detailed the diffusion of specific culture traits into the Musconetcong Valley from elsewhere, particularly the Delaware Valley and New England. For the larger area of New Jersey, Wacker (1975) did not discover universally close links between culture and landscape. Agglomerated settlements, for example, showed little link to cultural background, because of the role played by central authority. However, the impact of first settlement was again present with several of the aboriginal features, notably routeways, which continue to be evident today.

The above examples of full-length studies are a useful indication of landscape analyses that follow the Sauer tradition. There are, however, many more studies that focus on either a particular cultural variable, such as ethnicity, or a particular landscape variable, such as field patterns.

Landscape Studies: Principal Cultural Variables

Many cultural geographic studies focus on particularly influential variables, notably ethnicity and religion. This is essentially the landscape equivalent of delimiting single-factor formal regions. Some cultural variables are undeniably more effective at changing landscape than are others, and this section discusses landscape evolution in these terms.

The close links between ethnicity and landscape in the Ozark region of Missouri were analyzed by Russel Gerlach (1976) on the assumption that cultures, in this case ethnically defined cultures, determine landscape change. The significance of ethnicity was measured by comparing ethnic and nonethnic groups and landscapes. Clear differences were evident in agricultural activity, occupance, religion, and a number of social variables. The ethnic impact on landscape resulted primarily from the tendency of members of ethnic groups to settle in close proximity to one another, the importation of distinctive culture traits, and the existence of distict ethnic attitudes and perceptions. Cultural inertia played a role in the initial creation of landscape, although this was soon affected by processes of trial-and-error learning. Although Gerlach (1976, p. 175) discovered distinctive areas, it was acknowledged that all ethnic groups in the area faced two opposing forces: "On the one hand sentiment strongly favored ethnic retention, and, on the other hand, many advantages awaited those who chose to break with their ethnic past." The distinctiveness of any ethnic landscape is, then, at least partially a measure of its conservatism.

A study of German and non-German Texas farmers showed that the Germans were partially assimilated (Jordan, 1966). The visible cultural landscape varied little between German and non-German, but significant differences were evident with respect to intensity, productivity, and locational stability. A similar conclusion was reached by Sonya Salamon (1985) in a comparative analysis of two ethnic farming communities, one of German origin and the other of Northeastern United States origin. It was shown that there were significant differences in both farm size and organization, with the German farms being smaller and more diversified. A third analysis of Germans and non-Germans showed that Germans were less inclined to expand farms, in the Great Plains, because of an association with subsistence activities (Flora & Stitz, 1985).

Several themes underly such studies. Most important is the question of what happens to ethnic cultural traits in a new area. This question was posed in a rather different form in chapter 5, where the central concern was one of identifying what factors influenced behavior in a new area. Here, the question is posed in terms of trait retention, modification, or elimination with clear differences between ethnic groups.

Some especially distinctive landscapes are associated with religious groups such as the Ozark Amish and Mennonite landscapes, which are characterized by dispersed settlement, a particular farmstead architecture, a greater than typical variety of crops, and a conservative lifestyle reflected in such features as dress and transportation. Distinctive landscapes are most likely to emerge and be maintained where the group abides by certain common rules of organization (Gerlach, 1976).

A classic American case of institutionally based rules is that of the Mormons in Utah. These rules have combined to create a distinct Mormon landscape, which has ten major elements (Francaviglia, 1970). These are wide streets, roadside irrigation ditches, barns and granaries in town, unpainted farm buildings, open fields around town, hay derricks, "Mormon" fences, distinct architecture, use of brick, and Mormon ward chapels. Richard Francaviglia (1970) argued that any town landscape with five of the above ten elements can be safely classed as Mormon, and he then proceeded to map the visual landscape of the Mormons, which is especially clear.

Similar religious landscapes, that is similar in the sense that they diverge markedly from surrounding areas, are evident over smaller areas, wherever closely knit and centrally organized groups have located. For western Canada, Donald Gale and Paul Koroscil (1977) described the landscape of Doukhuber settlements and Richard Friesen (1977) described that of Mennonite settlements. In both cases, the visual landscape was a direct consequence of particular religious beliefs and institutional controls.

For many parts of the world, a most important variable affecting landscape in a host of ways is that of land subdivision. "Few decisions have a more lasting influence on the cultural landscape than those concerning land survey" (Jordan, 1977, p. 141). Surveys are liable to have lasting impressions on the boundaries of property, road networks, and wider aspects of cultural economic occupance. Therefore, this is not an aspect of culture comparable to those already discussed; rather, it is an institutional variable that can have singularly important effects, even to the extent of minimizing the effects of other cultural variables.

The impact of land policies on landscape in southern Africa was detailed by A. J. Christopher (1971) and Donald Holtgrieve (1976) demonstrated the cultural impacts of land speculation. One especially detailed analysis was of the conflict between earlier Mexican and later American land claims in California (Hornbeck, 1979). In all three cases, the author related aspects of land policy and survey to resultant cultural landscapes. One of the more popular examples in North America is the long lot system established by the French in Quebec and Louisiana. This method of subdivision stands in sharp contrast to prevailing rectangular systems and is a vivid indicator of a cultural impress. An important role played by a method of land subdivision is that of obliterating certain potential impacts of local cultures. Land policies are typically imposed from outside and are in many New World instances effectively derived from the European hearth. Thus they constitute a cultural variable that can actually have the effect of minimizing a local cultural impact.

The landscape studies discussed in this section are representative of a major research endeavor by cultural geographers, namely a focus on landscapes created by groups possessing at least one distinctive characteristic. Several variables help to explain the creation of distinct landscapes and their temporal stability. These include such issues as group identity, the impress of central authority, and the nature of contact with other groups. The following section considers the question of the cultural landscape in terms of the typical landscape variables analyzed.

Landscape Studies: Principal Landscape Variables

A focus on material culture elements visible in the landscape has been a hallmark of North American cultural geography. Probably the most successful exponent of this type of study is Kniffen, who employed this focus largely to demonstrate certain generalizations involving questions of regionalization and diffusion. A study of Louisiana house types enabled Kniffen (1936) to delimit "culturogeographic" regions and a study of covered bridges resulted in useful generalizations about the diffusion process (Kniffen, 1951). More recently, Kniffen (1974, p. 254) wrote that "the material forms constituting the landscape are the geographer's basic lore. The cultural geographer deals primarily with the occupance pattern, the marks of man's living on the land. He finds his data, his evidence, in buildings, fields, towns, communication systems and concomitant features."

Other cultural geographers have focused on some particular features of the material landscape, again with cultural generalizations in mind. In a detailed study of American log buildings, Jordan (1985) showed that a major influence on mid-American log construction was the cultural tradition of settlers from the Fenno-Scandian area. This was essentially because the techniques that such settlers brought to America were easily transferred to other settlers. Furthermore, the earlier that settlers arrived, the greater was their cultural impact. In a similar fashion, Jordan (1982) studied graveyards in Texas as an indicator of cultural patterns and delimited three types: southern, Hispanic, and German. Distributions were then explained as a result of diffusion processes. As a final example of such work, Peter Ennals (1972) classified nineteenth-century southern Ontario barns and analyzed both origins and evolution. Each of these studies focused on a particular aspect of the visible landscape, and yet each succeeded in generating useful generalizations about cultural landscape evolution. One criticism at this stage is that there is rarely any consideration given to the specific social or belief setting or to the related issue of the function and meaning of such objects in the landscape. A substantial attempt to correct this problem is that by John Stilgoe (1982) in an analysis of the American landscape between 1580 and 1845. This work related landscape features to people and explained the value of such features much in the tradition of John B. Jackson.

CULTURAL CONTACT AND TRANSFER

The remainder of this chapter focuses first on cultural contact and transfer, then on diffusion independent of migration, and finally on processes of internal transformation. The history of anthropology is one of changing emphases; an early concern with contact, a later recognition that diffusion played a role in change, and a belated acknowledgment of the importance of internally generated change. This intellectual development resulted essentially from assumptions about native North American cultures. A transition from viewing contact as cause of change to viewing diffusion as cause of change required a "more tolerant view of Indians as being flexible enough to make use of new ideas" (Trigger, 1985, p. 65). Similarly, the transition to recognition of the importance of internal transformation required reappraisal of the vitality of native cultures. This section comprises the discussion of migration, diffusion, and internally generated change. Inevitably, both of the related themes of culture contact and transfer have already been touched on in chapter 5 as well as earlier sections of this chapter. This section is, however, the first occasion on which these themes are explicitly elaborated. Many aspects of cultural landscapes can be traced to the contact between two or more groups and the transfer, or lack of transfer, that resulted. These are also themes especially attractive to anthropologists interested more in culture change than in landscape change. The anthropological focus has typically been on acculturation, which may be defined as the process that results "when groups of individuals having different cultures come into continuous first-hand contact, with subsquent changes in the original culture patterns of either or both groups" (Herskovits, 1938, p. 10). This broad definition includes diffusion, which is covered in the following section. For the present purpose, the key components of acculturation are culture change and assimilation, the latter being the potential end product of the larger process. Furthermore, the principal geographic concern is with acculturation as reflected in landscape or, more generally, in spatial organization.

A prime consideration in any discussion of contact and subsequent developments relates to the motivations of the incoming group. Contact may be accidental, a consequence of movement but without any specific intentions on the part of the incoming group. Many contacts between hunting and gathering societies fall into this category. In such cases, the result of contact was often a gradual agreement, through experience, on territorial limits. Contact may result from the movement of groups exploring or settling. Much of the European overseas expansion from the fifteenth century onward is of this type. The result of this contact is often aggression, exploitation, or acculturation. A third cause of contact is the deliberate movement of a group in order to convert or exploit. Much of the Spanish Conquest and subjugation of Central America is of this type. Some examples of culture contact and culture transfer are now discussed.

European Expansion: Unintentional Change

Early European contacts with North American natives were often one incidental component of the European exploratory process. Characteristic motivations for movement were primarily economic, such as a desire for precious metals or for shorter routes to the east. Contact was inevitable, but was rarely a matter of central concern. Despite this, it has typically been assumed that contact was the first occasion on which native societies experienced change. This conventional wisdom is now seen as incorrect. Aboriginal societies were not static and the contact experience continued, rather than initiated, change.

Indeed, recent archaeological evidence has suggested that many of the apparent results of contact were not dramatic revisions of earlier culture but logical extensions of already occurring change. For the Huron groups in Ontario, for example, there was "a significant revival of intentional trade in the late prehistoric period and it was along the networks that supplied traditional prestige goods that European materials first seem to have reached the interior of eastern North America" (Trigger, 1985, p. 162). This is not to deny that Europeans and European goods generated change, but it is important to place such change in the wider context of aboriginal culture. A basic problem here is that traditional ethnographic descriptions do not describe cultures prior to contact, but rather cultures soon after contact. Archaeological data are required for precontact descriptions and this means that much of the twentieth-century work by anthropologists needs to be either reinterpreted or, at least, carefuly evaluated (Trigger, 1985, p. 57). This process of reevaluation was one part of a shift of interest in archaeology in the 1950s, from seeing diffusion and migration as the primary causes of culture change to seeing internally generated change as primary. Emphasis is now on cultures as adaptive systems; a development fostered especially by Lewis Binford (1983). This movement away from cultures as collections of separate traits to cultures as "integrated behavioral patterns relating peoples to their environment" is now well established (Trigger, 1985, p. 70).

Much of the early culture change that occurred in many European-native contact situations was not intentional. Natives accommodated those aspects of European culture that were in accord with their own world view. Lethal epidemics, which so often affected natives, were beyond the control of both groups. A number of examples are now noted.

For the Haida of the Queen Charlotte Islands, British Columbia, European contact prompted major population losses, an altered settlement pattern, and some amendments to the seasonal cycle of activities (Henderson, 1978). European-introduced diseases, especially smallpox, decimated the Haida. Loss of population prompted adjustments to settlement with both abandonment and fusion of villages. These changes were dramatic in their impact; they were unintentional and rapid and occurred repeatedly between 1774 and the 1860s. The altered settlement pattern also represented a Haida attempt to adjust locations to better function within the fur trade. Impacts on the seasonal cycle were more limited. John Henderson (1978, pp. 17–18) argued that the cycle served important functions for the Haida, which resulted in a strong resistance to change. The Haida adopted new activities but retained their seasonal schedule. This is a good example of change occurring only if such change was acceptable to the natives. Other possible changes, such as a sedentary way of life that was forcefully advocated by missionaries, were rejected because they were not in accord with Haida desires. A second example, that of the Choctaws in Mississippi, highlighted similar points (McKee, 1971). An extensive contact period from 1698 onward involved Spanish, French, English, Americans, and missionaries. The Choctaw were most responsive to the French and the missionaries but persisted throughout as a sedentary agricultural group. Again, it is evident that the aboriginal group was selective in determining the change that took place. David Wishart (1976) arrived at similar conclusions regarding the fur-trade–generated contact for the early nineteenth-century northern Great Plains.

The key general observation here is that contact necessarily prompted change, but that the specifics of such change were determined by the receiving group. North American natives typically accepted those aspects of European culture that caused the least disruption. At the same time, they rejected efforts by the Europeans to impose radical changes. Stewart Raby (1973, p. 36) emphasized that, by 1900, "the Indian bands of southern Saskatchewan . . . had by no means been converted into the competitive agrarian individualists sought by their white guardians. Much had been said to them of the virtues of agriculture. Farming, and not the supposedly demoralizing pursuits of hunting and fishing, was identified as work." Even those aspects of the contacted culture that were accepted were often initially used in a different way (I. W. Brown, 1979). In a similar fashion, it is evident that European society often failed to satisfy native aspirations; with reference to Australian aboriginals, Henry Reynolds (1982, p. 129) noted that "young blacks who went willingly towards the Europeans fully expected to be able to participate in their obvious material abundance. Reciprocity and sharing were so fundamental in their own society that they probably expected to meet similar behavior when they crossed the racial frontier."

The basic conclusion is that much unintentional change occurred while some attempts at enforced change yielded little result. The unintentional change that did occur was typically determined by the receiving culture, whether it was aboriginal or European, and did not radically alter the structure of society. A major exception was the depopulation caused by disease.

The understanding of the consequences of contact, however, are far from complete. Contemporary ethnic history rages with controversies (Trigger, 1982). One of the best examples of a controversial interpretation is the view that the native overexploitation of both fur-bearing animals and game was caused not by a developing dependence on European goods but rather by the aboriginal belief that animal spirits were responsible for the ravages of disease (Martin, 1978). This belief prompted the natives to reject traditional beliefs, embrace Christianity, and deliberately exterminate the animals. Critics have advanced many counter-arguments (Krech, 1981).

European Expansion: Intentional Change

In some areas of the expanding European world, aboriginal culture change was effectively demanded by the incomers. In addition to exploratory and economic motives, there were active attempts to alter native lifestyles. A clear example of this type is evident in Guatemala. Spanish movement into Guatemala was not one aspect of an incidental process, but rather a deliberate attempt to both conquer and subjugate, which generated conflict and change. "Subjugation by imperial Spain . . . was a traumatic experience for the native peoples of Guatemala, more so because disruptions caused by military confrontation were reinforced for centuries thereafter by the operation of Spanish promoted forces that radically altered the nature and appearance of Indian life'' (Lovell, 1985, p. 58). The initial contact, which was military, occurred between 1524 and 1541 and took the form of a ruthless Spanish takeover of the land and the people. This was followed by conscious efforts to impose a Spanish way of life on the conquered groups. Conquest succeeded by culture change was the characteristic sequence in areas contacted by the Spanish. Culture change was imposed by a process of obligatory resettlement, which invariably severed ties with ancestral lands, and by the demands placed on native labor. The resultant relations between Spanish and Indian were those of oppressor and oppressed; an institutionalized exploitation was characteristic. Native culture and landscape changed with the Spanish hacienda system involving new tools, crops, and animals. All of the above occurred in Guatemala, but the most drastic change was that of population decline. Massive demographic collapse occurred throughout Spanish America with drops of over 90 percent in perhaps 150 years being typical (Lovell, 1985, p. 176).

The Guatemalan example is characteristic. Spanish Conquest of the Andean region was also a well-organized vigorous process of military subjugation followed by conversion to Christianity and labor exploitation. The Indians were controlled and surpluses were extracted from the Indian economy by means of the encomienda. Overall, throughout Spanish America, processes of intentional change were in effect and had a major impact on native cultures. Necessarily, many of the details of change varied spatially and were not formally imposed by the Spanish, but the overriding impression is one of massive forced change.

Probably the most effective explanation for the changes that occurred in areas of European overseas expansion involves recognition of both the role played by disease and the fact that the contacting cultures were technologically unequal. Any technologically advanced society that attempted to impose change was typically able to do so, even if the details of changes were not identical to the intentions. The technological inferiority of the contacted groups gradually resulted in their becoming dependent on the newcomers. It must also be remembered that Europeans believed in their own moral superiority, and natives were treated accordingly.

DIFFUSION

Explanations of culture change tend to emphasize either internal transformation or external stimuli, migration, and diffusion. Geographers do not typically distinguish between migration and diffusion, other than to see the former as one component of the latter. Not so with anthropologists for whom migration and diffusion are quite separate doctrines. Nineteenth-century anthropology explained cultural change largely in terms of migration, and it was not until the early twentieth century that diffusion, independent of migration, was argued to play a role. Thus, in addition to disagreements about internally versus externally generated change, there are also disagreements about the details of externally generated change. The previous discussion of contact focused on migration, and the current discussion reviews the importance of diffusion as cause of culture change. Anthropological recognition of diffusion was prompted by awareness that non-European cultures might be receptive to new ideas without these ideas being imposed. The anthropological distinction between migration and diffusion requires some elaboration. The long-standing acceptance of migration can be understood as follows. "If we accept the idea, implicit in nearly all creation myths, that man and his culture went forth together by immutable bonds, then obviously we can imagine the movement of culture from one place to another only when its human carriers move from one place to another" (Adams, 1978, p. 1).

Acceptance of migration resulted in diffusion being interpreted as evidence of migration. It was only when a culture concept emerged that was independent of specific populations that diffusion independent of migration became a feasible scenario. This is usually ascribed to Edward Tylor, and diffusion became regarded as a cause of culture change by the early twentieth century. Within anthropology, the consequence can be characterized as a battle between migrationists and diffusionists, with the key argument concerning the relative importance of movement of people and movement of ideas. Both Kroeber and Lowie, among others, regarded diffusion as the principal means of culture change.

Not surprisingly, the anthropological debate has occurred largely without reference to work in other disciplines, notably sociology and geography. Anthropologists have failed to appreciate the sociological distinction between awareness of an innovation and later acceptance of that innovation and have generally made little use of the work of Everett Rogers (1962). Similarly, anthropologists have not pursued the concepts and techniques developed by Hagerstrand (1953, 1967) focusing on communication and distance. Despite these limitations, the anthropological literature is replete with examples of diffusion as a cause of change.

For the cultural geographer, there are two principal strands to diffusion research (L. A. Brown, 1981, p. 16). The traditional cultural geographic view has close ties with early twentieth-century anthropology, especially with Kroeber, and is one component of the landscape school. The spatial view evolved in the 1960s as one component of the spatial analytic emphasis and derived from the work of Hagerstrand (1953, 1967).

The traditional view focused on diffusion as an explanation of cultural origins and cultural region as well as cultural landscape evolution. Carter (1978, p. 56) wrote that "diffusion is the master process of human culture." Within a fairly consistent theme was embraced a wide variety of material landscape features. Examples of features analyzed included house types (Kniffen, 1965; Jordan, 1983), covered bridges (Kniffen, 1951), grid pattern towns (Stanislawski, 1946), agricultural fairs (Kniffen, 1961), place names (Leighly, 1978), tobacco production (Seig, 1963; Raitz, 1973), and religious settlement (Crowley, 1978). The typical analysis was of a single material landscape feature, sometimes investigated detached from any larger cultural contact. The issue of single versus mulitple invention might be debated; the social, often ethnic, characteristics of receiving groups were often considered; and a strong emphasis was placed on description and mapping of features through space and time. The importance attached to diffusion by cultural geographers is evident in the standard texts: Broek and Webb (1978) viewed diffusion in a global perspective, Spencer and Thomas (1973) made many references to diffusion throughout their text, and Jordan and Rowntree (1986) included cultural diffusion as one of five themes applicable in principle to most aspects of cultural geography. In the most general sense, diffusion was and is viewed as a process affecting both cultural and cultural landscape evolution (Kirk, 1975). The distinction between migration and diffusion is rarely necessary as the central interest is in the effects and not in the process per se. The links between migration and diffusion were effectively summarized by Christopher Salter (1971, pp. 3–4) who wrote that ''the cultural geographer views man's mobility with a tripartite perspective: the catalyst for movement, the effect of movement on trait or people in motion, and the consequences of such movement.''

The spatial approach to diffusion emerged in the 1960s with strong theoretical, quantitative, and eventually behavioral interests, but it is in effect a logical growth from the traditional approach. Indeed, one of the earliest American discussions of the pioneering work of Hagerstrand was provided by John Leighly (1954), a discussion that clearly indicated both the cultural and the conceptual aspects of that work. Hagerstrand (1953, 1967), first published in Swedish in 1953, was not generally known in the English-speaking world until the 1960s, at which time the cultural content of the work was deemphasized at the expense of the revolutionary conceptual and technical aspects. It needs to be remembered that a central concern for Hagerstrand (1953, 1967) was the process of diffusion as a factor affecting landscape evolution and that the analysis was explictly in the Swedish and, to a lesser extent, the German geographic traditions (Pred, 1967, p. 305). Earlier work by Hagerstrand (1951) had focused on migration and the evolution of cultural regions. The pioneering content of the diffusion research requires some elaboration as it was developed in the 1960s.

First, the role of chance in the process of diffusion, and hence in landscape creation, was explicitly acknowledged by use of a procedure known as Monte Carlo simulation, which allows for the likelihood of any given event to be interpreted as a probability. Second, a number of generalizations were identified and labeled empirical regularities. These included the neighborhood effect, or distance decay effect; the hierarchical effect whereby innovation acceptance proceeds down the urban hierarchy; the notion of individual resistance to acceptance; and the S-shaped curve that describes a process of acceptance over time, which is initially slow, then rapid, and then finally slow once more. Third, an integral part of both the neighborhood and hierarchical effects was the idea that a communication process preceded and essentially explained the subsequent details of the innovation adoption process. Fourth, surrogate data were employed in lieu of communication details. Geographers following in the Hagerstrand tradition largely ignored the cultural content, rather centering their interest on the mechanics of the diffusion process. Work by rural sociologists was used to further develop the ideas of communication and adoption processes. It was appreciated that the adoption process proceeded through stages such as awareness, interest, evaluation, trial, and adoption. It was similarly appreciated that individuals varied in their innovativeness. The links with sociology, especially rural sociology, increased while the links with anthropology were minimal. One example of a Hagerstrand type analysis was that by Leonard Bowden (1965), which was concerned with the diffusion of irrigation wells in Colorado. In this study, the diffusion process was a central concern, the cultural landscape a lesser concern. Other diffusion analyses dealt with such diverse issues as cholera (Pyle, 1969), modernization (Riddell, 1970), and Negro ghettos in American cities (Morrill, 1965). The most detailed discussion of such work is contained in L. A. Brown, (1981), a volume that also reviewed market and infrastructure studies, economic history-based studies, and development studies.

Since circa 1970, some weaknesses of Hagerstrand type analyses have been identified and new research directions pursued. Weaknesses include a tendency to view innovations in isolation, not altogether a new weakness, and a tendency to ignore the effects of diffusion. One fruitful area for further work concerns diffusion as it impacts on the use of resources in space and over time. The impact of innovation diffusion on a given culture is not merely the presence of that innovation. Rather, some innovations are time saving and cause substantial shifts in the daily time budgets of household members. Other innovations are time demanding, such as a village school in an agrarian society. Analyses oriented in this fashion are less diffusion-process oriented and more culture-change oriented. A second new direction concerns the extent to which innovativeness is spatially variable. Geographers immersed in the spatial analytic tradition have assumed that all groups are equally receptive to an innovation. Anthropologists and cultural geographers are now correcting this simplification. A related development concerns the increased sophistication of behavioral interests with their necessary acknowledgment of individual differences in cognition. Viewed in simple terms, the process of innovation diffusion is one type of learning process (Norton, 1974). M. A. Brown, (1981, p. 126) noted that

> Hagerstrand's 1953 work can be viewed as behavioral in that it is primarily concerned with the processes by which individuals came to know about and accept innovations, and it recognizes individual differences in these processes. The reliance upon a simulation methodology, however, limited Hagerstrand's ability to test his ideas concerning adoption as a learning process.

It is now recognized that the relevance of behavioral variables varies with the innovation in question, the adoption unit, and the particular group. It is appropriate to suggest that groups such as the poor, less educated, handicapped, aged, and unemployed have access to fewer behavioral alternatives. A third new direction argues that it is necessary to take into account social, economic, and political conditions over which most individuals exercise little control. This radical view thus demands an understanding of the state and institutions and argues that different diffusions necessitate different explanations, that is, they have different causes.

One example that integrates the second and third directions relates to the situation whereby valuable innovations are preempted by early adopters. This may be typical in Third World areas when early adopters are entrenched elites who can transform initial profits into permanent profits by a variety of means such as political lobbying. Donald Freeman (1985) discussed the examples of coffee, pyrethrum, and processed dairy products in Kenya. The impact on the cultural landscape is the strengthening of landed elites within a general pattern of rural poverty. The impact on the adoption process is that the number of potential adopters is drastically reduced.

L. A. Brown, (1981, p. 17) noted that ''the directions of contemporary diffusion research in the cultural geography tradition are not apparent to this author.'' In an important sense, the traditional approach has helped to correct some of the deficiencies of the spacial approach, particularly those deficiences relating to culture and landscape change and to the role played by social and other preconditions. In a penetrating analysis of the spatial and traditional interests, James Blaut (1977) argued that the traditional interest, particularly the various works of Kniffen, provides a firm foundation for further development of theory primarily because of the breadth of the research interests. A later analysis (Blaut, 1987, p. 43) critically reviewed the underlying assumption that ''the natural state of affairs in any region is to have a center from which innovations emanate and a periphery toward which they diffuse.'' The preferred alternative involved assumptions of human, and therefore spatial, equality. The result of such revised thinking is a new set of hypotheses about culture history including, for example, the suggestion that large areas of Asia, Africa, and Europe were simultaneously involved in the origin of agriculture.

CULTURAL EVOLUTION

Interest in cultural evolution has been essentially restricted to anthropology, where it has experienced much criticism. Cultural evolution concepts were advocated by Herbert Spencer, Taylor, and Lewis Morgan and later criticized by Franz Boas and Lowie. The only substantive evidence of evolutionist thinking in geography was in connection with environmental determinism (Wagner, 1977). Recent advocates of the concept in anthropology include Leslie White, Julian Steward, and Marshall Sahlins and Elman Service. Some of the above developments were discussed in chapter 2. It is appropriate now to distinguish between general evolution and specific evolution. General evolution "is concerned with the progress of culture through successive levels of development," whereas specific evolution "involves the diversification of cultural forms by adaptation" and examines "the relationship of particular cultures to their environment" (Newson, 1976, p. 244). The former is primarily associated with White and the latter with Steward. Neither type of evolution precludes the possibility of change generated by culture contact and the Law of Cultural Dominance states that where two or more cultures are present in a region, the most effective culture will spread over the greatest distance. Effective is defined in terms of the ability to exploit energy resources (Sahlins & Service, 1960, p. 75). The merits of adopting an evolutionist perspective in cultural geography are argued by Linda Newson (1976, p. 254) to be as follows. "Adopting the specific evolution perspective, the development of a culture in relationship to its environment may be traced, whilst the same culture may be viewed in terms of evolutionary stages if the general evolutionary approach is employed." A major distinction between ecological and evolutionary approaches is that the former focuses on relations between culture and land whereas the latter can consider relations between cultures.

There is a close tie between the above ideas and those of adaptation and preadaptation. Cultural adaptation is the process of change in a culture following some other physical or human change (Denevan, 1983, p. 401). A good example of adaptation is that of Florida's Seminole Indians in the nineteenth century, who demonstrated a "remarkable ability to accomplish a swift succession of successful ethnoecologic changes" (Craig & Peebles, 1974, p. 83). The particular explanation in this case was twofold: an unrelenting pressure from enemies and the presence of Negro slaves. Cultural preadaptation argues that "the most important adjustments to a new environment develop *before* entering the new environment" (Newton, 1974, p. 144). Thus cultural preadaptation is one aspect of general evolution. The specific example developed by Milton Newton (1974) is that of an upland South culture that repeatedly preempted the frontier zone between 1775 and 1825.

The general ideas briefly discussed under the heading of cultural evolution have close ties with ecological thinking and are not insistent on any antidiffusionist stance. It is being recognized that a considerable anthropological literature is available to cultural geographers offering distinctive and potentially valuable viewpoints.

CONCLUDING COMMENTS

One distinguishing feature of cultural geography throughout the twentieth century has been the explicit interest in space and time. This interest is in marked contradistinction to regional geography and spatial analysis. The interest in temporal change has typically meant a close link with historical geography such that much research can be correctly classified as both cultural and historical. One of the distinguishing features of much of the cultural research is the emphasis on landscape, sometimes expressed as a regional interest. As noted, Sauer and others chose not to rigorously distinguish between landscape and region; this is especially evident in the ideas developed by J. E. Spencer and Ronald Horvath (1963) concerning the evolution of agricultural regions. A consideration of twentieth-century geography is strongly suggestive of the beneficial consequences of including time and of eschewing artificial distinctions, such as those between landscape and region.

Much traditional and contemporary cultural geography includes an emphasis on evolution, and thus, an evolutionary emphasis is not necessarily an ideal theme for a single chapter in a cultural volume. It is acknowledged that much of the material in other chapters also incorporates an evolutionary emphasis, and indeed, that some of the material in this chapter, for example, that concerned with world regions, lacks explicit time content. Despite these inconsistencies, it is argued that, overall, an interest in evolution is the dominant theme for much of this chapter's material whereas the material in other chapters is characterized by some other dominant emphasis.

An interest in evolution continues to be apparent in much cultural geographic research but it is clear that new influences are helping to generate new outlooks. Much contemporary research is centered on either a strongly social or strongly ecological thrust. Both of these emphases, especially the latter, have been a part of mainstream cultural geography for some time, but their rise to research prominence is relatively recent. It is these two emphases that are considered in chapters 7 and 8. The interest in evolution continues, but it is not always as evident as it has been in this chapter.

7

Understanding Landscape: Symbolism and Social Processes

As was the case in chapters 5 and 6, the current chapter embraces both conceptual and empirical work, discusses work from several disciplines, and strives to identify and detail a particular research emphasis in cultural geography. The central concern is with work typically labeled social geography in the British tradition, but that is currently becoming more closely integrated with the landscape school. This integration reflects a broadening of both of the traditional research interests. Social geography has benefited from input from sociology and social anthropology and the landscape school has increasingly begun to acknowledge social and institutional variables. As a consequence, there is an emerging commitment to symbolic interpretations of landscape and to group-centered analyses. In terms of particular research thrusts three major contributions are evident. First, Swedish geographers, under the inspiration of Torsten Hagerstrand, have evolved novel concepts regarding the social causes of landscape formation. Second, British geographers, partly inspired by other social scientists, have argued for alternative interpretations of landscape relying on both radical and humanist concepts. Third, geographers are demonstrating increased concern with social rather than material landscapes. Together, these contributions provide a new dimension to cultural geography although the interest continues to be in both space and time, thus reinforcing the traditional cultural focus on evolution. The first section of this chapter discusses the emergence of the symbolic and social emphases in terms of earlier contributions and of current emphases.

Once the character and credibility of the approach is established, attention turns to representative conceptual and empirical work. The second section of this chapter focuses on the concept of vernacular regions, and this is followed by sections on language, religion, ethnicity, and class. There are also sections on the social geography of the frontier and the social geography of settlement. Some concluding comments terminate the chapter.

Like chapters 5 and 6, this chapter is notable for variety. The several inspirations mean that a number of intellectual traditions are represented but the common threads of a combined commitment to society and landscape evolution are very much in evidence.

SOCIAL GEOGRAPHY

Development

It has already been suggested that social geography is the British counterpart to North American cultural geography. This is correct in the sense that North American geography departments have not typically taught or researched social issues whereas British departments have similarly neglected cultural themes, and in the sense that there is a general overlap of methods and topics. The different experiences are most easily explained in terms of the different intellectual origins of the two interests. North American cultural geography has clear European origins, but was essentially "created" by Carl Sauer and has not been "exported" elsewhere. British social geography, on the other hand, has origins in French sociology, in the Chicago school of human ecology, and in British human geography. Different inspirations generated different intellectual pursuits. The origins and early development of social geography are now considered.

As with cultural geography, there has been a tendency to equate social geography with all of human geography. Quite possibly such a broad view is derived from Vidal who linked social relations with genres de vie and hence with particular *pays* or regions. More generally, this tendency reflects the diverse origins of the term. In a review of the earliest occurrences of the term social geography, Gary Dunbar (1977) concluded that it was first used by French sociologists of the Le Play school in the 1880s and by Elisée Reclus in the 1890s. Neither of these early uses proved especially influential, with the Le Play sociologists becoming secondary in influence to Emile Durkheim while Reclus, as noted in chapter 3, did not exert a major impact. Few geographers have acknowledged these early inputs, one exception is Wreford Watson (1951). A detailed statement by G. W. Hoke (1907) also had little influence.

By the 1930s, social geography was developing as a distinct subdiscipline in Britain following a programmatic statement by P. W. Roxby (1930) and following the publication of social geography books by members of the Vidal school. The result was a social geography that was essentially concerned with the social patterns in a regional context. Characteristic works focused on population, occupational structures, and religion. Similar to cultural geography in the 1920s, this new field was explicitly antienvironmentalist. Raymond Pahl (1965, p. 81) suggested that social geography was concerned with the "processes and patterns involved in an understanding of socially defined populations in their spatial setting.''

It is clear, then, that social geography has origins in the European sociological and British geographic traditions. Interestingly, it appears to have also been influenced by American sociology in the form of the Chicago school of human ecology. The work of Walter Firey (1947) on Boston is especially significant because it laid great stress on social values, specifically symbolic values. This inspiration is largely urban in character and underlies the largely urban content of social geography in marked contradistinction to the rural focus of cultural geography. Social geography by the 1960s was an uncertain field with rather disparate intellectual stimuli, unlike cultural geography at that time, which had a very clear identity with one school of thought and with the evolution of landscape concept. The less precise content of social geography allowed it to participate more fully in the conceptual and quantitative upheavals of the 1960s whereas cultural geography, as already noted, largely abstained from such involvement. In the 1960s and 1970s social geography became more quantitative, more behaviorally oriented, and more relevant, and thus even more detached from cultural geography.

Thus, the development of the field of social geography is quite different from the case of cultural geography. Both the details and the general pattern vary. Prior to the 1970s, limited interaction took place and each discipline failed to make any real impact in the areas dominated by the other. Given this conclusion, it is perhaps surprising that there is currently a convergence of the two. The explanation appears to be linked to the dissatisfaction evident in both fields in the 1960s and early 1970s. Cultural geography in North America lacked vigor, because of limited contact with other areas of geography, whereas social geography in Britain continued to be overly diverse and lacking a central focus. The result was that both sets of interests sought new perspectives and new intellectual stimuli. To a significant extent, both areas have turned to similar developments for inspiration. These two searches have confirmed the underlying similarity of the two fields and further served to unite them. The general nature of the recent developments has been identified in chapter 4. Particular aspects are now considered.

Current Emphases

The traditional separation of cultural and social geography partly resulted from the reluctance of British geographers to discuss culture and the parallel reluctance of North American geographers to discuss society. The search for new concepts is prompting both groups to rethink priorities. This rethinking is also prompted by an increasing recognition of the role of space in sociological analyses and architectural analyses. Attempts are now being made by a variety of scholars to construct ''theories of social space'' (Bourdieu, 1985) and to deal with the ''problem of space'' (Hillier & Hanson, 1984). It is increasingly being acknowledged by scholars outside of geography that societies are spatially distributed and that societies assume definite spatial forms. "Spatial order is one of the most striking means by which we recognize the existence of the *cultural* differences between one social formation and another, that is, differences in the way in which members of these societies live out and reproduce their social existence" (Hillier & Hanson, 1984, p. 27).

Of greater relevance in the present context, there are two sets of concepts that are proving most influential. The first set of concepts are those currently evolving, primarily from Swedish geographers, under the leadership of Hagerstrand. The essence of time geography is that humans are not beings isolated from any wider context but rather are individuals on life paths. "In fact he discovered history and again created a link between history and geography by expanding the scope of the old concept of milieu. In this way he gathered up the threads of Vidal's thought" (van Paassen, 1981, p. 20). Hagerstrand, in common with earlier geographers such as Carl Ritter, Friedrich Ratzel, and Vidal, thus integrates geography and history. A major prompting for the emergence of time geography was Hagerstrand's dissatisfaction with the atemporal and dehumanized spatial analysis of the 1960s. As noted in chapter 6, Hagerstrand himself contributed significantly to spatial diffusion research at that time, but the spatial and quantitative aspects of his diffusion work were overemphasized at the expense of significant cultural content. The enunciation of time geography is at least partly an attempt to redress the balance. There are three key notions. It is assumed that human life is both spatially and temporally structural, that human life has both physical and social dimensions, and that human activities are subject to constraints. The general concern is with social life and especially the principle of neighborliness. Examples of applications are abundant and include work by Tommy Carlstein (1982) on preindustrial societies and by Allan Pred (1981a) on nineteenth-century cities. Both of these works, explicitly framed in time geographic perspective, are penetrating analyses of individual and/or social change. There is little concern with landscape per se, but the strong focus on change and society renders the concepts attractive to both cultural and social geographers. At present, the greater interest has come from social geographers who have also identified close links between time geography and structuration concepts. This second set of concepts, structuration, is now considered and the possible ties to time geography noted.

It appears that social geography is becoming increasingly sociological and sociology is increasingly acknowledging the role of space. These developments are evident in the formulation of structuration concepts by Anthony Giddens and the geographic response to these concepts. Structuration is a complex set of ideas that attempts to integrate the work of a wide variety of thinkers, including Durkheim, Sigmund Freud, Karl Marx, and Max Weber, into a rigorous framework. Central to structuration is the notion of interdependence of human agency and social structure in time and space. Furthermore, both agency and structure are temporally and spatially specific. The first of these two ideas is a particular interpretation of a long-standing debate between the relative merits of structuralist and individualist views. The structuration view sees social structures as being constituted by human agency and being, at the same time, the medium of this constitution. Thus, the first idea is an attempt to assess the status of individuals within society, an issue raised more generally in chapter 4. The second idea is undoubtedly a welcome recognition of the relevance of both time and space in sociological analyses. These two central ideas are especially evident in Giddens (1979). They have proved attractive to social geographers in general, but especially to those involved in time-geographic research, such as Carlstein (1981) who assessed structuration most favorably. The general links between the two are apparent with their shared emphasis on space and time and the shared focus on social interaction. Nicky Gregson (1986), however, recommended that geographers approach Giddens cautiously. Drawing on an observation by John Agnew and James Duncan (1981), to the effect that the importation of ideas from another discipline requires a full and careful prior evaluation, Gregson (1986, p. 201) concluded that "if we are to incorporate Giddens social theory into human geography in the future a critical approach to his work will prove vital." To a certain extent such a conclusion had been anticipated by Giddens (1983), who counseled against perhaps inappropriate integrations of time-geographic and structuration concepts, although this key theorist has also observed that "there are no logical or methodological differences between human geography and sociology!" (Giddens, 1984, p. 368). This is a stimulating, but not universally acceptable, assertion.

The two central ideas of structuration noted above have been assessed both conceptually and empirically by geographers. Pred (1984) was critical of geographers for viewing place as inert when it should correctly be viewed as an historically contingent process, as a transformation of space and of nature, which cannot be detached from the transformation of society. North American cultural geographers might well balk at any suggestion that they have viewed place as inert. Works already discussed by Donald Meinig (1969), on Texas, and by John Henderson (1978), on the Haida, are not conceptually sophisticated by time-geographic or structuration standards, but they are both clear examples of related spatial and social change. This suggests that the empirical aims of some current developments in social geography are not far detached from those of a more traditional cultural geography. This suggestion is supported by recent work from J. S. Duncan (1985, p. 187) who modified structuration concepts and then applied the modified concepts to a structuration process in Sri Lanka involving citizens and officials "both shaping and being shaped by the ideological framework of the society."

The above brief account of time geography and structuration clearly demonstrates an increasing convergence of some sociology and some social geography and, to a lesser degree, some sociology and some cultural geography. It is a little misleading, however, to suggest that such convergences are limited to these concepts. Less specific evidence is available from North American and British geographers and these two sources are now noted.

Recognition that spatial and social behavior are inextricably entwined was central to the social geography textbook authored by John Jakle, Stanley Brunn, and Curtis Roseman (1976). The conceptual structure of the book was derived significantly from symbolic interactionism and permitted a definition of social geography as the study of "human spatial behavior and the derived geographical patterns from the point of view of society: the summation of a population's symbolic interactions" (Jakle, Brunn, & Roseman, 1976, p. 7). The authors advocated social geography as preferable to cultural geography, because of the implied emphasis on communication processes through which symbolic inter- actions take place. But it is evident that their basic premises are appropriate to much cultural geography. There are emphases on the inevitable integration of social and geographical identities, on the social structure of space, on the spatial structure of society, and on social and spatial change. A textbook on England and Wales likewise acknowledged that individuals are constrained in their be- havior by the character of the groups to which they belong (Dennis & Clout, 1980, p. 2).

Similar ideas are central to much of the work of the cultural geographer Philip Wagner (1972, 1974) who saw distinct landscapes and societies evolving in response to communication processes often generated by social institutions. A related needed emphasis on the spatial aspects of social change was noted by David Robinson (1979, p. 1) for work on colonial Latin America. Finally, there are several examples of research that take "material culture and look at its spatial expression, at how material items dispense and coalesce across the earth's surface to form distinctive configurations that reflect different histories and different societies" (Richardson, 1974b, p. 197).

The above literature is representative of a "new" social geography, which is characterized by a healthy diversity of ideas and a willingness to import useful ideas from other disciplines. The links with cultural geography are evident such that either adjectival geography is a generally acceptable term. Perhaps surpris- ingly, however, this type of work has not been widely quoted by some social geographers who appear to be, on occasions, reinventing key concepts. For example, one recurring feature of contemporary social geography is the correct insistence on a social-spatial integration. Somewhat misleadingly, however, there is a tendency to derive inspiration for such integration almost solely from time- geographic and/or structuration concepts (see Gregory & Urry, 1985, p. 3). A popular recent assertion is that "it is not just that the spatial is socially con- structed; the social is spatially constructed too" (Massey, 1984, p. 6) This theme was implicit in the textbook by Jakle, Brunn, and Roseman (1976, p. 9) who wrote that "in describing people socially it may be necessary only to describe the places that they occupy."

Conclusions

This section on social geography has attempted to indicate origins, development, and current trends. It is emphasized that cultural geography is essentially North American whereas social geography is essentially British. This unfortunate state of affairs is partly explained by circumstances of origin and partly by the impact of other disciplines. Regardless of terminological differences, today there is a shared interest in revitalization. An emerging North American social geography and a rejuvenated British social geography are closely linked to recent social theory and are identifying traditional cultural concerns of landscape and change. Much recent social geography is explicitly derived from the landscape tradition, with culture being conceived as social practice and landscape being conceived as place (P. Jackson, 1986, p. 120). The current situation is far from resolved, but a reasonable interpretation sees a continuing integration of human-geographic and social theory, the latter meaning both sociological and anthropological concepts. While the theoretical issues continue to be debated, empirical work continues unabated. This empirical work centers on the notions of symbolism and society and, collectively, is adding appreciably to our understanding of landscape. This work is now discussed under a series of thematic, as opposed to conceptual, headings. The work discussed varies in conceptual sophistication, but the central themes are always evident.

VERNACULAR REGIONS

Inclusion of this section in the current chapter requires some explanation. Most authors of work on vernacular regions indicate the links with psychology and specifically with perception. Indeed, a popular synonym for "vernacular region" is "perceptual region." Clearly, then, this section could have been conveniently integrated into chapter 5. It was preferred, however, to delay discussion until now for several reasons. Vernacular regions are, it is suggested, much more than portions of an area perceived to have a regional identity by those within and/or those without. They are regions to which a particular meaning is attached and thus possess a social and likely symbolic identity. It is argued that this social identity is a useful distinguishing characteristic and that the empirical work on vernacular regions is enriched when linked to the concepts identified in the current chapter. "Perceptual or vernacular regions are those perceived to exist by their inhabitants and other members of the population at large . . . the vernacular region is the product of the spatial perception of average people" (Jordan, 1978, p. 293). This characteristic definition emphasizes the concern with perception, although an appraisal of related work uncovers explicit interest in social landscapes. This section considers vernacular regions as aspects of both perceptual and social landscapes.

A major concern in most work on vernacular regions is with region delimitation. Given the concern with perception, it is not surprising that the typical delimitation exercise is based on data collected from individuals by such means as questionnaires. Terry Jordan (1978) gathered data from 3860 students in an analysis of regions in Texas, Karl Raitz and Richard Ulack (1981) interviewed college students in their Appalachian study and received 847 responses, and Art Lamme and Raymond Oldakowski (1982) had responses from 356 individuals attending the Florida State Fair in a Florida analysis. The most substantial data collection was that of Ruth Hale (1971, 1984) who corresponded with weekly newspaper editors, county agents, and postmasters and received 6800 responses. In these typical studies the basic premise is that "if one is interested in regions as they exist in the minds of people, one must go to the people" (Lamme & Oldakowski, 1982, p. 101). The results of such studies are stimulating and suggestive, but it is necessary to question the validity of the data-gathering exercise. Necessarily, the samples are biased and the views of particular groups are not incorporated. To what extent these nonrandom samples render the results misleading is difficult to assess. Clearly, if the aim is to delimit regions perceived by "average people," then the data-collection process needs to ensure that average people are questioned (Jordan, 1978, p. 293). The problem of identifying the appropriate respondent is thus a substantial one. A second difficulty in data collection relates to the specific questions asked. It is often not a straightforward matter to collect information consistently, because different individuals interpret identical questions differently. Also, many of the views held by individuals cannot be accurately reported by those individuals and many respondents try to please interviewers. These and many other detailed issues plague much social science research (Simon, 1978, pp. 273–308). These two sets of criticisms are not intended to detract from the merits of this type of research objective, rather to emphasize the need to interpret results cautiously and to keep the data-collection process always in mind.

An alternative procedure for delimitation was pioneered by John Reed (1976), and has since been used by Wilbur Zelinsky (1980). This involves calculating the ratio between a specific regional term such as *Dixie* and a term such as *national* or *American* as these appear in telephone directories. The argument is that the greater the relative incidences of the regional term, the more likely it is that a given area belongs to that region. A combination of this procedure and questionnaires was used by James Shortridge (1980) in a Kansas analysis. Criticisms of this alternative approach are that the research is predetermining the regional name and that, once again, the information collected may not be truly representative.

What types of result are achieved by such research? It is typically possible to map the vernacular regions. Todd Zdorkowski and George Carney (1985) mapped past and present Oklahoma regions by means of including a question on name changes through time. Usually it is possible to identify major or dominant regions, secondary regions, and local regions. Some researchers identified regions with directional names (Jordan, 1978; Shortridge, 1980; Raitz & Ulack, 1981), and a general interest in topographic factors is evident. Both positive and negative perceptions are often analyzed. Jordan (1978, p. 302) noted a Texan preoccupation with such adjectives as big and golden; Raitz and Ulack (1981, pp. 116–118) observed a tendency to reflect values in regional names and a tendency to avoid the term *Appalachia*, because of the negative image associated with it. Finally, an attempt may be made to indicate the intensity of regional identity; for North America, Zelinsky (1980) observed strong regional feelings, particularly in the southeast, and weak sentiments in the northeast.

The results achieved are often compared to previous regional identifications, perhaps to typically acknowledged culture areas. Zelinsky (1980, p. 13) saw close parallels between the vernacular and culture areas usually labeled South, Midwest and New England, and Lamme and Oldakowski (1982, p. 108) observed a close link between the vernacular regions and an established cultural divide in Florida. For Kansas, Shortridge (1980, p. 91) found such a comparison difficult, because of a paucity of conventional cultural analyses, and Hale (1971) observed that regions as well established as the Corn Belt did not coincide with a vernacular region. It can be argued that vernacular regions are those that are of real importance simply because they are those that people believe in and identify with, unlike the more abstract regions delimited by planners and others. If this is the case, then the need to ensure that "correct" regions are identified becomes all the more crucial.

Vernacular regions are, however, of interest not only as perceived and possible planning regions, but also because of their association with place. The recognition that a given area has a particular identity such that it is named implies that the identity is important, that the area has meaning to the occupants. An alternative way to express this is to state that distinct vernacular regions are occupied by distinct groups, which thus renders vernacular regions of sociological as well as geographical interest. For the Ozark region, Joan Miller (1968) was able to use folk materials to delimit a distinct region and to identify the self-sufficient family farm as the principal way of life. Distinct values may thus be shared by the inhabitants of a vernacular region, and an especially clear link between people and place is implied. Vernacular regions are perhaps occupied by a group that shares characteristics, a principal characteristic being the very identity with place. This argument will not always apply. Many vernacular regions are institutional creations, such as tourist and promotional regions, whereas others, such as the Bible Belt, are perhaps too large and too varied.

The notion of vernacular regions accords well with sociological concepts of types of space. It may be appropriate to regard the French Riviera as a vernacular region, or what Daniel Gade (1982) called elitist space. Similarly, Richard Jackson and Roger Henrie (1983) identified vernacular regions, or sacred spaces, in a Mormon context. The idea of a vernacular region, therefore, needs to be interpreted in a variety of ways. As is the case with formal regions, we need to identify the reasons for the existence of the region carefully and, if appropriate, to consider what type of space, in sociological terms, the region contains. Such investigations can only add to the understanding of the region and the region-occupant relationship. In a related way, there is merit to temporal analyses. The evolution of, and changes experienced by, a region are necessarily related to culture change as a whole. The rise of a distinct French Riviera was a response to the requirements of a particular class in French society and its desire to identify with a given environment. In much the same fashion, urban neighborhoods and communities can be regarded as vernacular regions created by particular groups to help express their identity.

The analysis of vernacular regions is valuable. In addition to the established analyses, largely based on questionnaire data at the national, regional, or state level, it seems likely that geographers will focus explicitly on particular social categories of vernacular regions and on analyses within urban areas. One interesting question, however, remains unanswered. Vernacular regions are those perceived as regions both from within and without. But to what extent these perceptions are actually similar is little considered. There may be agreement as to the existence of a given region, but is there agreement as to the character of the region? The simple answer is no. It is probable that those living within a region will differ somewhat in their assessment of regional identity, and that the differences between those within and those without will be substantial. For the residents of a vernacular region, that region is perhaps home; for nonresidents it is someone else's home. The example of the Bible Belt is instructive. For many of those within, it is a regional name of which they are proud; Oklahoma City proudly proclaims itself to be the "Buckle on the Bible Belt." But for many without, it is a term of derision as suggested by such phrases as the "Bible and Hookworm Belt" and the "Bible and Lynching Belt." The typical analysis has not considered this issue of differing perceptions and appraisals, and yet it is important on both conceptual and applied levels. It seems necessary to go beyond perceived regional existence to the broader issue of perceived regional identity. If vernacular regions are to be used for planning purposes, then such an extension is crucial.

SOCIAL GROUPS AND LANDSCAPE

We now approach a fundamental question. What is the appropriate basis for delimiting meaningful groups for cultural geographic research? The characteristic approach has been to focus on such cultural universals as language, religion, and ethnicity and a more recent approach has been to focus on class. The general argument for use of such variables is that they approximate the more general idea of culture and hence can be related to such research themes as landscape evolution. Furthermore, all four permit analyses at conventional geographic scales; geographers do not often focus attention on small groups such as families. It is recognized that much human behavior is a result of group membership, and the correct identification of a principal cultural variable may go a long way to explaining landscape.

Once again, it is appropriate to refer to the ongoing social science debate between the relative merits of individual and group analyses. Analyses of individuals can be criticized for ignoring the social structures within which individual acts are framed whereas group analyses might appear to ignore individual will. This complex issue is far from resolution. One attempt to focus on the optimum scale suggested that it is ideology that links institutions to actors, that ideologies have symbolic components, and that the "landscape serves as a vast repository out of which symbols of order and social relationships, that is ideology, can be fashioned" (J. S. Duncan, 1985, p. 182). Interestingly, this idea is not so different from the claim made some years ago by Elaine Bjorklund (1964, p. 227) to the effect that "ideology constitutes the basis for making decisions and choices affecting the ways of life and works." The claim is elaborated in some detail and discussed within an empirical context. Other attempts to discuss suitable scales of analysis have typically advocated some group level.

It is evident that cultural geographers have not given this difficult issue much thought, preferring to accept and use the established variables for delimiting groups. There are two related issues here, one concerning the variable(s) used and one concerning the scale. Correct variables and correct scales may be argued on a priori theoretical grounds, as with Marxist arguments for class and group, or may be determined on the basis of research problem, as is the case with most cultural geographic analyses. This current section considers the four most popular variables that are used to delimit groups, namely language, religion, ethnicity, and class. Sociologists recognize other variables that often generate small groups, such as kin, but these have made minimal impact on geography to date.

Language

Language is a cultural variable and the principal means by which a culture ensures continuity through time. It is perhaps the most valuable single possession of the human race, because all of our complex cultures and technologies depend on our ability to communicate with one another. There are many human languages, each subject to changes in rules, content, and dialect. A useful distinction between language and dialect is that languages are mutually unintelligible whereas dialects are mutually intelligible varieties of one language (Edwards, 1985, p. 18). To impose some order on the distribution of languages, cultural geographers employ the concept of a linguistic family, that is a group of closely related languages that show evidence of having a common origin.

The Indo-European family is the largest and most widespread. This family includes most European languages and those of the Indian subcontinent. The dominance of this family in the world context is related to the process of colonial expansion, and today approximately one half of the world's population speaks an Indo-European tongue. Each language family is divided into groups that, in turn, are divisible into individual languages. Groups within the Indo-European family include Romance, which evolved from Latin and includes Spanish and

French; Germanic, which includes English and German; Slavic, which includes Russian; and Indic, which includes Hindi and Bengali. The common bond between all of these languages is their origin in Eastern Europe, perhaps some 5000 years ago. A second example of a language family is the Sino-Tibetan, with Chinese as the principal language and an areal coverage encompassing most of China and Southeast Asia. Necessarily, a definitive classification is not available; Charles Zimolzak and Chester Stansfield (1979, p. 106) mapped fourteen families and needed to include an "others" category. In addition to the large number of languages, each language is constantly changing. Content and dialect changes of the English language are evident within England through time (compare the English of Shakespeare's time to that of today) and between England and those areas settled by the British in recent centuries, such as the United States and Australia. There are also significant differences within a single political unit. In exceptional cases a new language may emerge relatively rapidly. Sometimes a lingua franca, which is a language used over a large area by people of different languages who need to communicate, is amended into a pidgin. A pidgin is a language with relatively few words, some borrowed from each of several other languages. Two areas where a pidgin has developed into a significant language are Louisiana and Haiti where French Creole is spoken. Most pidgin languages have emerged as a consequence of travel by Europeans.

From what has been said so far it might reasonably be assumed that the analysis of language is central to cultural geography. Such is hardly the case, judging by the extent which language has been used as a tool of cultural analysis. There are relatively few programmatic statements or empirical analyses despite the impetus provided by Wagner (1958). The major exception to this generalization is the work on place names. Some aspects of the cultural geography of language are now considered.

There are close relationships between language and religion and ethnicity. The success of English as a world language today is closely related to the power of Christianity as a proselytizing religion, and the spread of Arabic is closely related to the fervor of the Muslim faith. In a rather different vein, the survival of Latin as a language resulted from its use by the Roman Catholic church. At the most general level, there is a spatial conformity between language and ethnicity although large-scale movements of people can disturb this relationship. Many of the localized ethnic groups in areas of both old and new settlement speak a nonmajority language, either because of isolation or because of a conscious attempt to retain a distinct identity. Certain languages have, through time, retreated into difficult and often isolated locales and have established a linguistic refuge area (Jordan & Rowntree, 1986, p. 154). The long-term movement of the Khoi and San peoples into the desert of southwest Africa in the face of Bantu migrations is one example. The Celtic fringe of western Europe is a second. In both of these cases the language-ethnicity relationship is close. The close links between these three variables means that a given group is often delimited on a multivariable basis. It is typically correct, for example, to regard an Amish settlement in North America as a language group, a religious group, and an ethnic group.

Language is also intimately associated with ideas of nationalism. In medieval Wales, the words for language and for nation were synonomous. In many parts of the world today, minority language groups argue for a separate political identity on the basis that a different language does indeed mean a different culture. In Wales, the Welsh language and Welsh culture are inextricably entwined such that "the language may be considered the matrix which holds together the various cultural elements which compose the Welsh way of life" (Bowen & Carter, 1975, p. 2). A similar logic is evident in Ireland where survial of the Gaeltacht, the area where Irish is spoken, is "synonymous with retention of the distinctive Irish national character" (Kearns, 1974, p. 85). In other countries, minority languages strive for more than survival such that national political problems may result. There are linguistic issues in Canada, Spain, Belgium, Cyprus, and India, which in turn have ignited some level of conflict. Language has been used as a rationale for national expansion. Adolf Hitler, for example, was able to argue for German expansion on the basis of language, a consequence of the long history of German migrations since A.D. 800, the *Drang nach Osten* or eastward movement. All of these brief examples highlight the perceived centrality of language to cultural and national identity.

A relatively well-researched area is that of language impact on landscape, especially as evident in place names. In addition to research on place names per se, there is work on place names as a measure of the impact of a group on landscape. With reference to Finnish place names in Minnesota, Matti Kaups (1966) noted that the number of names a group could bestow was related to physical landscape and to the arrival date of the group—the first effective settlement concept. Place names can also be employed as a surrogate for culture spread and as a basis for delimiting regions.

A major developing area of interest relates to language and society. "The analysis of language is relatively new intellectual terrain for social geographers" (P. Jackson, 1984, p. 106). This is hardly surprising because language has also been largely ignored by sociologists despite the importance attached to language over fifty years ago by George Mead (1959). The relatively recent emergence of sociolinguistics, the sociology of language, reflects an increasing sociological concern, a concern that is currently being transferred into geography. The challenge for geographers is considerable, as traditional areas of interest are being reinterpreted in light of emerging sociological concepts and controversies. Implicit in sociolinguistics is a concern for identity, both individual and group. This is important for geographers interested in language-ethnicity and language-nation issues. For many researchers, language is the basic criterion for delimiting an ethnic group or nation, although *ethnic* is a poorly defined term and some claim that the linguistic criterion for nationalism has been of importance only in Europe and the Middle East (A. Smith, 1971, pp. 18–19).

Sociolinguists have clarified some basic points concerning language and society that are of interest to geographers. Two functions of language are noted. Language is both a means of communicating and a symbol or emblem of groupness. It is this latter function that renders language potent for ethnic and nationalist sentiments. The symbolic function is evident among many New World immigrant groups (Eastman, 1984). In some instances, language may operate largely as a symbol and not serve a communication function, as is the case with Irish. Furthermore, the role of language as a social act is emphasized, with language often mirroring social stratification. An obvious, but little analyzed, association is that between a particular dialect or accent, a particular social class, and a particular region. Words and pronunciations say much about social and spatial origins. They are able to create a group solidarity and prompt respect or prejudice from outsiders. Thus, membership in a language, dialect or accent group is important as a factor related to both attitudes and behavior. A final contribution from sociolinguistics is the recognition that communication assists in creating the social reality of an area. Social realities are constructed and maintained by communication. This symbolic interactionist view thus acknowledges the centrality of language as a variable affecting the spatial pattern of society and the social character of space.

The centrality of language to geography and other social sciences is being increasingly acknowledged. Geographers have not, as yet, responded as successfully as have sociologists, with their development of sociolinguistics, but there are clear indications that linguistic geography is both a vital and a vibrant area for research. A traditional cultural geographic interest in landscape is continuing (Noble & Dhussa, 1983) as is the interest in region delimitation (Withers, 1981). Language continues to be used as a surrogate for culture (Pryce, 1975), and there is growing appreciation of the links between language, identity, ethnicity, and nationalism—an appreciation that is being fostered by work in sociolinguistics (Edwards, 1985).

Religion

A second variable conventionally used by geographers as a means of delimiting cultural regions and/or delimiting groups is religion. Religion may have intimate relationships with the evolution of landscape and society, and indeed, for some cultures religion is the binding element. David Sopher (1967, p. vii) wrote ''although geographers have long recognized that religious ideas and organization may play an important role in the way man occupies and shapes the land, important geographic studies focusing on this theme only recently have begun to appear.'' Sopher (1967) then proceeded to discuss relationships between environment and religious systems and institutions in terms of environmental effects on religion as well as religious effects on environment, the religious organization and occupation of space, and the diffusion and present distribution of religions. In a book on the geography of religion in England, John Gay (1971, p. 1) did not pursue these ideas preferring a detailed description of religions and an attempt at an explanation of denominational allegiance. Sopher (1981, p. 511) acknowledged that his earlier outline had become "outdated in several respects," but also observed little change in themes or techniques and a failure to integrate with spatial analysis, a failure already noted as characteristic of most cultural geography. The following discussion considers five research themes, namely, sacred space, denominational geography, religious impact on landscape, religion and ecology, and finally, religion and social and economic change.

The notion of sacred space is one aspect of an important principle: all human landscape has a cultural meaning. Although this notion is an old one, it was particularly elaborated within sociology in the early twentieth century and has received only sporadic attention from geographers such as Erich Isaac (1964), John K. Wright (1966), and Yi-fu Tuan (1978). An oft-quoted contribution is that of John B. Jackson (see 1984) who has discussed in detail those landscapes that we create and without which we would be unable to operate as members of society. Sacred space may be conveniently defined as that space that is esteemed by a particular individual or group. It is one example of symbolic landscape. A simple tripartite classification recognizes sacred, profane, and mundane space. Profane space lacks value for a particular individual, group, or culture; mundane space is where humans live and operate, but it lacks special symbolic quality. Such a categorization of space does not imply any absolute distinctions, and it is important to emphasize that all known space has meaning with the notion of sacred space merely recognizing that some areas have particular and more intense meanings attached to them. This is an important point. Place "provides an emotional anchorage to individuals and groups" (E. Cohen, 1974, p. 55). Sacred space implies particular attachment to place, although the degree of sacredness is highly variable. Necessarily, this notion is not limited to religious space; however, religion is a major factor and has the capability to endow space with sacred meaning. A useful typology suggested three types of sacred space (R. H. Jackson & Henrie, 1983, p. 95): "Mystic-religious space is associated with religious or other experiences inexplicable through conventional means. Homelands are sacred space because they represent the roots of each individual, family or people. Historical sacred spaces represent sites which have been assigned sanctity as a result of an event occurring there."

All sacred spaces vary according to a number of characteristics. They are capable of eliciting a number of emotions such as pride, nostalgia, and spiritual devotion. The intensity of the emotion depends on how "sacred" the space is. Some sacred spaces are sacred for only one person, others for small groups, and others for larger groups and cultures. Some individuals perceive their place of birth and/or their area of upbringing as sacred while others do not. A sacred space may be long-lasting or quite ephemeral depending on the type, the number of people involved, and the degree of sacredness. Sacred spaces vary in size and in their impact, if any, on landscape. Many sacred spaces are recognized as such even by those who do not themselves share the emotion involved— Jerusalem and Mecca would qualify as such. Indeed, there seems to be merit to the suggestion that only such widely recognized places be accorded sacred status, because there does indeed seem to be a major distinction between such places and, for example, the home of an individual. Regardless, the notion of sacred space is a useful one and, because of the increasing link between sociology and geography as well as the increasing humanistic focus in geography, this concept is being recognized and applied. One analysis of spaces sacred to Mormons is now noted.

The Mormons are a cohesive, and perhaps an atypical, religious group with a particular organization that they were able to utilize in order to settle and transform a difficult area. The Mormons are often seen as a separate culture and their area of settlement as a cultural region with a distinct landscape (Meinig, 1965; Francaviglia, 1970). R. H. Jackson and Henrie (1983) hypothesized that a number of spaces were sacred to the Mormons and tested their hypotheses by means of questionnaires. The most sacred spaces for Mormons were the Salt Lake Temple, the future city of Zion, and the Sacred Grove, all of which are mystic-religious sites for the group. The homeland space seen as most sacred was the state of Utah whereas such spaces as present and childhood home were significantly less sacred. The sacred historical sites were those associated with Mormonism rather than any hypothesized national space. This innovative study concluded that for the Mormons the most sacred of spaces are those associated with their religion. Useful extensions of this type of study might profitably focus on spaces that are seen as sacred, not just for an individual or group but also by individuals or groups. It is suggested, for example, that people see all churches as sacred to someone.

Geographers have also considered sacred space in the more general context of pilgrimages, especially the Moslem pilgrimage to Mecca. Although this pilgrimage is not obligatory it is, for many, a lifelong goal. Many pilgrims also visit Medina to the north with both Mecca and Medina being forbidden to non-Moslems, a restriction that serves to emphasize their sacredness to Moslems. An explicit interest in the symbolic meaning of pilgrim activities was central to an analysis of pilgrim behavior on Shikoku Island, Japan (Tanaka, 1977).

A second research theme evident in the geography of religions is the concern with denominational variations. This interest stems both from a general assumption of a close relationship between denominations and other social variables and from the wide variety of denominations. Zelinsky (1973, p. 51) noted that "members of a single family may belong to two or more churches simultaneously; a given individual may join several different churches in the course of a lifetime" and saw this as clear evidence of a marked American individualism. Studies of denominational membership by Zelinsky (1961, 1973, pp. 94–100) and by Shortridge (1976, 1977) confronted major data problems, but nevertheless generated useful conclusions. Although church membership is common, a concern with religion proper is not. Major religious occasions are clearly becoming less and less sacred and there is an increasing correspondence between intensity of religious feeling and patriotism. Zelinsky (1973, p. 95) argued that "Americanism has, in a most fundamental sense, become the true religion of Americans.'' A specific attempt to examine the spatial dimensions of this civil religion used data on bicentennial participation and identified the interior north of the United States as a region with an especially ''high commitment to public celebration of American civil religion.'' A focus on more conventional religions by Shortridge (1977) created a regionalization of U.S. religion that included three areas of conservative Protestantism, the South, Utah, and parts of the northern plains; two areas of extreme Catholicism, French Louisiana and the Spanish southwest; and two areas of liberal Protestantism, the Midwest and the West Coast. A general concordance is evident between these religious regions and established cultural regions. Analysis of denominations are popular in the United States, but less evident elsewhere.

Another type of denominational study has focused on only one denomination and raised questions such as the relation between a denomination and patterns of diffusion and spatial distribution (Meyer, 1975). Denominational analyses of this type can, of course, center on a wide range of geography-religion relationships, but most notably on the impact of landscape.

The impact of religion on landscape is sometimes dominant, sometimes non-existent. According to Richard Francaviglia (1970, 1979) there is a distinctive Mormon landscape comprising potentially ten landscape features. These are noted in chapter 6 and ''simply stated, if any town has 5 or more of the above elements, it will be a Mormon town'' (Francaviglia, 1970, p. 60). It is rather difficult to accept this proposed general basis for designating a town as Mormon, because it treats each of the features equally. It is also evident that the Mormon landscape is not really reflecting a particular ideology, but rather a strong institutional factor (Sopher, 1981, p. 515). The role of religion as an institutional factor is also apparent in many other landscapes created by religious groups such as the Amish and Mennonite. In some instances, however, ideology is clearly reflected in landscape. For western Canadian Doukhubor settlements, the belief in a simple and equal life is evident in a landscape devoid of symbols and with communal homes for up to one hundred people (Gale & Koroscil, 1977). Ideology is also reflected in the Bhuddist temple landscape of Japan (Tanaka, 1984), in the Hindu temple landscape of Calcutta (Biswas, 1984), and in the Jewish synagogue landscape (Shilhav, 1983, p. 325). In these examples, religious ideas are evident in landscape and changing ideas prompt changing landscapes. Unlike many of the North American religious landscapes, which are gradually losing identity, the Eastern examples are retaining their distinctiveness. There is a North American tendency for previously different religious groups to become more and more American in character.

In addition to the institutional and symbolic aspects of religious landscape creation, geographers have also considered the more general landscape-religion links. The area north and northwest of San Antonio, Texas, was settled mainly by Germans whose religious culture has survived to the present, resulting in distinctive patterns of ''church affiliation, residential segregation by sect, religious spatial organization, ecclesiastical architecture and burial practices'' (Jordan, 1980, p. 109). Many studies of this type use religion as one of possibly several cultural variables, less attention being paid to the ideological issues.

A fourth research theme, little pursued by geographers, concerns religion and ecology. There is a clear difference between the attitudes to land central to Christianity on the one hand and several Eastern religions on the other hand, although the ecological impact of these differences is less clear (Sopher, 1981, pp. 517–518). One function of most religions is to help establish a sound human and land relationship, and in Christianity the tradition is that humans can dominate nature in contrast to an Eastern emphasis on unity. This simple argument can be used to explain massive ecological impacts in areas of Christianity and the less dramatic changes in the East. The argument is, however, subject to much debate; Tuan (1968) noted a lack of accord between religious ideals and ecological reality. The religion-ecology link is unquestionably too complex to be characterized in simple terms. Religions change and hence attitudes to land change. Religions vary enormously within and there may be many alternative views; the attitude to land held by Protestants is less temperate than that held by Catholics. The relationship is not a simple one-to-one link as there may be many other related variables. Ecological impact will vary according to economic requirements and level of technology.

Despite these cautionary statements there are some excellent examples of attitudes to land affecting landscape and society. For the Mithila region of north India, the central religious tenet is unity of humans and nature. "The Maithilis believe in a oneness of life as manifested in all things. Plants, animals, clouds, the sky and water share the life force equally with man" (Karan, 1984, p. 89). These beliefs have influenced landscape, folk art, folk songs, and social organization. Studies of this type appear more valuable than generalizations referring to major religious traditions.

The final research theme to be considered in the context of religion is that of religion and development, both social and economic. Little geographic work has appeared in this area despite most religions impacting on the larger societies and economies of which they are a part. Jordan and Lester Rowntree (1986, pp. 189–197) produced a wealth of examples where religious practices affect crops, animal husbandry, and fishing. These include the impact of Christianity on vine cultivation, the absence of pigs in Islamic and Judaic areas, and the fish taboos practiced by most Hindus. Religion also affects social organization with the Hindu caste system in particular determining the social role to be played by each person, a system that is now illegal. One of the more persuasive conceptual discussions of the effects of religion on economic and social life was provided by Weber who attempted to demonstrate the complex interplay between a particular set of beliefs, the Protestant Ethic, and specific action, the rise of capitalism. Weber argued that a particular set of beliefs were necessary for the evolution of capitalism; indeed that economic and social development generally depended primarily on sets of beliefs. For capitalism, the necessary beliefs were the outlooks on work and wealth typical of Protestant groups. A similar argument was advanced by the French historian, Élie Halévy, who proposed that Methodism incorporated attitudes to work that the industrial classes adopted in the nineteenth century, particularly an attitude of individual discipline, and that these seemed to prevent the growth of revolutionary ideas. Neither of these broad proposals has been tackled in a substantive geographical manner.

Religious groups have relevance in a geographic context, but past research is so varied that clear themes are difficult to disentangle. Religion is one, sometimes dominant, cultural variable. The five themes discussed above are of varying importance judging by the interest shown by geographers, but each is relevant to the broader understanding of landscape and social change. Much of the research noted would traditionally be labeled cultural and much social. An attempt has implicitly been made to emphasize the integration of the two. As a basis for delimiting groups, religion is valuable but geographers must not forget the often close links with other cultural variables. These points are tellingly made by Roger Stump (1986, p. 3) who noted that religion is a critical component of social identity and that "the geography of religion can be more usefully defined as a motif running through the larger discipline of cultural geography."

Ethnicity

Defining groups according to an ethnic criterion is particularly difficult, essentially because there is not a generally accepted definition of the term. An examination of sixty-five studies of ethnicity noted that fifty-two of them offered no explicit definition (Isajiw, 1974). Minority or social subgroups are often defined as ethnic, especially in the North American immigrant context, but John Edwards (1985, p. 6) argued that majority groups can also be considered ethnic. In addition to the question of scale, there is much discussion in social science concerning ethnic group boundaries and content. Fredrik Barth (1969) focused on boundaries and their changes and emphasized that ethnic distinctions do not depend on absence of social interaction across boundaries. Other social scientists have argued that the key subject matter is the content of the ethnic group. A third general issue concerns the distinction between the objective characteristics of an ethnic group such as language and religion, and an involuntary characteristic such as ethnicity.

This brief background is enough to indicate that ethnicity is a complex and uncertain basis for group delimitation. Ethnic groups might often be most effectively categorized by some other variable or variables. Indeed, it often appears the ethnic is used in place of cultural or social as descriptive terms: "ethnics are custodians of distinct cultural traditions . . . the organization of social interaction is often based on ethnicity" (Raitz, 1979, p. 79). There is one additional complication, the tendency to equate ethnicity and race. The race concept is fraught with problems. Scientifically speaking, it is concerned with hereditary differences in physical characteristics existing between groups of humans. Social geographers often relate ethnicity and race, seeing ethnicity as "the linkage of a particular cultural mode with a particular genetic stock'' (Peach, 1983, p. 104). Aside from being conceptually naive, such a view also raises thorny questions about discrimination.

Given the diverse interpretations and usage of ethnicity, it is inevitable that a wide variety of research can be considered under this heading. Three research themes are noted: first, the experience of ethnic, immigrant, minority groups in North America; second, inequalities evident between groups; and third, group identity and social interaction.

Analyses of North American minorities have considered issues of acculturation, assimilation, and differentials in skills. The whole question of adjustments to a new country and a new society has been pursued for both rural and urban areas. The experiences of Polish settlers in the Canadian prairies suggested that a successful adjustment to the Canadian way of life was only achieved as a result of a harsh trial-and-error process (Matejko & Matejko, 1978). This is a not uncommon conclusion. Other rural ethnic studies include those by Aidan McQuillan (1978) comparing three groups, Robert Ostergren (1980) on Swedish migration patterns, and Alan Brunger (1982) on Catholic Irish settlement in Ontario. Most such studies tackled a specific research problem and used ethnicity as a convenient means of classification.

Studies dealing with discrimination and inequality are increasing in both number and conceptual sophistication. Much discrimination results directly from racist attitudes. Ideas about race and racial bases for civilization have a long history. Racist thought grew rapidly after the Reformation because of the impact of European expansion and the spread of polygenetic theories of human origins. By the late eighteenth century, racism was a usual explanation for observed cultural differences. The greatest advances in such ideas were made by the Frenchman Joseph Arthur de Gobineau writing in the mid-nineteenth century. Gobineau argued especially for a Germanic Aryan race. A second influential writer was the Englishman Houston Stewart Chamberlain who similarly saw race as the sole explanation of progress and saw Germanic people as the superior group. Racist ideas have not left us today. A review by Peter Jackson (1985) focused in some detail on racial and ethnic segregation while David Ley (1983b, pp. 264–276) reported many cases of ethnic segregation in an urban context. One analysis of the inequitable distribution of health-care facilities in Auckland and Wellington, New Zealand, showed that the presence of ethnic groups was a major explanatory factor (Barnett, 1978). It is in such studies of discrimination that the ethnic basis for group definition is perhaps most useful. This was forcefully argued by Michael Smith (1969) who noted that some groups may be excluded from some opportunities and resources either for legal or operational reasons.

Ethnic group identity and the social interaction within and between groups are being increasingly analyzed. The introduction to an edited collection of papers, under the theme, ''Social Interaction and Ethnic Segregation,'' emphasized the reliance placed on American sociology, especially the work of Robert Park, concerning the links between spatial and social distance (P. Jackson & S. J. Smith, 1981). During the assimilation process, ethnic groups are continually adjusting their social interaction. A change in spatial behavior, perhaps prompted by a change of residence, typically increases social interaction between the ethnic and host populations thus furthering assimilation (Jakle, Brunn, & Roseman, 1976, pp. 159–162). Residential propinquity, in both rural and urban settings, limits social interaction between ethnic groups and hosts (Brunger, 1982).

Although these three areas of research are important and expanding, it is still necessary to question the use of an ethnic variable as a central component of research. The term remains poorly defined and sometimes is essentially based on language, sometimes on religion, sometimes on race, and sometimes on social or class issue. The need to recognize that human populations are divided into groups along with the practical requirements of research prompt the use of an ethnic label when perhaps an alternative label might be more desirable.

Class

This fourth and final basis for group delimitation is one little used to date by geographers, but for both conceptual and empirical reasons it is appropriate to suggest that there will be increasing applications. James Blaut (1980) argued that from the perspective of a radical researcher, classes are the appropriate variable for delimiting cultures, and Pred (1981a) noted that certain individuals or classes typically exert power over others, a situation drastically affecting the behavior of groups. Work focusing on class has often also focused on the conflict between classes. A study of skilled workmen in Hamilton, Ontario, between 1860 and 1914, looked both at class as culture and at conflict (Palmer, 1979). In a very different analysis, Peter Cromar (1979) considered the impact of particular power groups on various economic activities. These types of study recognize the need to go beyond conventional interpretations of culture and conventional bases for group delimitation if the research problem so requires. Much recent work on issues such as urban managerialism (Leonard, 1982) and on institutional forces (Flowerdew, 1983) can be interpreted along similar lines.

For the sociologist, class is often either a status structural category or an expression of self-identity. Neither view is adequate from a radical viewpoint, which contends that class and class struggle cannot be separated. The geographer Mark Billinge (1984), used structuration and other concepts in an analysis of class struggle in late eighteenth- and early nineteenth-century England, but there is little indication at present that such analyses will have a significant impact. Geographers have typically considered class devoid of theoretical content, essentially on the basis of socioeconomic status. Explicitly conceptual uses of class as a variable are likely to become more evident.

Summary

This extended section on several of the variables used to define groups has introduced a massive amount of research. Language, religion, and ethnicity are popular cultural variables with a large literature; in Jordan and Rowntree (1986) each is assigned a chapter. No attempt has been made here to cover the full range of research topics, but rather to identify research themes that are relatively novel and that are often clearly integrating the traditionally different schools of cultural and social geography. The bases on which groups are defined are important as the initial classification may affect the outcome of research. In some cases, group definition is determined pragmatically; in other cases, it reflects a theoretical imperative. Each of the four variables discussed is in some instances a useful surrogate for culture, although ethnicity in particular has serious definitional problems. In many cases, there is a close accord between the variables; the exception is class—most language, religious, or ethnic groups comprise several classes.

One additional variable might have been considered, namely the state. Although often related to language, it can be treated quite independently as Colin Williams and Anthony Smith (1983) indicated in an account of the national construction of social space. As a variable affecting behavior, the state is currently being widely acknowledged (Johnston, 1981). Although clearly not a cultural variable in the conventional sense of that term, it may be that much of our social behavior and our landscape-forming activities are primarily determined not by our membership in a language, religion, ethnic group, or class, but rather by the political unit, or possibly units, to which we belong (Grice & Drakakis-Smith, 1985). One immediate reaction to such a suggestion might be that the real determinants of behavior are smaller groups. This is the usual view argued by the symbolic interactionists and evident in much current social geography (Ley, 1987). P. Jackson (1986, pp. 122–123), for example, asked for "a sensitivity to the political significance of regional distinctiveness and the diversity of local experience."

A useful conclusion to this section is to suggest that, despite an abundance of conceptual and empirical support for the smaller-than-the-state group, it is likely that future research will increasingly acknowledge the role of the state as a major "cultural" variable. This assertion is, of course, little more than a restatement, in modified form, of social organism or superorganic ideas and the latter have been extensively used by Zelinsky (1973) in a provocative and stimulating cultural and social geography of the United States.

THE SOCIAL GEOGRAPHY OF THE FRONTIER

There is a voluminous literature within the general field of historical geography with close links to social geography, for example, work in historical demography. It is not appropriate either to review or to integrate this material in the present volume, and attention is restricted to one research theme, that of the social geography of the frontier. This theme is currently receiving much attention and a major contribution to our understanding of social evolution is evident. The basic research question concerns the development of society in a frontier area, usually a New World frontier settled by Europeans.

The present geographic concern with what are often labeled as settler societies is on "changes in human behavior in rural communities as they move through the historical process of establishment, growth, maturity, and decline under the driving force of modernization" (Swierenga, 1982, p. 497). Traditionally, environmental theories have dominated, with those of Frederick Jackson Turner and Walter Prescott Webb being paramount, but there has also been a rural history interest in the cultural change from community to society. James Malin (1967) emphasized the cultural forces behind individual behavior and James Henretta (1978) focused on individual families. Social geographers are now contributing actively to this field with specific reference to the character of settler societies. Cole Harris (1977) saw societal change in terms of increased accessibility to land, other researchers focused on the significance of Europeans entering more or less complete societal vacuums and developing the local resources (Baran, 1957), and a third view emphasized that fragments of essentially metropolitan European societies became distinctive settler societies because of isolation (McCarty, 1973). One crucial prerequisite for the evolution of a settler society was the "fragility" of earlier societies (Denoon, 1979, p. 512). This, once again, echoes the first effective settlement logic. Graeme Wynn (1983, p. 363) argued that fluid settler societies evolving at a time of technological change could not typically rely on traditional practices and thus earlier European ways had to be amended; "everywhere localism was assaulted by the centralizing tendencies of modern technology." There are exceptions of course. French-Canadian society is usually regarded as different from English-Canadian and U.S. societies because of the feudal origins, the close ties to land, the military defeats suffered, the role of the Church, the French language, and the commitment to survival (Isbister, 1977). There appears to be merit in the idea that French Canada was a fragment of European society. In a rather different vein, a comparison of early New Zealand and Australian pastoralism showed that the evolution of a colonial capitalist society did not result from class conflict but rather from the dynamics of pastoral production, specifically, the development of aggressive tactics for land acquisition (Fairweather, 1985).

Social historians and social geographers are tackling questions of societal change in the frontier context. Various concepts are evident, but the range of empirical studies is not yet adequate to generate definitive conclusions, if such are to emerge. This one research interest will likely develop to include long-term analyses of change through the phase of early settlement to the present. It is also likely that there will be continuing integration of sociological theory and geographic empiricism, an integration largely lacking at present.

THE SOCIAL GEOGRAPHY OF SETTLEMENTS

Most studies in social geography are in an urban setting, as is evident from the discussion so far. Much of the literature assumes that social geography is essentially an urban orientation; Emrys Jones and John Eyles (1977, p. 2) wrote that their social geography book "is largely about urban society . . . reflecting the weight and distribution of studies in social geography. This does not unduly distort the real situation because we live in a predominantly urban society, and most of our problems lie in the city." In a similar vein, Richard Dennis and Hugh Clout (1980) approached the social geography of England and Wales within the central theme of urbanization. Books focusing on other than urban social geography typically find it necessary to justify their content, with one key argument being that rural areas are socially different from urban areas (Phillips & A. Williams, 1984, p. 3). To an important extent, this association of social and urban and the related separation of urban and rural is unfortunate. It is evident that the processes operating in rural and urban areas are not significantly different. This section considers some aspects of the social geography of settlements without centering on any urban-rural distinction. The following theme is central to much of this discussion: settlement is an expression of society. Studies of community, segregation, housing, and various institutional factors often reflect this theme.

Settlement patterns are large and complex artifacts, aspects of material culture that mirror humans themselves. Humans construct societal stages, settlements, according to three considerations: the allocation of activities, the cultural design of society, and the available resources (Richardson, 1974a, p. 35). The societal stage produced in turn has the ability to affect human behavior. Thus we can interpret settlement patterns as "a set of instructions that locate people in sociocultural time and space" (Richardson, 1974a, p. 36). Extending this logic, we might contend that human behavior is caused by first, large group membership, such as the state; second, small group membership, as implied by symbolic interactionist logic; and third, by such aspects of material culture as settlement patterns. All of these change, but it is the third that is likely to change most slowly.

Community studies, as practiced by sociologists, use both questionnaire data and participant observation procedures, usually to produce a descriptive statement. Geographers have paid more attention to community structure in preindustrial situations (Langton, 1975), in industrial situations (Dennis, 1976), and in contemporary situations (Dennis & Clout, 1980) whereas historians have paid considerable attention to in-depth analyses of particular cities (see Muller, 1978). Closely related are studies of urban territoriality (Ley & Cybriwsky, 1974) and of housing and segregation. There are links, for example, between such variables as housing tenure on the one hand and family, ethnic, social, and economic status on the other hand. It is also recognized that local communities and housing areas have both a subjective and an objective identity. In terms, then, of human occupance, settlements are characterized by varying degrees of social segregation. These can be explained in terms of economic variables, such as the market processes of ecological models, social variables such as those noted by Firey (1945) and by reference to Marxist theory (Harris, Levine, & Osborne, 1981).

An overriding issue in most social analyses of settlement relates to the roles played by particular individuals and institutions. Pahl (1969) is undoubtedly the leader in the development of the managerialist approach, which is concerned with the actions of specific agents determining urban structure. These agents, often called gatekeepers, include real estate agents, lawyers, mortgage lenders, and local officials. In various ways all of these are in a position to limit access to housing and to generally impose constraints on the behavior of individuals. The conceptual logic is basically that of Weberian sociology. The approach can, however, be logically extended to include institutions in addition to individuals. Thus, various levels of government can influence who builds where and what homes are available to whom. It is now generally acknowledged that institutional frameworks are able to exert significant influences on residential structure. Larry Bourne (1981) has reviewed many factors affecting housing supply and allocation.

Studies of gentrification have also focused on institutional forces including community organizations, neighborhood groups, and city planners (J. H. Johnson, 1983; Cybriwsky & Western, 1982). The complex arguments and research associated with the managerial thesis and the role of institutions cannot be fully reviewed here; Simon Leonard (1982) has reviewed the managerial thesis and Ley (1983b) covers much of the general ground. Enough has been said, however, to acknowledge the complexity of decision making in both rural and urban environments. The attention being paid by geographers to relevant factors is raising questions about the scale of analysis: individual, small group, large group, or state. This continuum is being increasingly recognized and the conceptual background for particular scales being increasingly researched.

CONCLUDING COMMENTS

Two topics are summarized in this section: first, the issue of the symbolic character of landscape and second, the issue of groups. Landscape as symbol has been introduced in chapter 5 and several times in this chapter and it is now opportune to summarize this theme, which is one of the principal examples of the developing cultural-social integration. All landscapes have a meaning, perhaps a value, for their creators. Similarly, many landscapes reflect these meanings or values. Both of these points were tellingly made by Wagner (1974). This theme was explicitly discussed in the context of both language and religion, but it can be approached from other directions.

According to Meinig (1979b, p. 164), a "mature nation has its symbolic landscapes. They are part of the iconography of nationhood, part of the shared set of ideas and memories and feelings which binds people together." Such a view incorporates the notion of sacred space and the notion that certain landscapes are indeed particular places. Meinig (1979b) tackled the latter and noted that little is known about such landscapes either in terms of origin or detailed expression. It seems possible, however, to correlate symbolic landscapes with regions, and this suggests that landscapes themselves result from social and cultural processes. Thus, new symbolic landscapes, and of course new actual landscapes, are being created on a continuous basis. In a similar fashion, it is possible to identify landscapes that are in some way particularly valued (Lowenthal, 1978).

Symbolic landscapes, then, reflect and express society and culture. All landscapes are symbolic, some more evidently so than others. One attempt to provide a basis for interpreting some such landscapes was that of O. F. G. Sitwell and S. E. Bilash (1986), employing concepts from linguistics and physiological psychology. A second empirically focused attempt, which also integrated cultural and social geography, is evident in work on urban areas interpreting culture in terms of symbols and signifying systems (Agnew, Mercer, & Sopher, 1984). This type of research is not too far detached from symbolic archaeology, which requires that attention be paid to the cognitive aspects of human behavior.

A recurring issue in this volume is that of social scale; the current chapter identifies several variables that can be used to delimit groups, both small and large. Current work in cultural and social geography emphasizes a number of scales and variables for group delimitation. Individuals, families, extended families, friendship circles, voluntary associations, involuntary associations, institutions, and governments are all considered. A penetrating analysis of the Munich environment recognized five types of groups: groups with specific attributes, lifestyle groups, groups with specific behavior, groups of specific perception, and groups of specific environmental sensibility (Geipel, 1981). The increasing awareness of sociological concepts is one factor generating the interest in groups and group size. Karl Butzer (1978) referred in some detail to the sociological idea that communities shape attitudes.

Symbolic landscapes and social scales are being investigated by cultural and social geographers alike. It is in these two areas of interest that the suggested convergence of the two traditionally separate subdisciplines is most evident. It is hardly surprising that it is important conceptual questions that are being shared, for both areas of investigation have been conceptually weak until recently. It is now being readily acknowledged that the landscape school of cultural geography can benefit from a broadened perspective that sees culture in other than idealist terms and that studies culture in both symbolic and material expressions. Social geographers are likewise broadening their horizons beyond the urban scene and recognizing the limitations of spatial analytic type research. Conventional cultural geographic themes such as language, religion, and ethnicity have been interpreted here in a broader human context, and it has been recognized that cultures manifest their beliefs in many ways, both material and symbolic. The integration of cultural and social geography is welcome, because it encourages a broader viewpoint, a more diverse set of concepts, and more varied research problems. The emergence of new concepts, new to geography that is, has succeeded in breaking down old and now unjustifiable barriers. The prospects for continued and varied research are good.

8

Understanding Landscape: Ecological Emphases

The ecological approach to cultural geography has a long and erratic history. Unlike the various evolutionary approaches, most notably the landscape school, it has not been characterized by an early seminal statement and a subsequent legacy of empirical research. Rather, the ecological approach has origins in physical science, has parallels in various other social sciences, and has failed to establish a clear and distinct identity. The same comment applies equally to the experience of other social sciences. In geography, this situation prevails despite the occasional key development, such as the 1922 address by Harlan H. Barrows (1923), the application of systems concepts in the 1960s, the link with time geography in the 1980s, and the relatively constant association with mainstream cultural geography. Ecological interests were introduced in chapter 2 as one aspect of concerns in related disciplines, in chapter 3 as one aspect of the rise of cultural geography, and in chapter 4 as one contribution to contemporary social theory. The word *ecology* is derived from two Greek terms: *oikos*, which means "place to live" or "house," and *logos*, which means the "study of." Ecology, then, is the study of organisms in their homes. More explicitly, ecology is concerned with the analysis of the relationships among living organisms and their relationship to the totality of physical factors that make up their environment. It has already been emphasized that this is a potentially all-embracing theme with a strong interdisciplinary focus. In anthropology in particular, an ecological approach has been seen as correcting the limitations of both enviromentalism and possibilism. It is appropriate to commence this chapter with the acknowledgment that this approach is perhaps the most sophisticated way to interpret the human and land relationship. There are six sections to this discussion. First, it is necessary to detail and discuss the origins and development of ecological interests in the various social sciences in order to place the geographic work in the appropriate context. Second, the impact on cultural geography is assessed by reference to stimuli from both anthropology and sociology. The third section introduces the idea of cultural adaptation. Fourth, the links between systems logic and ecology in geography are considered and the overall failure of this linkage is noted. Fifth, specific examples of relevant geographic research are discussed. The final section is a brief conclusion.

HISTORICAL DEVELOPMENT: OTHER DISCIPLINES

It is conventional to trace the origins of ecology to Charles Darwin and specifically to the third chapter of *The Origin of Species* (1859), which considered the various adaptations and interrelationships of organic beings and enviroment. Humans were implicitly included. The first use of the term ecology was by Ernst Haeckel in 1869, but it was again Darwin, in *The Descent of Man* (1871), who formally included humans along with other living things (see Stoddart, 1986, pp. 167–168). These origins remain central to ecology today with the primary focus being the relationship of a given organism both to other organisms and to their surroundings. The core argument is that these relationships are basic to existence. Given this broad focus, it is easy to appreciate that there are many academic ecologies, such as plant ecology, animal ecology, and human ecology. Of all the various ecologies it is probably human ecology that has the most tenuous links to the parent discipline of biology and that has the most uncertain identity. The uncertain identity has resulted from the situation whereby human ecology evolved in more than one academic discipline, unlike the other ecologies. Human ecology aspires to be interdisciplinary, but is possibly better described as multidisciplinary. This has disadvantages in that the field of human ecology can be described as "a strange nonfield, a hybrid attempt to understand the ecology of one species, the being *Homo sapiens*" (Young, 1983b, p. 2). According to David Stoddart (1986, p. 168), "from about 1910 'human ecology' was used for the study of man and enviroment, not in a deterministic sense, but for man's place in the 'web of life' or the 'economy of nature.' " From 1910 to the present, then, human ecology has survived, and in some cases thrived, in a number of disciplines. Unquestionably, however, it has failed to surface as a synthetic human ecology, and it remains distinctly attached to different disciplines. This section considers the seminal statements in sociology, anthropology, and psychology respectively.

Seminal Statements

The founding figure in sociology is Robert E. Park, the leading member of the Chicago school of thought. Along with Ernest W. Burgess, Roderick McKenzie and Louis Wirth, Park advocated and practiced an ecological approach. The first detailed account appeared in the textbook by Park and Burgess (1921) referred to in chapter 2, although Park (1915) had outlined ecological ideas some years earlier. What was the essential content of the early sociological argument?

Philosophically, the work of Park has both positivist and humanist overtones. It was the former that proved most attractive to geographers in the 1960s, and the latter that is proving more attractive today (P. Jackson & S. J. Smith, 1984, p. 65). Of continuing attraction has been the emphasis on mapping and regionalizing. For the Chicago school of sociology, human ecology centered on the spatial location of humans and of human institutions as they interact. Spatial distributions were mapped and explained in terms of various competing causal processes, such as those of competition, segregation, dominance, invasion, and of succession. These processes were explicitly defined and discussed by McKenzie (1926). Equilibrium was seen as the normal state and processes of change were regarded as disruptions.

The most fundamental process was competition. Humans compete for space, a competition that was reflected in differential urban land values, which in turn, influenced location decisions. One result of the competitive process was segregation, the evolution of distinctly different urban areas. The process of dominance referred to the fact that specific activities were able to locate in the most desirable areas; within the city it is the central business district that is dominant. The concepts of invasion and succession referred to the changes in land use in a given area. In the Chicago context, these processes were particularly evident as one ethnic group "invaded" an area and "succeeded" the previous residents. The logical outgrowth of these ideas was the elaboration of a model of the city that comprised a series of concentric zones of land use. These zones were seen as the eventual spatial outcome of the various processes.

The early sociological emphasis on spatial issues was a novel and major contribution. Park was undoubtedly influenced by Darwin and by plant ecologists, but personal background was also crucial.

> I expect that I have actually covered more ground tramping about in cities in different parts of the world, than any other living man. Out of all this I gained, among other things, a conception of the city, the community, and the region, not as a geographical phenomenon merely, but as a kind of social organism (Park, 1952, p. 5).

The emphasis was on the intimate relationships between humans and other humans and between humans and their environment. Humans were seen as organic creatures and therefore were affected by the general laws of the organic world. Hence, the appropriateness of a biological analogy. The analogy was amended to allow for both nonsocial and social factors; nonsocial (biological) factors gave rise to communities, while social factors gave rise to society. It was, of course, the social factors that distinguished human from other ecologies.

The origins of an ecological approach in anthropology lie in the work of scholars such as Alfred Kroeber and Clark Wissler. Kroeber (1928), for example, observed a neglect of ecological considerations in earlier ethnological studies. But it was a student of Kroeber, Julian Steward, who was responsible for the seminal statements in anthropology. These statements appeared in a series of empirical analyses in the 1930s but it was not until 1955 that an explicit outline of the methodology appeared. In an analysis of primitive societies Steward (1936, p. 331) identified a strong functional relationship between culture and ecology, which was "something akin to cultural law." A study of natives in the Basin-Plateau region noted that patrilineal sociopolitical groups were "conditioned to a definable extent by human ecology" (Steward, 1938, p. 256). The general concern in both of these empirical analyses was with human adaptation to nature. As expressed by Steward (1955), the ecological approach in anthropology recognized the unity of humans and nature and noted that each was to be defined in terms of the other.

Three procedures were needed (Steward, 1955, pp. 40–41): first, the analysis of the interrelationships between environment and exploitative or productive technology; second, the analysis of interrelationships between behavior patterns and exploitative technology; and third, the analysis of the extent to which behavior patterns affected other sectors of culture. In any ecological analysis it was necessary that detailed local studies precede generalization.

There are clear distinctions between this cultural ecology and the earlier derivation of human ecology in sociology. Although both have their intellectual origins in plant and animal ecology and although both added humans to the ecological equation they are quite different from one another and there has not been any beneficial linking of the two. The sociological conception was urban and western in orientation whereas the anthropological conception was rural and preindustrial. In addition to the ecological stimulus, Steward was also infuenced by a legacy of earlier anthropological work. Park, on the other hand, effectively created a human ecology with minimal inspiration from within sociology.

The ecological thrust in psychology owes most to the pioneering work of Kurt Lewin who "started a chain of events that continues to develop today, marked by prolific scholarly output in psychological ecology and enviromental psychology" (Young, 1983a, p. 17). This thrust is discussed in behavioral context in chapter 5. In general, the contribution from psychology is not clearly related to comparable pioneering statements in sociology and anthropology. The one link is that, unlike most psychology, the approach of Lewin explicitly acknowledged the relevance of a nonpsychological, that is a social and physical, environment. The details of the work, however, are not comparable to other disciplines and contribute little to the human ecologies being discussed in this chapter.

Development of an Ecological Approach

In sociology, anthropology, and psychology an ecological approach has continued through to the present. In addition, there has been evidence of similar approaches in other disciplines, notably history. These various developments are now considered.

Human ecology in sociology developed as a major research field very rapidly (Alihan, 1938; House, 1936). Factual surveys and detailed mapping exercises combined to produce a series of empirical statements in the 1920s and early 1930s. Most of these were analyses of Midwestern U.S. cities, especially Chicago. Inevitably, empirical and conceptual criticisms emerged. The most substantive empirical criticism was that of Homer Hoyt (1939) who proposed a different model of urban structure, one which emphasized the relevance of radial routes. Another empirical criticism is more relevant here—the introduction of other variables, specifically those of sentiment and symbolism (Firey, 1945). Boston was used as the study city, and it was argued that various symbolic associations and sentimental attachments could become identified with particular city areas and that these variables could counter the ecological processes. This contribution was effectively an introduction of culture into the human ecological framework.

The most substantive theoretical criticism centered on the community-society dichotomy, arguing that it was simply inappropriate. The result was a generally declining interest in environment as a variable related to human behavior. This decline might also be attributed to Durkheimian sociology. Despite some continuing research by Chicago school sociologists, the principal direction of work from circa 1950 onward was increasingly aspatial. Furthermore, the ecological thrust was modified to include selected ecological variables. Perhaps the clearest statement of the amended sociological human ecology was that by Amos Hawley (1950), which discussed first, human differentiation, using such factors as age, sex, labor, and so forth; second, community structure, which was based on differentiation; and third, spatial structure. Most modern work has used Hawley (1950) as the appropriate revision of earlier concepts. The most recent restatement was that by Gordon Ericksen (1980), which was critical of previous approaches because of their deemphasis of humans. The prospects for a viable sociological approach remain in some doubt.

It is in anthropology that an ecological approach seems to have found the most convivial home. The pioneering work of Steward has been continued, albeit in amended form, by many anthropologists. In addition to literature loosely labeled as cultural ecology, there is also an emerging interest in ecological anthropology. Ecology is usually seen as a more appropriate perspective than either environmentalism or possibilism. Environmentalism is criticized for being overly naive, and possibilism is seen as little more than an acknowledgment of complex causation. Roy Vayda and Andrew Rappaport (1968) developed the work of Steward to the extent of arguing for a unified science of ecology, not merely a cultural ecology, Fredrik Barth (1956) introduced the idea of an ecological niche in an analysis of ethnic group distribution, and Betty Meggers (1954) discussed the limits set on cultural evolution by environments to the extent of arguing for cases of determinism. These three developments are suggestive of the diverse expansion of cultural ecology, a diversity evident in Robert Netting (1977), who considered that any theoretical or methodological overview was not practicable. A book dealing with ecological anthropology argued for "numerous unifying concepts and principles" (Hardesty, 1977, p. vii). The concepts included adaptation, human energetics, and the ecological niche. Following this theme, Emilio Moran (1982) tackled the question of how humans adapt to various ecosystems. The adaptation concept is further detailed in the following section.

The initial stimulus to ecological psychology provided by Lewin has prompted a cross-cultural approach involving new cultures and new environmental contexts. Therefore, the principal development within psychology has been a focus on the cultural and environmental bases of behavior, the argument being that individuals develop differently in response to their environmental and cultural, or ecocultural, context. A primary focus of this research is to ascertain what kinds of behavior are associated with what kinds of population. Culture can then be seen as "a group's adaptation to the recurrent problems it faces in interaction with its environmental setting" (J. W. Berry, 1984, p. 87). This approach in psychology is clearly related to cultural ecology in anthropology.

Attention so far has been restricted to three disciplines, but this does not exhaust the list and this section concludes with a reference to work in history. Two historians in particular, James Malin and Walter Prescott Webb, have succeeded in integrating history and ecology. From this perspective, the task of history is essentially that of reconstructing human history in the wider context of being but one part of natural history. For Malin, this is effectively a focus on human and land relations through time, with humans always seen as the primary determinant. Thus, no region is seen as being superior or inferior to any other region; each offers resources to humans who have the required technology. "Natural resources can not be exhausted until man's contriving brain and skillful hand are exhausted" (Malin, 1967, p. 474). A good collection of works by Malin (Swierenga, 1984) includes examples of concepts, specific case studies in the American grasslands, and quantitative applications.

This theme was strongly pursued by Donald Worster (1984) in a cogent argument advocating more nature in the study of history. Worster (1984, p. 4) began his argument where James Malin and Walter Prescott Webb left off, referring primarily to Karl Wittfogel and the argument that "the fundamental relation underlying all social arrangements . . . is the one between humans and nature." The second major inspiration was the cultural ecology from anthropology, notably Steward, Rappaport, and Marvin Harris. Worster (1984) concluded by suggesting a number of specific research themes that could be tackled by a combination of history and ecology, most notably the rise of capitalism and the frontier. One historian (Cronon, 1983) has provided an account of the ecological and environmental changes caused by Europeans since their arrival in New England. Three components of the ecosystem were identified (Indians, Europeans, and the environment) and their interrelationships prior to 1800 analyzed. The less-destructive pre-European relationship was discussed in terms of perception of land and mobility. The European impact on the other ecosystem components was destructive as a result of their commercial basis, technological level, disease introduction, and general habitat destruction.

The principal conclusion emerging from this overview of ecological emphases in human sciences is that there have been several interpretations of the physical concepts and that these interpretations are themselves rather distinct. There has been little indication of a unified human ecology. The sociological, anthropological, and psychological views have all impacted on geography, and in addition, some geographers have attempted to delimit a more specifically geographic human ecology. The following section discusses the development of ecological concepts within geography.

HISTORICAL DEVELOPMENT: GEOGRAPHY

At first sight, it appears reasonable to suppose that if human ecology does have one natural disciplinary home it is in geography. Perhaps surprisingly, however, geography, despite extending some invitations, has not proven to be a congenial abode for human ecologists. The views of mid-nineteenth–century geographers, such as Alexander von Humboldt and Carl Ritter, centered on human and land relations, and these relations were also central to various European and American views that emerged in the early twentieth century. Unfortunately, geographers tend to have perpetuated divisions in their discipline, not only a physical-human division, but also a regional-ecological division and, later, a spatial-ecological division. There seems little doubt that the failure of geography to center on an ecological approach is at least partially a consequence of an internal identity crisis. Regardless, geography has flirted with human ecology on several occasions. Perhaps the first occasion involved Friedrich Ratzel, who was effectively arguing that anthropogeography and human ecology were one and the same.

The seminal statement is, of course, that of Barrows (1923, p. 3), a statement primarily aimed to define the field of geography as the study of "mutual relations between man and his natural environment" and thus as "human ecology." A careful distinction was made between adjustment to, as opposed to influence of, environment, the former being seen as the proper object of study. An explicit distinction was made between geography and history, with the historian beginning "his studies with what our remote ancestors saw" whereas the geographer begins his studies "with what we ourselves see" (Barrows, 1923, p. 6). But at the same time, Barrows (1923, p. 12) noted that historical geography should focus on both past and changing human-land relations. It was concluded that geography as a discipline needed to exclude much physical content and to center on a human ecological focus.

Overall, the statement by Barrows created little impact. Two major exceptions were an introductory geography text that was subtitled "An Introduction to

Human Ecology'' (White & Renner, 1936) and a second text by the same authors (White & Renner, 1948). Geography was defined as ''the study of human society in relation to the earth background'' (White & Renner, 1948, p. v). Two concepts of geography were implicitly rejected: the idea of the earth as the home of man and the idea of geography as influences of natural environments. Both of these were seen as inappropriate interpretations of human ecology. Most important, geography was thus seen as one of the social sciences. Nevertheless, this view competed unsuccessfully with chorology to become the core of geography and it was not closely integrated with the landscape school, at least partly because of the exclusion of physical content and because of the ambivalence regarding time.

The second landmark statement by a geographer is probably that by Warren Thornthwaite, a student of Carl Sauer. Thornthwaite (1940, p. 343) developed the view that human ecology must transcend all of the present academic disciplines, and that the development of a science of human ecology must involve cooperation of geography, sociology, demography, anthropology, social psychology, economics, and many of the natural sciences as well.'' This perception of human ecology as a cooperative enterprise is quite different to the earlier statement by Barrows.

The view of geography and human ecology by nongeographers was one of noting major differences in emphasis. James Quinn (1950, p. 339) suggested that geographers were concerned with direct human-land relations whereas ecologists were concerned with interrelationships. Hawley (1950, p. 72) also identified this distinction and added that geography, regional geography that is, was atemporal while human ecology was not. A more positive view was conveyed by Leo Schnore (1961) in an enlightening interpretation of then current human geography in ecological terms; work in economic, urban, and population geography was cited for the ecological content.

By the 1960s, geographic human ecology remained as an uncertain field and as an uncertain method. An attempt at identity was made by W. B. Morgan and R. P. Moss (1965) focusing on the concept of community, a concept already well established in sociology. Community was seen as a society occupying a particular region and these communities were to be studied with reference to biological and not physical relationships, thus leading to ecological analyses. In an important sense, this proposed scheme was similar to that of Barrows.

The contemporary ecological approach to geography continues to turn to traditional sociological literature, as evidenced in the social geography books by David Ley (1983b) and Richard Dennis and Hugh Clout (1980), and to that of ecological anthropology as evidenced by Marvin Mikesell (1978), for example. There are occasional statements that are radically different, such as that by Jim Norwine and Thomas Anderson (1980, p. vii), which centered on the environment as a factor ''impacting man's destiny,'' but these are exceptions. Perhaps the most fruitful recent development is one that has taken place in a variety of disciplines, including geography, centering on the notion of adaptation. This is far from new, but it has developed substantially in recent years and merits further consideration.

CULTURAL ADAPTATION

Cultural adaptation has recently emerged as a particular interest within the larger concern of ecology. For some authors, the two terms are essentially synonymous, but for others the idea of adaptation is just too close to environmentalism. The historian Malin, for example, was initially strongly influenced by Webb in emphasizing human adaptation to fixed and stable environments and only later did he acknowledge that the human mind was a crucial variable (Swierenga, 1984, p. xxii). In an analysis of the Mormon landscape, William Speth (1967) argued that an adaptation focus lay midway between the two extremes of environmental and cultural determinism. Increasing interest in the ecologically inspired idea of adaptation certainly renewed debate about the dangers of determinism, specifically the environmental variety. Gordon Lewthwaite (1966, p. 22) argued for a reconsideration of the role played by environment; John Mogey (1971) argued that all human behavior is social. It is important to appreciate that any discussion of cultural adaptation is clouded by this contentious issue. This section now proceeds to consider several of the recent contributions to the cultural adaptation concept. These contributions include geographic, anthropological, sociological, and psychological content.

In all cases, adaptation is viewed as a process; this is in marked contradistinction to early developments in anthropology centering on types of culture and culture stage. A central question is why humans behave as they do in the environment. This question, and the process of adaptation, have been tackled in various ways. The geographer Mogey (1971) proposed an adaptation concept closely linked to the concept of society.

For Mogey (1971), human life is social life and humans are society; the two cannot be logically separated. In order to survive, all societies have social mechanisms permitting them to adapt to environment. These mechanisms include techniques and objectives and are learned. Each society has a different set of social mechanisms, and for any given society, these are always subject to change. Following this logic, Mogey (1971, p. 80) was able to refute environmentalism. Even major natural disasters do not lead to social change; indeed, many societies are adapted to specific disasters. Adaptation, then, becomes a social matter. Mogey (1971) specifically identified the community as the appropriate social unit for study—the social unit in which the process of adaptation operates. Necessarily, different communities utilize different adaptive processes. Differences between communities stem from two factors, technology and values. The former is a conventional variable for classifying groups, and the latter involves questions of the pattern and acquisition of status. Six propositions were thus advanced by Mogey (1971, p. 92).

1. The community is the unit of social structure through which environments affect human behavior. This process is called adaption or adaptation.
2. Any adaptive innovation requires modification both of the value system and also of the techniques of the community if it is to be acceptable.
3. In equalitarian communities rates for the appearance of adaptive innovations will be low.
4. The mere presence of a status system which supports a set of leaders does not guarantee the ready acceptance of innovations.
5. Adaptive innovations are frequent and acceptable in communities with bureaucratic organizations because they have values based on achievement and a status hierarchy that demands performance.
6. Bureaucratic organizational systems have their own internal rigidities which may impede their performance in the process of adaptation. More work on the interrelations of value systems and techniques in political, religious and family systems is clearly essential.

This original contribution is similar to some of the ideas expressed in chapter 5 of this volume concerning the behavior of colonizers. Mogey (1971) was careful to avoid a form of sociological determinism and regarded the above ideas as propositions, not conclusions. There is little evidence as yet that these ideas are being used by others; in their comprehensive volume on social geography, Peter Jackson and Susan Smith (1984) make no reference to these ideas.

Adaptation at the scale of the individual has been discussed by John Berry (1984). This work proposed an ecocultural psychology, centering on adaptation to the recurrent problems posed by environments, which required that "individual behavior may, and indeed *must,* be seen in its total ecological and cultural context" (J. W. Berry, 1984, p. 91). Adaptation, from this perspective, "refers to the reduction of dissonance within a system—the increase of harmony among a set of interacting variables" (J. W. Berry, 1984, p. 100). Harmony can be increased in three ways: adaptation by adjustment, adaptation by reaction, and adaptation by withdrawal. The first is probably the most characteristic form of adaptation and, indeed, many researchers regard adaptation and adjustment as synonymous. Adjustment involves changes in behavior designed to reduce conflict with environment, reaction involves a retaliation against the environment effectively to make the environment adjust, and withdrawal involves a conflict reduction by human removal from the source of conflict. It is useful to note that these three versions of adaptation are comparable to work in psychology, which recognizes a movement toward, against, or away from a stimulus (Lewin, 1936). This perspective on adaptation sees all adaptations as being particular solutions to particular environments.

Recent work by the anthropologist John Bennett (see 1984) centered on adaptation as human behavior. "To understand behavior one must view it both as a set of psychological processes which are probably universal or nearly so, and as a set of novel behavioral responses adapted to particular times and situations"

(Bennett, 1984, p. 246). Thus, particular human institutional and historical precedents are factors influencing adaptation. The question arises as to precisely what is the adaptive potential in human behavior. Individual and group behaviors can be seen as adaptations, but the processes are different for the two scales. What may be a sound adaptive response for an individual may not be so for the group. Further confusion arises from the fact that sound adaptive responses for both individual and group may not be so for the environment. These distinctions raise the question of environmental abuse, for it may be that human adaptation is focused more on adaptation to one another than it is to environment. Bennett (1984, pp. 251–253) suggested that from an individual viewpoint, the key factor in adaptation is coping whereas from a group viewpoint, the key factor is the presence of institutions. In both instances adaptation is likely to involve some rational choice process. These considerations led Bennett (1984) to a detailed account of resource use and scarcity, a theme not pursued in the present context.

A second major anthropological contribution to cultural adaptation is that by David Hardesty (1977, 1986). In this work, adaptation was acknowledged to be the central concept in ecological studies, because it is the process by means of which sound human-environment relationships develop. Adaptation was also closely linked to evolution and three levels were distinguished: behavioral, physiological, and genetic. The concern here is with the behavioral level. "Behavior is the most rapid response that an organism can make and, if based upon learning rather than genetic inheritance, is also the most flexible" (Hardesty, 1977, p. 23). The two types of adaptive behavior are idiosyncratic, that is unique individual responses usually studied by psychologists, and cultural, that is shared responses usually studied by anthropologists. Cultural adaptation occurs because of changes in technology, organization, and ideology, all aspects of culture. How do these changes foster adaptation? The usual response has been to assert that they provide solutions to the problem posed by environment, but Hardesty (1977, p. 24–31) added three other processes: changes in the cultural variables improve the effectiveness of solutions, provide adaptability, and provide awareness of environmental problems. Regardless of specifics, adaptation is characterized by continual changes in human-environment relations. Hardesty (1986) proposed a model of adaptation, which can be summarized as follows. The focus is on individuals and their fitness to adapt, with fitness being linked to cultural baggage and learning. It is acknowledged that space is culturally meaningful, with ideology being the key determinant as to what is meaningful. Adaptation itself frequently occurs because of some revolutionary, as opposed to evolutionary, change in ideology. These ideas are closely linked to various developments in geography (see Hardesty, 1986, p. 16) and it seems likely that this approach may impinge on a variety of cultural and social geographic research.

Some researchers have tackled specific research problems in a genuinely interdisciplinary fashion. An analysis of rural violence in one valley of Colombia explictly employed a range of concepts to argue that "the spatial organization of society cannot be meaningfully comprehended without an understanding of the totality of ecological relationships in which specific societies are involved, adaptively, through cultural means'' (Schorr, 1974, p. 272). Violence was shown to have several causes with the result that its occurrence is random and frequent and thus normal. Because it is normal, the local populations have adapted their spatial arrangements, behaviors, and attitudes to the expectation of violence. Thomas Schorr (1974) described the structure of space and the material landscape of the valley, but stressed that these could only be comprehended when related to human behavior. This argument applied at a variety of scales, the valley region as a whole and specific family residence locations. The overall result is an adaptive organization that emphasizes security given the reality of violence. This thoughtful analysis of one specific problem is a clear indication of the need to adapt not only to nonhuman but also to human surroundings.

A second example with a strong interdisciplinary content focused on the cultural organization of space in Taos Pueblo (Katz, 1974). The Taos Indians have a compact settlement pattern with a resultant high rate of interaction and there has resulted three distinctive adaptations. These adaptations are in the form of particular spatial organizations. One adaptation involves maintaining an acceptable social distance between individuals by means of exercising restraint, another involves displays of hostility, the third involves procedures for ensuring adaptation to a specific aspect of the social environment.

The final discussion under this heading returns to contributions by geographers. One geographer in particular, Karl Butzer, has argued that a version of cultural adaptation could be a key explanatory procedure for the cultural geographer (Denevan, 1983; Hardesty, 1986) while several others have made reference to cultural adaptation (Porter, 1965; Grossman, 1977; Hansis, 1984). An especially useful appraisal of the adaptation concept noted that human survival was dependent on there being available a supply of adaptive responses (Denevan, 1983). The appropriate scale of analysis is the ecological population and the basic research aim is that of accounting for "the sources of variation and the processes of selection" (Denevan, 1983, p. 401). This type of contribution is essentially derivative of anthropology and state and class are included as relevant variables in the process of adaptation. The tendency in both anthropology and cultural geography has been to focus on traditional societies where such variables appear to be least relevant. The geographic contribution to the debate on cultural adaptation is stimulating, but limited relative to that by anthropologists. It is, however, interesting to note that, just as both sociological and anthropological versions of human ecology have influenced geographic versions, so have these same two disciplines influenced geographic analyses of adaptation. Mogey (1971) incorporated significant sociological content while William Denevan (1983) incorporated significant anthropological content.

This section on cultural adaptation demonstrates some of the diversity of current emphases in various social science disciplines. There is as yet little evidence of a coherent and unified focus, a situation that ought not to elicit surprises given that this is precisely the situation for the wider theme of human ecology. As is the case with ecology, there have been numerous references to adaptation, implicit and explicit, in both cultural and social geographic literature. It remains to be seen whether or not future research sees the concept as central.

HUMAN ECOLOGY AND SYSTEMS ANALYSIS

> Of the three conceptual frameworks geographers have utilized in their efforts to probe the relationships of man and environment, the ecological approach is at once the simplest and most complex, the most fascinating and the most difficult to accomplish. Whereas landscape relies on man's footprints, and perception examines images to identify salient man-nature processes, ecology attempts to attack the processes frontally and thus faces the problem of an overwhelming set of variables and forces. (English & Mayfield, 1972, pp. 119–120)

The above statement succinctly summarizes the inevitable complexity of the ecological approach, an approach that explictly acknowledges the multiplicity of variables and their complex linkages. Cultural adaptation has been one attempt to impose some order on this confusing scenario. Another attempt has involved the application of systems concepts, concepts that have long been associated with human and other ecologies.

Any self-sustaining collection of living organisms and their environment is an ecosystem, sometimes called an ecological system. This concept was first introduced in 1935 by an English botanist, Arthur George Tansley. Ecosystems can be viewed at a variety of scales, from the world to perhaps one pond. One clear potential advantage to the ecosystems approach is that it acknowledges, for any given environment, the complexity, indeed the totality, of interrelationships between all organisms. The system is always seen as being in a dynamic balance with environment, that is, the system is constantly adapting in response to changing conditions. Nonhuman ecosystems can be analyzed in detail involving consideration of energy flows and matter cycles in particular. Human ecosystems need to be viewed more cautiously as the biological limits to behavioral patterns are less rigid. Despite this comment, geographers and others have attempted to apply the concept to human systems.

David Stoddart (1965) noted four interesting properties of the ecosystem concept. First, it is monistic in that it integrates living things and environment and permits acknowledgment of the various interactions between elements. In the broadest sense, this property can be seen to be in accord with the ambitious aims of mid-nineteenth–century and later cultural geographers. The emphasis on unity is in direct opposition to the various dualistic approaches, especially environmentalism. Second, the ecosystem concept implies a structure that can, in principle, be investigated. Third, ecosystems are functioning structures; there are communications taking place within the system. Fourth, any ecosystem is in fact one example of a general system. This means that all of the properties of a general system apply also to the specific ecosystem. The first applications of ecosystems were biological, but only occasionally included humans as one component of the system.

A human ecosystem analysis allows, in principle, a study of human modification of environment, both accidental and deliberate, and of the consequences of modification. Very often it is the case that increasing human involvement leads to species destruction and ecosystem imbalance. Environmental scientists often study human populations, resources, and human use of the earth in broad ecosystem terms. These studies remain fairly faithful to the original botanical concept and have not been prevalent in the social sciences. The characteristic social science emphasis has been one of accepting the ecosystem in broad terms and tailoring it to the specific requirements of the disciplinary focus.

Pioneering statements from a human science perspective by the economist Kenneth Boulding (1950, 1968) described society as an ecosystem, as one example of the more general concept of a system. A more influential statement was that by Clifford Geertz (1963). Using a cultural ecology framework, land use change in Indonesia was analyzed by reference to systems logic. For Geertz (1963), the prime advantage of such an approach was the explicit initial acknowledgment of complexity, of a network of mutual causality. In this sense, the concept was essentially used as a point of view and little use was made of the variety of analytical procedures developed for biological and general systems (Hardesty, 1977, p. 15). Other anthropologists have applied systems logic more explicitly, for example, Rappaport (1963) in an analysis of human involvement in island ecosystems. The central assertion, which is evident from both geographic and anthropological work, is that human populations can be treated in much the same way as any other population. Rappaport (1963, p. 170) concluded that "the study of man, the culture bearer, cannot be separated from the study of man, a species among other species." This is not a universally accepted conclusion.

The attraction of a systems framework for the cultural geographer is evident. This attraction was explictly outlined by Don Foote and Bryn Greer-Wooten (1968) while a detailed introduction to geographic systems in general is that of Alan Wilson (1981). Despite statements of this type, the ecosystems concept remains a treacherous one to employ. Geographers have not had the same success as have anthropologists, and even the anthropological research has been heavily criticized (see Hardesty, 1977, p. 15). Why is it that the ecosystems concept, as one aspect of the wider ecological focus, has had less impact in geography than in anthropology? One possible reason is quite simply that geography can be regarded as a cluster of interests rather than as a discipline with a central subject matter focus that can effectively permit the application and evaluation of new procedures. For geography, the result is that ecological analyses often look remarkably like their counterparts in anthropology. There is, of course, nothing wrong with this at all. The only problem is that it further reinforces the identity crisis of twentieth-century geography. With these comments in mind, this chapter now proceeds to discuss and evaluate geographic examples of ecological research. These examples include the themes of adaptation and of eco-system as appropriate.

HUMAN ECOLOGY AND CULTURAL GEOGRAPHY

Human ecology literature in geography is characterized by a number of pro-grammatic statements and a relative paucity of research. The research literature referred to by geographers includes sociological, anthropological, and geographic examples. Urban and socially inclined geographers refer to the urban sociology research emanating initially from the Chicago school; rural and culturally inclined geographers refer to the cultural ecology school in anthropology and related work. It seems appropriate to assert that geographers have not succeeded in establishing a similar major school of thought. This failure is related to the uncertain identity of geography and to the fact that geographic claims to an interest in ecological matters, regardless of how central ecology may appear, have been erratic. The usual procedure appears to be one of claiming that an ecological approach is *the* approach with some geographers seeing the need for such an aproach as self-evident. While such may be the case, it is also proper to recognize that there is yet little evidence of the centrality of ecology to geography. This section includes discussions of urban ecology, cultural ecology, and other contributions.

Urban Ecology

Both the social urban geographer and the human ecologist are interested in space and in adaptive processes. The first interest sees spatial differences resulting from social processes, and the second is concerned with human-land and human-human processes. The initial stimulus from the Chicago school of sociology has persisted and radically affected later geographic work. Despite obvious limita-tions, such as the omission of a cross-cultural perspective and of any reference to symbolism, that school remains central to geography. In a detailed analysis of the English town Sunderland, Robson (1969) fused the spatial interests of the geographer and the structural interests of the sociologist to produce an account of urban spatial structure and its causes. A concentric pattern of social areas was evident in north Sunderland whereas a sectoral pattern was evident in the south, unlike the ideal ecological distribution of concentric zones around the entire city. The distortion of the ideal was prompted by industrial considerations and by the desire of the social elite to be close to the city center. The processes of invasion and succession were both evident. The ecological emphasis was a major thrust in the urban geography of the 1960s, because of the then willingness of geography to borrow from other disciplines and the emphasis being placed on quantitative techniques. Factor analysis in particular was well suited to ecological analyses. Overall, there are few links between the human ecology practiced in the urban context and that practiced in the guise of a cultural ecology. Because of the links with positivistic spatial analysis, the urban ecology is somewhat rejected today.

Cultural Ecology

In geography, the second principal application of ecological concepts is typically labeled cultural ecology and is essentially comparable to anthropological interpretations. Geographers have largely failed to carve a specific niche for themselves within cultural ecology. Urban ecological studies, with their intellectual heritage in sociology, are quite different from cultural ecological studies, with their intellectual heritage in anthropology. James Clarkson (1970) emphasized this distinction by discussing ecology and spatial analysis as though they were necessarily different, which is most assuredly not the case in urban social geography. For Clarkson (1970), ecology was essentially related to innovation diffusion and economic development.

The close links between cultural ecology in geography and in anthropology are suggested by the frequent inclusion of anthropological research in geography articles and books (see English & Mayfield, 1972). But there are also a variety of studies by geographers that are explicitly in the cultural ecology tradition. In several cases, such as those of Burton Gordon (1954), Homer Aschman (1954), and Donald Innis (1958) the work was completed under the guidance of Sauer, a further indication of the breadth of the landscape school. Two substantive studies by geographers are now noted followed by reference to a particular research problem.

Shifting cultivation has proven an attractive research area for both ecologically inclined anthropologists and geographers. David Harris (1971) focused on swidden cultivation as a functioning, human-modified ecosystem, with reference to the upper Orinoco rain forest in Venezuela. A detailed description of agricultural practices was provided and several conclusions reached. Polycultural swiddens were shown to be cultivated longer than monocultural swiddens; the latter were less stable and more mobile, and to be more likely to have their abandonment caused by weed invasion. An important general conclusion was confirmation of the "ecological fitness" of swidden cultivation (D. Harris, 1971, p. 494). This research also prompted the conclusion that the failure of a maize-dominated system to penetrate the South American tropical forest may have been caused by ecological as well as cultural barriers; specifically by the difficulty of burning the cleared vegetation adequately in an area with a minimal dry season.

A different type of ecological analysis concerned a village in Malaysia and provided an historical description, a spatial-functional description, and a human-land analysis (Clarkson, 1968). Interesting relationships were evident between farming technology, land use, and social organization such that the three combined as some form of integrated system. The Malayan Chinese village studied displayed a stable social system even when other key ecological variables changed. "The Chinese had the mental and material equipment necessary to establish a complex, but stable and flexible, eco-system involving vegetable gardening'' (Clarkson, 1968, p. 155). The influence of cultural values, such as the high regard for family-centered activities, on the ecosystem was clearly demonstrated. The work of Clarkson (1968) is one example of a geographic contribution to intensification theory, particularly, as developed by Ester Boserup (1965). The leading geographer in this area has been Harold Brookfield (see 1973) and the typical focus has been on relations between agriculture and population density.

One particular research theme that has benefited from the application of ecological approaches is that of the origin of agriculture. This fascinating problem intrigues scholars from many disciplines, at least partly because it was perhaps the first major cultural, as opposed to biological, revolution. Ecological questions are at the heart of the agricultural origin problem, specifically the relative roles played by environment and culture.

The central argument in the ecological theory is that preagricultural societies, hunters and gatherers, did not need agriculture. Evidence suggests that the population-resource balance was satisfactory and was sufficient to counter any need for agriculture. Furthermore, because of their characteristic mobility, experimentation with crop planting was not feasible. A hunter-gatherer group could not be expected to anticipate the long-term advantages of agriculture and thus make the required short-term sacrifice of minimizing mobility. Ecological theory proposes that a specific situation is required that will counter the negative consequences of the lack of mobility. Various ecological theories are available that allow for precisely such a situation. Climatic change is central to some such theories. One of the better, if largely speculative, set of ideas was developed by Sauer (1952) in his suggestion that agriculture originated in areas where mobility was minimized because resources were plentiful. The resultant leisure time prompted experimentation with planted seeds. Most of the ecological arguments presuppose preadaptation; this is not accepted by all scholars. Philip Wagner (1977) argued for a ecological determinism while George Carter (1977) saw individual genius as the key cause.

The use of ecological concepts in this research problem is general rather than specific. Detailed systems analyses are not characteristic. The characteristic approach is to argue for some environmental and cultural relationships, the details of which explain the problem at hand. Geographers have contributed, along with scholars from many other disciplines, to this research problem.

Other Contributions

Time geography, a relatively recent development that is discussed in chapter 7, has been closely linked to ecology in recent work by Tommy Carlstein (1982). The ecological groundwork is laid early with both human time and human space being regarded as resources; according to Carlstein (1982, p. 4), this is one means of integrating spatial and ecological analyses in geography. The concept, ecotechnology, was defined to emphasize that "technology is an intermediary factor between ecology, on the one hand, and economy, on the other" (Carlstein, 1982, p. 8). An analysis of preindustrial societies focused on intensification theory and carrying capacity.

Another thrust has come from the possibly surprising area of historical geography. Indeed, in terms of the impact on related disciplines, this work is especially significant. Arthur Ray (1971, p. 9) produced an "historical study in ecological cultural geography" in his account of Indian exploration in the forest to grassland transition zone in western Canada between 1680 and 1850. In a similar fashion, Conrad Heidenreich (1971) analyzed the area of Huron settlement in Ontario in a manner that was partially derivative of anthropological research.

All of these geographic contributions are closely linked to research in other disciplines. Even the most novel of the geographic emphases, time geography, is intimately linked to anthropology and, to a lesser extent, structuration theory in sociology.

CONCLUDING COMMENTS

This chapter contains a fundamental contradiction. It is evident that there is no consensus in the social sciences as to what an ecological approach comprises. At the same time, it is evident that much useful research has been conducted under the general ecological umbrella. Much conceptual confusion is accompanied by reasonable research success.

Ecological approaches are best viewed as simply one more way of investigating both human-human and human-land relations. An analysis dealing with these relationships is an ecological analysis. But not all ecological analyses are conceptually simple. Adaptation approaches and systems analyses are two of the many concerns that are typically more rigorous. The multidisciplinary, and sometimes interdisciplinary, character is evident, and it would be misleading to create the impression that ecology is at the center of any one social science. It is employed in geography, sociology, anthropology, psychology, and history, but it is not the dominant concern in any of these fields. Superficially, geography would appear to be the most natural home of ecology because of the physical and human content and the long-standing idea that the discipline can serve as some sort of bridge between physical and human sciences. The reality, however, appears to be that geography is both physical and human but only rarely does it combine these two.

The multidisciplinary character of human ecology has typically resulted in a lack of concept clarification across disciplines. Ecology appears, in one sense, to be waging a losing battle against ever-increasing specialization. A universal approach appears irrelevant to many in the contemporary academic world. The approach has experienced major victories in sociology, anthropology, psychology, and geography but these achievements are rarely closely related. Geography appears to have been the one discipline to have actively exploited contributions from each of the other disciplines; impacts from sociology and anthropology are noted in this chapter and impacts from psychology are more evident in chapter 5. In an analysis of the human ecology tradition to geography Philip Porter (1978) noted five post–1950 themes, none of which is exclusively the domain of geography. The first is the evolution of cultural systems, a research area primarily anthropological in character. The second is perception and natural hazards research, areas covered by psychologists, although much of the hazards research has original geographic contributions. The third concerns population pressure and limits to growth questions; these are not distinctively geographic issues and the geographic input is less than the anthropological input. The fourth concern is with medical ecology, an area of research where geographers clearly work on the periphery. The final concern is with political economy, again a theme where the geographic input is secondary. These comments are not intended to denigrate the geographic work, rather to emphasize that there is not really any distinctively geographic human ecology. One response to this conclusion is, of course, to simply state that such is precisely what the ecological approach offers, a method of analysis that can be successfully utilized by various of the traditional disciplines. The negative aspect is that the multidisciplinary character does not necessarily mean increased communication. One clear exception is the agricultural origins problem to which anthropologists, geographers, and others have all contributed in a relatively integrated dialogue.

The geographic use of the ecological approach has been erratic. Explicit attempts to define the ecosystem as a geographical model, such as that by Stoddart (1967) have not been successful, either conceptually or as inspirations for empirical research. Stoddart (1967, p. 538) explicitly proposed the idea of a geo-system as a replacement for ecosystem and argued that ''systems analysis at last provides geography with a unifying methodology, and using it geography no longer stands apart from the mainstream of scientific progress.'' This argument has won few converts. Physical geography has been approached from an overall systems viewpoint, but human geography in general has been much less affected. Among the many possible reasons for the failure of a systems approach to effectively reorient geography is, quite simply, the fact that geographers do not seek yet another unifying methodology. If anything, the contemporary need is for a unified subject matter, not method.

An appraisal of ecological approaches is instructive. Despite the fact that, in principle, the ecological argument is at the very heart of geography, the details of the approach have not emerged as dominant. Once again, a key reason is that the human-land theme is geography has not succeeded itself in becoming a dominant paradigm since the demise of environmentalism, and consequently, an ecological thrust within the human-land theme could hardly be expected to emerge as a major method. A second reason is that the ecological approach has been subject to so many interpretations and geographers have been attracted to different interpretations. An approach that is itself so diverse is necessarily likely to have difficulty becoming a dominant method in any discipline. A third reason is that ecological approaches have never succeeded in developing as a school of thought within geography comparable, for example, to the landscape school. Perhaps the appropriate context in which to place and assess the approach is simply as one of several ways of looking at human-land relations and at landscape. In this volume, it is but one of four delimited. Viewed from this perspective, ecology has made positive and lasting contributions to our understanding, and it is important not to be too concerned with assertions and counter assertions concerning the need to define geography ecologically.

9

Retrospect and Prospect

This final chapter serves three principal functions. First, some summary and concluding statements are presented. This section is relatively brief as each of the earlier chapters has included a "Concluding Comments" section. Second, aspects of the development of cultural geography are reconsidered. This section considers the criticism that most methodological writing merely re-covers established discourse and reconsiders the impact of selected concepts. Third, some final comments, including avenues for future research, are noted in a suggestive rather than definitive fashion.

GENERAL CONCLUSIONS

The introduction to this volume attempted a fairly precise delimitation of cultural geography as a subdiscipline of human geography. In a general sense, this was an atypical interpretation of cultural geography for both teaching and research purposes. The majority of North American texts centered on cultural geography treat it as synonymous with human geography, as noted by William Norton (1981). Text exceptions to this generalization include Peter Haggett (1983) and Robert Stoddard, Brian Blouet, and David Wishart (1986). The latter authors stated that "because culture works as a guiding force behind much of human behavior, it can be argued that cultural geography and human geography are one and the same. In practice, however, cultural geography is a subset of human geography, just as are population and political geography (Stoddard, Blouet, & Wishart, 1986, p. 87)." In addition to viewing cultural geography as a subdiscipline, and thus narrowing the potential content substantially, this volume has argued from the outset for increased integration of two typically separate fields, cultural and social geography. It was asserted in the introduction, and it is hoped, demonstrated in subsequent chapters, that a cultural-social distinction is more confusing than helpful. The combination of these two assertions about cultural geography has enabled this volume to produce a distinct and meaningful discussion of cultural geography as a subdiscipline integrating two previously rather separate research traditions. The subdiscipline delimitation and the subject matter are by no means perfect, but it is hoped that both the conceptual and empirical content have confirmed the appropriateness of the two initial assertions.

With regard to methodology, the approach has been a catholic one. This does, of course, have disadvantages as the content occasionally leaps from method to method, variously praising and condemning. But there is one basic merit and that concerns the most fundamental of questions about geography. Quite simply, there is more than one geographic method and method is a poor rationale for discipline or subdiscipline delimitation. The methods used by cultural geographers are various and are not restricted to cultural geography. The four approaches to the understanding of landscape discussed are behavioral, evolutionary, symbolic, and ecological. These are not cultural geographic methods, rather they are methods employed by cultural geographers. This fourfold classification is far from ideal. It is quite clear that specific research topics can be assigned to perhaps more than one of the four and that there are close links between classes. No attempt has been made to argue that this is the correct classification, if such exists; rather, it is recognized that the contents of chapters 5 to 8 are separated for at least partially pragmatic reasons. Each of the four approaches to landscape combines both conventional cultural and conventional social content, although chapter 6 is essentially cultural and chapter 7 is essentially social.

One central theme has been evident in this volume, namely a concern with landscape evolution and with relevant variables. This traditional theme has been supported by detailed reference to human-land relations. Visible and symbolic landscapes have been distinguished in an acknowledgment of the complexity of the term *landscape*. A rationale for such a central theme developed gradually through chapters 2, 3, and 4 in a fairly broad-ranging appraisal of geography and other social sciences. Chapters 2 and 3 focused on human-land concepts that are effectively concepts of culture. Chapter 4 centered on current interests in cultural and social geography, admitting the relative newness of many concepts, but also confirming the persistence of both landscape and Vidalian schools. Definitive conclusions were not reached at the end of chapter 4. It was suggested, rather than asserted, that landscape evolution remains a central interest, but that the approaches to that theme, or subject matter, have changed through time and are now more process oriented than previously. The subject matter is now typically tackled with a far greater awareness of social scale, one of the benefits of cross-fertilization with other social sciences (see Norton, 1987).

The four empirically oriented chapters do not provide an overview of what some geographers might regard as comprising cultural geography. Even if the specific delimitation is accepted, questions of content remain. Perhaps the one that most merits comment is the apparent exclusion of folk and popular culture analyses. The Terry Jordan and Lester Rowntree (1986) text includes a chapter for each of these topics and the chapter contents accord well with the overall thrust of that text. In the current volume, these two areas of analysis are not excluded, rather they are contained as appropriate within the four themes, although it is granted that relatively little of the popular culture research is selected for inclusion. This is thought to be quite acceptable in a volume that does not have as a primary aim the inclusion of a fully representative literature.

An attempt has been made to stimulate both the teaching and researching of cultural geography. These are far from separate matters. Viewing cultural geography as a subdiscipline presupposes that it succeeds, for teaching purposes, an introductory human course and hence a course in cultural geography is an "advanced" offering requiring the consideration of basic methodological questions as well as the presentation of the facts of cultural geography. With an appropriate course of lectures, or study manual, it is felt that this volume, although clearly not written as a text per se, can serve that purpose most effectively. Signposts are erected; suggestions are made—appropriate procedures for a post-introductory course.

One final general conclusion is in order. The cultural geography proposed here is itself dynamic. Knowledge is ever changing and the very character of cultural geography makes it especially susceptible to change. It is the explicit links with other disciplines that are so relevant in this context. Cultural geographers cannot afford to lose sight of the methods and practice of the other social sciences. This is not a straightforward task as there is a constantly shifting conceptual scenario in particular, but the task is no less necessary because of this complexity. Current advances in sociology, anthropology, and psychology in particular need to be assessed in terms of potential contributions to an understanding of landscape evolution.

THE SUBDISCIPLINE OF CULTURAL GEOGRAPHY

One of the purposes of this volume has been to present an account of cultural geography as it relates to the parent discipline and to other disciplines. By and large this account has been presented in fairly conventional terms, that is to say by investigating sources and generally interpreting them at face value. This procedure can be criticized because it "merely recovers the commonplaces and established discourse of the discipline" (Pickles, 1985, p. 16). The alternative is to ensure that not only do we research past statements as a means of ascertaining what was said, but we also research these statements as a means of rethinking the issues.

During the earlier methodological discussion, certain figures and statements are highlighted. This section now reconsiders a number of the major issues. One such issue concerns the general character of American geography prior to the mid–1920s. The Association of American Geographers, organized in 1904 under the strong guidance of William Morris Davis, was the center of a rejuvenated geography, rejuvenated by physiography. In addition, there was a second favored field, that of anthropogeography as formulated by Friedrich Ratzel. This was essentially one specific interpretation, environmental determinism. Major books favoring this view were published by Ellen Semple (1903, 1911) and by Albert Brigham (1903). By 1914, this second view of geography had "forced its way to front ranks in American geography" (Pfeifer, 1938, p. 3). A third view penetrated American geography at this time; this concerned region delimitation, especially of physiographic region (Fenneman, 1916).

This early threefold identity of American geography was subject to two major statements in the 1920s by Harlan H. Barrows (1923) and Carl Sauer (1925). To a certain extent these two antienvironmentalist statements had their groundwork laid in the 1920 translation of a volume by Jean Brunhes. Translated volumes by Lucien Febvre and Paul Vidal de la Blache appeared later in 1925 and 1926 respectively. In addition, the writings of the anthropologist Robert Lowie, Alfred Kroeber, and Clark Wissler were accessible. Together, these various works questioned environmentalism and introduced the culture area concept. Both Barrows and Sauer advocated the cultural landscape analysis and emphasized geography as a social science. The Barrows statement proved less influential than that by Sauer.

The view of geography argued by Sauer was, as we have seen, the seminal English-language statement. Geography was to be the study of landscape, but landscape itself was simply a better term than either region or area, better because area was not an exclusively geographic concept whereas region implied a definite magnitude (Pfeifer, 1938, p. 7). The aim of geography was to establish the genetic qualities of landscape. Sauer was effectively proposing a form of historical regional geography, with regions being natural and human landscape complexes. Sauer explicitly opposed any geographic, physical-human, dualism.

After the mid-1920s, and the statements from both Barrows and Sauer, geography progressed along divergent lines. Environmentalism continued to be influential with a new 1933 edition of a classic (Semple, 1903) and books by George Miller and Almon Parkins (1928) and Ellsworth Huntington and Sumner Cushing (1934), for example. But there was also a growing landscape or regional approach; either term sufficed in the 1930s. There was work explicitly associated with Sauer and there was work more typically labeled regional. These two, however, were markedly similar. A course taught by Sauer titled "Culture Regions of the World" combined cultural evolution with a discussion of culturally delimited regions (Sauer, 1940). Much 1930s regional geography may not have referred to Sauer but it was roughly comparable. As noted in chapter 6, Derwent Whittlesey (1929) elaborated a sequent occupance procedure not dissimilar from the landscape school and this term, *occupance,* tended to be favored. Regional studies often contained a significant evolutionary content (see James, 1929). In the broadest sense, the period prior to the publication of perhaps the first definitive antievolutionary statement, by Richard Hartshorne (1939), was marked by rather similar landscape and regional, or occupance, emphases.

It was the 1940s that saw the rise of an atemporal regional geography and the resultant separation of landscape and regional concerns. Hartshorne (1939, p. 107) did not exclude "historical studies of changing integrations . . . as long as the focus of attention is maintained on the character of areas changing in consequence of certain processes, in contrast to the historical interest in the processes themselves." Acknowledging the general similarity of landscape and regional interests is not by any means a radical interpretation (see Taafe, 1974). What is being emphasized is the initial (1925–1939) similarity of landscape and regional geography notably in terms of the role of time and the emphasis on the cultural landscape. The differences were those of emphasis; the regional school more typically incorporating an environmentalist view and being less concerned with causal processes.

The relative distinctiveness of cultural geography was thus assured in the late 1930s. That distinctiveness remained through to at least the 1970s. During this period, the regional and then spatial analytic paradigms dominated human geography and in both cases were explicitly atemporal and relatively little concerned with human-land relations. The present tendency, as evidenced especially in chapter 4, is toward the increasing centrality of traditional cultural and newer social concerns.

SOME FINAL COMMENTS

This volume has left much undone and has not necessarily resolved many of the questions posed. This final section attempts at least partially to rectify these two limitations. These final comments concern humans and land, landscape, and the future of cultural geography.

Humans and Land

The theme of humans and land is as central for cultural geographers today as it was for Sauer in the 1920s, and indeed, for many European geographers before then. The details of debate may have changed but the basic questions raised are little different. Under the heading of "Nature versus Culture," Yi-fu Tuan (1986, p. 11) noted that all humans distinguish between the two and insist on the need for culture to change nature. One of the easiest changes to accomplish is simply the naming of parts of nature. These changes are needed in order to enable humans to feel at home; in the most general sense culture is preferred to nature. "A principal aim of culture is to extend the realm of the familiar at the expense of nature and the strange" (Tuan, 1986, p. 16).

Human relationship with nature is not the only concern for some scholars; there are the linked additional concerns with human-human relationships and human-human world relationships. Several scholars have proposed that, in order to achieve the "genuine happiness" sought by Tuan (1986, p. 10), three reconciliations are needed: humans with nature, humans with humans, and humans with human world. Two such scholars are Karl Marx and Hannah Arendt (Dyck, 1979). Both argued that a meaningful human life can only be achieved if individuals are willing to commit themselves to groups; it is the social environment that provides the necessary context. From a completely different conceptual basis, the social anthropologist Anthony Cohen (1982, pp. 1–2) contended that social reorganization is the "means through which people order, value and express their knowledge of their worlds of experience." To belong to a cultural group is to see oneself as different from those outside of the culture. This is precisely what Fredrik Barth (1969) was referring to in the argument that group ethnicity is most meaningful at the outer spatial limits of the group. Belonging to a group also means ascribing positive values to the group; usually it is the everyday behavior that is so valued. Following this argument, culture becomes a source of identity for Cohen (1982), with identity being closely comparable to the meaningful human life discussed by Marx and Arendt.

The above comments say little about the appropriate basis for group delimitation. In some cases, the basis is spatial, as has often been noted with reference to local communities (see Sutter, 1973). Very often, regardless of any spatial variable, it becomes necessary to consider both the basis for delimitation and the most relevant scale. These two related questions have been raised on several occasions in this volume, most notably in chapter 7, and definitive answers are lacking. Relevant variables and relevant scales are likely to differ according to the specifics of the research problem. Particular assumptions need to be questioned. It has recently been argued, for example, that contrary to the view proposed by Marx, people from the same class took opposing sides in the political struggle in France in 1848 (Traugott, 1985). Cultural geographers need to be cautious in their approach to humans, culture, and the various relationships between humans, nature, other humans, and human landscapes.

Landscape

Cultural geographers continue to be confronted with a plethora of interpretations of the term *landscape* (Cosgrove, 1985). It is appropriate to begin this discussion by acknowledging that cultural geographers do not have a monopoly on the term. Human geography in general is likely to remain a spatially oriented discipline "whose ultimate concern is with those landscape features produced and modified by the corporate actions of social man" (Chorley, 1973, p. 158). Some human geographers have tackled landscape evolution from a theoretical perspective, centering on economic features. Richard Morrill (1979, p. 85), for example, created geometric landscapes "unsullied by time or the real environment." The essential purpose of such a procedure was to expose some order in the chaos of reality. It would be an intriguing extension of current cultural research to attempt something similar for cultural landscapes; the result just might be some improved cultural geographic theory (Norton, 1988).

Some scholars, however, have argued for the "primacy of economic factors in the development of cultural systems" (K. E. Lewis, 1984, p. 3). Culture evolves at least partially in response to the need to exploit environment for reasons of survival and improvement; these needs may be predominantly economic and hence the adaptations that take place are economic. This is a commonplace assumption in much cultural ecology. A contrary view, emphasizing the relative importance of cultural variables, was proposed with reference to the question of underdevelopment in a Malayan context. Joseph Spencer (1960 p. 43 wrote that "in the psychological changes that mark the acceptance of the changing elements of culture in Malaya lies a large degree of true "development.' " Finally, in this connection, George Kay (1971) argued for a combined cultural and economic approach to landscape emphasizing technology as a major determinant. This argument was derived significantly from a consideration of the five stages of technology proposed by Hans Carol (1964). The five are adaptation, domestication, diversification, mechanization, and automation. This discussion has served to emphasize the obvious, namely, that cultural landscapes are parts of larger human landscapes just as cultural geography is a subset of human geography.

The diverse role played by landscape in cultural geography can be further emphasized by a consideration of landscape as a tool for learning and of landscape as a prompt for thought and description. Humans can learn through landscapes and can communicate that learning to others. "We, as geographers, are blessed with the most exciting of educational mediums when we realize how much we can learn and teach through an aggressive use of our landscape" (Salter, 1977, pp. 1–2). Landscape can serve as a means to an end—the end being the understanding of humankind. Using landscape to learn allows geographers to ask about the landscape created and about human existence in landscape. Answers, and hence learning, are achieved by looking at subjective and objective space, at the modification of space, at the perception of use of space, and at the institutions humans create to dictate use of space. Most important, geographers must contribute an understanding of the use of space in the form of landscape evaluation and possible preservation. Ian Matley (1977) detailed the issue of preservation while David Lanegran (1986) provided an example of an effective geography and society cooperative effort concerned with the use of land and awareness of that use. Landscape as a tool for learning is explicit in much humanistic writing. For Edward Relph (1984, p. 213) it was "impossible to ignore landscape, for it frames our lives." An understanding of landscape can be presented as a description subsequent to the writer seeing and thinking about the landscape. Such an approach presupposes that landscapes cannot be objectively analyzed, but that a skilled individual description can educate others.

The Future of Cultural Geography

It seems reasonable to assume that cultural geography is to continue as one major thrust of geographic research and that the details of that thrust will continue to be various and will themselves change. It is useful to emphasize at the outset that there is no necessity for cultural geography; all disciplines and subdisciplines are merely human creations (Johnston, 1985, p. 5). Once they are in existence they tend to be perpetuated, if only because individuals and groups have capital invested in the field. As has been emphasized in this volume, the specific character of cultural geography is a function of the time and circumstances of origin, and at any one time, it is a function of location. Thus the first statements of Sauer reflected the need to oppose an earlier environmentalism whereas the specifics of subdiscipline content have varied markedly between, for example, the cultural geography of North America and the social geography of Britain. Thus, cultural geography is both "historically constituted" and "regionally constituted" (Johnston, 1985, p. 5). Recognizing that there is not any logical necessity for a discipline does not, however, remove the need to seek central foci and clarify content. Geography in general, and cultural geography in particular, continue along this difficult route. The statement made by an anonymous Polish geographer in the 1920s, to the effect that "I fear to give all my life to geography only to find at the end that there is no science of geography" (cited in Johnson, 1929, p. 192), must have been uttered many times since. One of the problems with continuing to seek or to clarify identity is a tendency to present old wine in new bottles. Richard Morrill (1986, p. 98) criticized recent suggestions concerning the need to view places in terms of a coevolution of spatial and social structures on the simple and logical ground that such a view was far from novel.

The cultural geographic search for an understanding of landscape continues, as does the related search for appropriate interpretations of the human and land relationship. There are humanistic approaches focusing on individuals, radical approaches focusing on the societal stucture within which individuals operate, suggestions for a positivist approach (V. P. Miller, 1971), and of course, a series of traditional approaches. The traditional approaches, especially in the North American tradition have focused "much more on artifacts than on people" (Johnston, 1986, p. 48). That deficiency is clearly being rectified by the cultural geography of the 1980s and beyond.

Bibliography

Adams, W. Y. (1978). On migration and diffusion as rival paradigms. In Duke, Ebert, Langemann & Buchner. (Eds.), *Diffusion and migration: Their roles in cultural development* (pp. 1–5). Calgary, Canada: University of Calgary, Archaeological Association.

Agnew, J. A., & Duncan, J. S. (1981). The transfer of ideas into Anglo-American human geography. *Progress in Human Geography*, 5, 42–57.

Agnew, J., Mercer, J., & Sopher, D. (Eds.). (1984). *The city in cultural context*. Boston: Allen & Unwin.

Alihan, M. A. (1938). *Social Ecology*. New York: Cooper Square.

Allen, J. L. (1975). Thomas Jefferson and the passage to India: A pre-exploratory image. In R. E. Ehrenberg (Ed.), *Pattern and process: Research in historical geography*. (pp. 103–113). Washington, D.C.: Howard University Press.

Aschmann, H. (1954). *The ecology, demography and fate of the Indians of the central desert of Baja California*. Unpublished doctoral dissertation, University of California, Berkeley.

Asheim, B. T. (1979). Social geography: Welfare state ideology or critical social science? *Geoforum 10*, 5–18.

Baran, P. A. (1957). *The political economy of growth*. New York: Monthly Review Press.

Barker, R. G. (1968). *Ecological psychology: Concepts and Methods for studying the environment and behavior*. Stanford, CA: Stanford University Press.

Barnett, J. R. (1978). Race and physician location: Trends in two New Zealand urban areas. *New Zealand Geographer, 34*, 2–12.

Barrell, J. (1972). *The idea of landscape and the sense of place 1730–1840: An approach to the poetry of John Clare*. Cambridge, UK: Cambridge University Press.

Barrell, J. (1982). Geographies of Hardy's Wessex. *Journal of Historical Geography, 8*, 347–361

Barrows, H. H. (1923). Geography as human ecology. *Annals, Association of American Geographers, 13,* 1–14.

Barth, F. (1956). Ecologic relationships of ethnic groups in Swat, North Pakistan. *American Anthropologist, 58,* 1079–1089.

Barth, F. (Ed.). (1969). *Ethnic groups and boundaries.* Boston: Little Brown.

Bennett, J. W. (1976). *The ecological transition.* New York: Pergamon.

Bennett, J. W. (1984). Human ecology as human behavior. In I. Altman, A. Rapoport, & J. F. Wohlwill (Eds.), *Human behavior and environment, Advances in theory and research: Vol. 4. Environment and culture.* (pp. 243–277). New York: Plenum Press.

Berdoulay, V. (1978). The Vidal-Durkheim debate. In D. Ley & M. Samuels (Eds.), *Humanisitic geography* (pp. 77–90). Chicago: Maaroufa Press.

Berry, J. W. (1984). Cultural ecology and individual behavior. In I. Altman, A. Rapaport, & J. F. Wohlwill (Eds.), *Human behavior and environment, Advances in theory and research: Vol. 4. Environment and culture* (pp. 83–106). New York: Plenum Press.

Berry, T. M. (1949). *The historical theory of Giambattista Vico.* Washington, D.C.: Catholic University of American Press.

Billinge, M. (1984). Hegemony, class and power in late Georgian and early Victorian England: Towards a cultural geography. In A. R. H. Baker & D. Gregory (Eds.), *Explorations in historical geography: Interpretive essays* (pp. 28–67). Cambridge, UK: Cambridge University Press.

Billington, R. A. (1966). *America's frontier heritage.* New York: Holt, Rinehart and Winston.

Binford, L. R. (1983). *Working at archaeology.* New York: Academic Press.

Biswas, L. (1984). Evolution of Hindu temples in Calcutta. *Journal of Cultural Geography, 4,* 73–84.

Bjorklund, E. M. (1964). Ideology and culture exemplified in southern Michigan. *Annals, Association of American Geographers, 54,* 227–241.

Blaut, J. M. (1977). Two views of diffusion. *Annals, Association of American Geographers, 67,* 343–349.

Blaut, J. M. (1980). A Radical critique of cultural geography. *Antipode, 12,* 25–29.

Blaut, J. M. (1987). Diffusionism: A uniformatarian critique. *Annals, Association of American Geographers, 77,* 30–47.

Boorstin, D. J. (1960). *American and the image of Europe.* New York: World.

Boorstin, D. J. (1962). *The image; Or what happened to the American Dream?* New York: Atheneum.

Boserup, E. (1965). *The condition of agricultural growth: The economics of agrarian change under population pressure.* London: Allen & Unwin.

Boulding, K. E. (1950). *A reconstruction of economics.* New York: John Wiley & Sons.

Boulding, K. E. (1956). *The image: Knowledge in life and society.* Ann Arbor: University of Michigan.

Boulding, K. E. (1968). General systems theory—The skeleton of science. In W. Buckley (Ed.), *Modern systems research for the behavioral scientist: A sourcebook* (pp. 3–10). Chicago: Aldine.

Bourdieu, P. (1985). The social space and the genesis of groups. *Social Science Information, 24,* 195–220.

Bourne, L. S. (1981). *The geography of housing.* New York: Halsted Press.

Bowden, L. W. (1965). *Diffusion of the decision to irrigate*. Chicago: University of Chicago, Department of Geography.

Bowen, E. (1981). *Empiricism and geographical thought*. Cambridge, UK: Cambridge University Press.

Bowen, E. H., & Carter, H. (1975). The distribution of the Welsh language in 1971. *Geography, 60*, 1–15.

Breisach, E. (1983). *Historiography: Ancient, medieval and modern*. Chicago: University of Chicago Press.

Brigham, A. P. (1903). *Geographic influences in American history*. Boston: Ginn & Company.

Broek, J. O. M. (1932). *The Santa Clara valley, California: A study in landscape change*. Utrecht, Holland: Oosthoek.

Broek, J. O. M. (1965). *Compass of geography*. Columbus, OH: Merrill.

Broek, J. O. M., & Webb, J. W. (1978). *A geography of mankind* (3rd ed.). New York: McGraw-Hill.

Brookfield, H. C. (1964). Questions on the human frontiers of geography. *Economic Geography, 40*, 283–303.

Brookfield, H. C. (1969). On the environment as perceived. In C. Board, R. J. Chorley, P. Haggett, D. R. Stoddart. (Eds.), *Progress in geography* (Vol. 1, pp. 51–80). London: Arnold.

Brookfield, H. C. (Ed.). (1973). *The Pacific in Transition: Geographical perspectives on adaptation and change*. London: Arnold.

Browett, J. (1981). On the role of geography in development geography. *Tijdschrifte Voor Economische en Social Geografie, 72*, 155–161.

Brown, I. W. (1979). Functional group changes and acculturation: A case study of the French and the Indian in the lower Mississipi valley. *Mid-Continental Journal of Archaelology, 4*, 147–166.

Brown, L. A. (1981). *Innovation diffusion: A new perspective*. New York: Methuen.

Brown, M. A. (1981). 'Behavioral approaches to the geographic study of innovation diffusion: Problems and prospects. In K. R. Cox & R. G. Golledge (Eds.), *Behavioral problems in geography revisited* (pp. 123–144). New York: Methuen.

Bruhn, J. G. (1974). Human ecology: A unifying science. *Human Ecology, 2*, 105–125.

Brunger, A. G. (1982). Geographical propinquity among Pre-Famine Catholic Irish settlers in upper Canada. *Journal of Historical Geography, 8*, 265–282.

Bryson, R. A., & Murray, T. J. (1977). *Climates of hunger: Mankind and the world's changing weather*. Madison: University of Wisconsin Press.

Bunkse, E. V. (1981). Humboldt and an aesthetic tradition in geography. *Geographical Review, 71*, 127–146.

Bunting, T. E., & Guelke, L. (1979). Behavioral and perception geography: A critical appraisal. *Annals, Association of American Geographers, 69*, 448–462.

Burgess, R. (1978). The concept of nature in geography and Marxism. *Antipode, 10*, 1–11.

Burton, I. (1963). The quantitative revolution and theoretical geography. *Canadian Geographer, 7*, 151–162.

Buttimer, A. (1978). Charism and context: The challenge of la geographie humaine. In D. Ley & M. Samuels (Eds.), *Humanistic geography* (pp. 58–76). Chicago: Maaroufa Press.

Butzer, K. W. (1978). Cultural perspectives on geographical space. In K. W. Butzer

(Ed.), *Dimensions of human geography* (Res. Pap. No. 186, pp. 1–14). Chicago: University of Chicago, Department of Geography.

Cameron, J. M. R. (1974). Information distortion in colonial promotion: The case of Swan River colony. *Australian Geographical Studies, 12,* 57–76.

Cameron, J. M. R. (1977). *Coming to terms: The development of agriculture in pre-convict Western Australia* (Geowest 11). Perth: University of Western Australia, Department of Geography.

Carlstein, T. (1981). The Sociology of structuration in time and space: A time geographic assessment of Gidden's theory of structuration. *Svensk Geografisk Arsbok, 57,* 41–57.

Carlstein, T. (1982). *Time, resources, society and ecology: On the capacity for human interaction in space and time: Vol. 1 Preindustrial societies.* London: Allen & Unwin.

Carol, H. (1964). Stages of technology and their impact upon the physical environment: A basic problem in cultural geography. *Canadian Geographer, 8,* 1–9.

Carroll, G. R. (1982). National city-size distributions: What do we know after 67 years of research? *Progress in Human Geography, 6,* 1–43.

Carter, G. F. (1948). Clark Wissler: 1870–1947. *Annals, Association of American Geographers, 38,* 145–146.

Carter, G. F. (1964). *Man and the land.* New York: Holt, Rinehart and Winston.

Carter, G. F. (1977). A hypothesis suggesting a single origin of agriculture. In C. A Reed (Ed.), *Origins of agriculture* (pp. 89–133). The Hague: Mouton.

Carter, G. F. (1978). "Context and methodology. In P. G. Duke, J. Ebert, G. Lange-mann, A. P. Buchner (Eds.), *Diffusion and migration: Their roles in cultural development* (pp. 55–64). Calgary, Canada: University of Calgary, Archaeological Association.

Chappell, J. E., Jr. (1980). Crucial deficiencies in cultural determinism. *Geographical Survey, 3,* 3–18.

Chase, W. G, & Chi, M. T. H. (1981). Cognitive skill: Implications for spatial skill in large scale learning. In J. H. Harvey (Ed.), *Cognition, social behavior and environment* (pp. 111–136). Hillsdale, NJ: Lawrence Erlbaum Associates.

Childe, V. G. (1956). *Society and knowledge.* New York: Harper.

Chisholm, M. (1978). Theory construction in geography. *South African Geographer, 6,* 113–122.

Chorley, R. J. (1973). Geography as human ecology. In R. J. Chorley (Ed.), *Directions in Geography* (pp. 155–169). London: Methuen.

Christopher, A. J. (1971). Land policy in southern Africa during the nineteenth century. *Zambezia, 2,* 1–9.

Christopher, A. J. (1973). Environmental perception in Southern Africa. *South African Geographical Journal, 55,* 14–22.

Christopher, A. J. (1984). *Colonial Africa.* Totowa, NJ: Barnes and Noble.

Clarkson, J. D. (1968). *The cultural ecology of a Chinese village: Cameron Highlands, Malaysia* (Res. Pap. No. 114). Chicago: University of Chicago, Department of Geography.

Clarkson, J. D. (1970). Ecology and spatial analysis. *Annals, Association of American Geographers, 60,* 700–716.

Claval, P. (1984). The historical dimensions of French geography. *Journal of Historical Geography, 10,* 229–245.

Cohen, A. P. (1982). Belonging: The experience of culture. In A. P. Cohen (Ed.), *Belonging: Identity and social organization in British rural cultures* (pp. 1–17). Manchester, UK: Manchester University Press.

Cohen, E. (1974). Environmental orientations: A multidimensional approach to social ecology. *Current Anthropology, 17*, 49–70.

Cosgrove, D. (1978). Place, landscape and the dialectics of cultural geography. *Canadian Geographer, 22*, 66–72.

Cosgrove, D. (1983). Towards a radical cultural geography: Problems of theory. *Antipode, 15*, 1–11.

Cosgrove, D. (1984). *Social formation and symbolic landscape.* London: Croom Helm.

Cosgrove, D. (1985). Prospect, perspective and the evolution of the landscape idea. *Transactions, Institute of British Geographer, 10*, 45–62.

Cosgrove, D., & Jackson, P. (1987). New directions in cultural geography. *Area, 19*, 95–101.

Craig, A. K., & Peebles, C. S. (1974). Ethnoecologic change among the Seminoles, 1740–1840. *Geoscience and Man, 5*, 83–96.

Cromar, P. (1979). Spatial change and economic organization: The Tyneside coal industry (1751–1770). *Geoforum, 10*, 45–57.

Cronon, W. (1983). *Changes in the land: Indians, colonists and the ecology of New England.* New York: Hill and Wang.

Crowley, W. K. (1978). Old order Amish settlement: Diffusion and growth. *Annals, Association of American Geographers, 68*, 249–264.

Crush, J. S. (1980). On theorizing frontier underdevelopment. *Tijdschrifte Voor Economishe en Social Geografie, 71*, 343–350.

Cullen, I. G. (1976). Human geography, regional science and the study of individual behavior. *Environment and Planning A, 8*, 397–409.

Curtin, P. D. (1964). *The image of Africa.* Madison: University of Wisconsin Press.

Cybriwsky, R. A, & Western, J. (1982). Revitalizing downtowns: By whom and for whom? In D. T. Herbert & R. J. Johnston (Eds.), *Geography and the urban environment: Vol. 2* (pp. 343–365). New York: John Wiley & Sons.

Darby, H. C. (1983). Historical geography in Britain, 1920–1980: Continuity and change. *Transactions, Institute of British Geographers, 8*, 421–428.

Darley, J. M, & Gilbert, D. T. (1985). Social psychological aspects of environmental psychology. In G. Lindzey & E. Aronson (Eds.), *The handbook of social psychology* (2 vols., pp. 949–991). New York: Random House.

Darwin, C. R. (1859). *On the origin of species by means of natural selection, or the preservation of favoured races in the struggle for life.* London: John Murray.

Darwin, C. R. (1871). *The descent of man, and selection in relation to sex.* London: John Murray, 2 vols.

Davidson, W. V. (1974). *Historical geography of the Bay Islands, Honduras.* Birmingham, AL: Southern University Press.

de Blij, H. J. (1978). *Geography: Regions and concepts.* New York: John Wiley & Sons.

Denevan, W. M. (1983). Adaptation, variation and cultural geography. *Professional Geographer, 35*, 399–406.

Dennis, R. J. (1976). Community structure in Victorian cities. In B. S. Osborne (Ed.), *The settlement of Canada: Origins and transfer* (pp. 105–138). Kingston, Canada: Queen's University.

Dennis, R. J., & Clout, H. (1980). *A social geography of England and Wales.* Elmsford, NY: Pergamon.

Denoon, D. (1979). Understanding settler societies." *Historical Studies, 18*, 511–527.

Dickinson, R. E. (1939). Landscape and society. *Scottish Geographical Magazine, 55*, 1–15.

Dickinson, R. E. (1969). *The makers of modern geography.* London: Routledge & Kegan Paul.

Dodge, S. D. (Ed.). (1937). Round table on problems in cultural geography. *Annals, Association of American Geographers, 27*, 155–175.

Downs, R., & Stea, D. (Eds.). (1973). *Image and environment: Essays on cognitive mapping.* Chicago: Aldine.

Drakakis-Smith, D. (1981). Aboriginal underdevelopment in Australia. *Antipode, 13*, 35–44.

Dunbar, G. S. (1974). Geographic personality. *Geoscience and Man, 5*, 25–33.

Dunbar, G. S. (1977). Some early occurrences of the term "social geography." *Scottish Geographical Magazine, 93*, 15–20.

Duncan, J. S. (1978). The social construction of unreality: An interactionist approach to the tourist's cognition of environment. In D. Ley & M. S. Samuel (Eds.), *Humanistic geography* (pp. 269–282). Chicago: Maaroufa Press.

Duncan, J. S (1980). The superorganic in American cultural geography. *Annals, Association of American Geographers, 70*, 181–198.

Duncan, J. S. (1985). Individual action and political power: A structuration perspective. In R. J. Johnston (Ed.), *The future of geography* (pp. 174–189). London: Methuen.

Duncan, J. S., & Ley, D. (1982). Structural Marxism and human geography: A critical assessment. *Annals, Association of American Geographers, 72*, 30–59.

Duncan, S. S. (1979). Qualitative change in human geography: An introduction. *Geoforum, 10*, 1–4.

Durham, W. H. (1976). The adaptive significance of cultural behavior. *Human Ecology, 4*, 89–121.

Dyck, J. H. A. (1979). *The individual and the group in social reality: An interpretation of the socio-political thought of Karl Marx and Hannah Arendt.* Unpublished master's thesis, University of Manitoba, Winnipeg, Canada.

Earman, J. (1986). *A primer on determinism.* Dordrecht, Holland: Reidel.

Eastman, C. (1984). Language, ethnic identity and change. In J. Edwards (Ed.), *Linguistic minorities, policies and pluralism* (pp. 259–276). London: Academic Press.

Edwards, J. (1985). *Language, society and identity.* Oxford, UK: Blackwell.

Elazar, D. J. (1984). *American federalism: A view from the States.* New York: Harper & Row.

Ellen, R. (1982). *Environment, subsistence and system.* New York: Cambridge University Press.

Ellen, R. (1988). Persistence and change in the relationship between anthropology and human geography. *Progress in human geography*, 229–262.

English, P. W., & Mayfield, R. C. (1972). Ecological perspectives. In P. W. English & R. C. Mayfield (Eds.), *Man, space and environment* (pp. 115–120). New York: Oxford University Press.

Ennals, P. M. (1972). Nineteenth-century barns in southern Ontario. *Canadian Geographer, 3*, 256–270.

Entrikin, J. N. (1976). Contemporary humanism in geography. *Annals, Association of American Geographers, 66,* 615–632.

Entrikin, J. N. (1980). Robert Park's human ecology and human geography. *Annals, Association of American Geographers, 70,* 43–58.

Ericksen, E. G. (1980). *The territorial experience: Human ecology as symbolic interaction.* Austin: University of Texas Press.

Evans, E. E. (1939). Donegal survivals. *Antiquity, 13,* 207–222.

Evernden, N. (1981). The ambiguous landscape. *Geographical Review, 71,* 147–157.

Evernden, N. (1985). *The natural alien.* Toronto, Canada: University of Toronto Press.

Fairweather, J. R. (1985). White settler colonial development: Early New Zealand pastoralism and the formation of estates. *Australia and New Zealand Journal of Sociology, 21,* 237–257.

Feldman, D. A. (1975). The history of the relationship between environment and culture in ethnological thought: An overview. *Journal of the History of the Behavioral Sciences, 11,* 67–81.

Fenneman, N. M. (1916). Physiographic divisions of the United States. *Annals, Association of American Geographers, 6,* 19–98.

Firey, W. (1945). Sentiment and symbolism as ecological variables. *American Sociological Review, 10,* 140–148.

Firey, W. (1947). *Land use in central Boston.* Cambridge, MA: MIT Press.

Flinn, M. V., & Alexander, R. D. (1982) Culture theory: The developing synthesis from biology. *Human Ecology, 10,* 383–400.

Flora, J. L., & Stitz, J. M. (1985). Ethnicity, persistence, and capitalization of agriculture in the Great Plains during the settlement period: Wheat production and risk avoidance. *Rural Sociology, 50,* 341–360.

Flowerdew, R. (Ed.) (1983). *Institutions and geographic patterns.* New York: St. Martins Press.

Foote, D. C., & Greer-Wooten, B. (1968). An approach to systems analysis in cultural geography. *Professional Geographer, 20,* 86–91.

Found, W. C. (1971). *A theoretical approach to rural land use patterns.* London: Arnold.

Francaviglia, R. V. (1970). The Mormon landscape: Definition of an image in the American West. *Proceedings, Association of American Geographers, 2,* 59–61.

Francaviglia, R. V. (1979). *The Mormon landscape.* New York: AMS Press.

Freeman, D. B. (1985). The importance of being first: Preemption by early adopters of farming innovations in Kenya. *Annals, Association of American Geographers, 75,* 17–28.

Friedl, J., & Pfeiffer, J. (1977). *Anthropology: The study of people.* New York: Harper & Row.

Friesen, R. J. (1977). Saskatchewan Mennonite settlements: The modification of an Old World settlement pattern. *Canadian Ethnic Studies, 9,* 72–90.

Gade, D. W. (1982). The French Riviera as elitist space. *Journal of Cultural Geography, 3,* 19–28.

Gale, D. T., & Koroscil, P. M. (1977). Doukhubor settlements: An experiment in idealism. *Canadian Ethnic Studies, 9,* 53–71.

Gastil, R. D. (1975). *Cultural regions of the United States.* Seattle: University of Washington Press.

Gay, J. (1971). *Geography of religion in England.* London: Duckworth.

Geertz, C. (1963). *Agricultural involution: The processes of ecological change in Indonesia.* Berkeley: University of California Press.

Geertz, C. (1965). The impact of the concept of culture on the concept of man. In J. R. Platt (Ed.), *New views of the nature of man* (pp. 93–118). Chicago: University of Chicago Press.

Geertz, C. (1973). The interpretation of cultures. New York: Basic Books.

Geipel, R. (1981). Which Munich for whom. *Lund Studies in Geography, 48,* 160–180.

Gerlach, R. L. (1976). *Immigrants in the Ozarks: A study in ethnic geography.* Columbia: University of Missouri Press.

Giddens, A. (1979). *Central problems in social theory.* New York: Macmillan.

Giddens, A. (1983). Comment on the theory of structuration. *Journal for the Theory of Social Behaviour, 13,* 75–80.

Giddens, A. (1984). *The constitution of society: Outline of the theory of structuration.* Cambridge, UK: Polity Press.

Glacken, C. (1967). *Traces on the Rhodian shore: Nature and culture in western thought from ancient times to the end of the eighteenth century.* Berkeley: University of California Press.

Glacken, C. (1985). Culture and environment in western civilization during the nineteenth century. In K. E. Bailes (Ed.), *Environmental history* (pp. 46–57). New York: University Press of America.

Gold, J. R. (1980). *An introduction to behavioral geography.* London: Oxford.

Gold, J. R., & Goodey, B. (1983). Behavioral and perceptual geography. *Progress in Human Geography, 7,* 578–586.

Golledge, R. G. (1981). Misconceptions, misinterpretations, and misrepresentations of behavioral approaches in human geography. *Environment and Planning A, 13,* 1325–1344.

Goodey, B., & Gold, J. R. (1985). Behavioral and perceptual geography: From retrospect to prospect. *Progress in Human Geography, 9,* 585–595.

Goodwin, C. P. V. (1974). *The image of Australia.* Durham, NC: Duke University Press.

Gordon, B. L. (1954). *Human geography and ecology in the Sinu country of Columbia.* Unpublished doctoral dissertation, University of California, Berkeley.

Gould, P., & White, R. (1986). *Mental maps* (2nd ed.). London: Allen & Unwin.

Gould, S. J (1981). *The mismeasure of man.* New York: W. W. Norton.

Grano, O. (1981). External influence and internal change in the development of geography. In D. R. Stoddart (Ed.), *Geography, ideology and social concern* (pp. 17–36). Totowa, NJ: Barnes and Noble.

Gregory, D. (1982). *Regional transformation and industrial revolution.* New York: Macmillan.

Gregory, D., & Urry, J. (1985). Introduction. In D. Gregory & J. Urry (Eds.), *Social relations and spatial structures* (pp. 1–8). New York: Macmillan.

Gregson, N. (1986). On duality and dualism: The case of structuration and time geography. *Progress in Human Geography, 10,* 184–205.

Grice, K., & Drakakis-Smith, D. (1985). The role of the state in shaping development: Two decades of growth in Singapore. *Transactions, Institute of British Geographers, 10,* 347–359.

Griffin, E., & Ford, L. (1980). A model of Latin American city structure. *Geographical Review, 70,* 397–422.

Gritzner, C. F. (1966). The scope of cultural geography. *Journal of Geography, 65*, 4–11.

Gritzner, C. F. (1981). Personal correspondence.

Grossman, L. (1977). Man-environment relationships in anthropology and geography. *Annals, Association of American Geographers, 67*, 126–144.

Guelke, L. (1982). *Historical understanding in geography.* New York: Cambridge University Press.

Guelke, L. (1983). Review of *Geography and geographers* by R. J. Johnston. *Economic Geography, 59*, 81–86.

Hagerstrand, T. (1951). Migration and the growth of culture regions. *Lund Studies in Geography B, 3.*

Hagerstrand, T. (1967). *Innovation diffusion as a spatial process* (A. Pred, Trans.). Chicago: University of Chicago Press. (Original work published 1953).

Haggett, P. (1983). *Geography: A modern synthesis* (rev. 3rd ed.). New York: Harper & Row.

Hale, R. F. (1971). *A map of vernacular regions in America.* Unpublished doctoral dissertation, University of Minnesota, Minneapolis.

Hale, R. F. (1984). Vernacular regions of America. *Journal of Cultural Geography, 5*, 131–140.

Hall, C. S, & Lindzey, G. (1978). *Theories of personality.* New York: John Wiley & Sons.

Hamill, L. (1984). Comment on quantitative methods for investigating the variables that underlie preference for landscape scenes. *Canadian Geographer, 28*, 286–288.

Hansis, R. (1984). Comments on adaptation, variation and cultural geography. *Professional Geographer, 36*, 216.

Hardesty, D. L. (1977). *Ecological anthropology.* New York: John Wiley & Sons.

Hardesty, D. L. (1986). Rethinking cultural adaptation. *Professional Geographer, 38*, 11–18.

Harris, D. R. (1971). The ecology of Swidden cultivation in the upper Orinoco rain forest, Venezuela. *Geographical Review, 61*, 475–495.

Harris, M. (1968). *The Rise of anthropological theory.* New York: Thomas Y. Crowell.

Harris, R., Levine, G., & Osborne, B. S. (1981). Housing tenure and social classes in Kingston, Ontario, 1881–1901. *Journal of Historical Geography, 7*, 271–289.

Harris, R. C. (1977). The simplification of Europe overseas. *Annals, Association of American Geographers, 67*, 469–483.

Harris, R. C. (1978). The historical geography of North American regions. *American Behavioral Scientist, 22*, 115–130.

Harris, R. C., Roulston, P., & DeFreitas, C. The settlement of Mono Township. *Canadian Geographer, 19*, 1–17.

Harriss, B., & Harriss, J. (1982). Development studies. *Progress in Human Geography, 6*, 584–592.

Hartshorne, R. (1939). *The nature of geography: A critical survey of current thought in the light of the past.* Lancaster, PA: Association of American Geographers.

Harvey, D. W. (1969). *Explanation in geography.* London: Arnold.

Harvey, D. W. (1975). *Social Justice and the City.* Baltimore, MD: Johns Hopkins University Press.

Harvey, D. W. (1979). Monument and myth. *Annals, Association of American Geographers, 69*, 362–381.

Hawley, A. H. (1950). *Human ecology: A theory of community structure*. New York: Ronald Press.

Haynes, R. M. (1980). *Geographical images and mental maps*. London: Macmillan.

Heidenreich, C. (1971). *Huronia: A history and geography of the Huron Indians, 1600–1650*. Toronto, Canada: McClelland and Stewart.

Henderson, J. R. (1978). Spatial reorganization: A geographical dimension in acculturation, *Canadian geographer, 12*, 1–21.

Henretta, J. A. (1978). Families and farms: Mentalite in pre-industrial America. *William and Mary Quarterly, 35*, 3–32.

Herskovits, J. M. (1938). *Acculturation*. New York: J. J. Augustin.

Heyer, P. (1982). *Nature, human nature and society: Marx, Darwin, biology and the human sciences*. Westport, CT: Greenwood Press.

Hillier, B., & Hanson, J. (1984). *The social logic of space*. New York: Cambridge University Press.

Hoke, G. W. (1907). The study of social geography. *Geographical Journal, 29*, 64–67.

Holtgrieve, D. G. (1976). Land speculation and other processes in American historical geography. *Journal of Geography, 75*, 53–64.

Holt-Jensen, A. (1982). *Geography: Its history and concepts*. Totowa, NJ: Barnes and Noble.

Hornbeck, D. (1979). The patenting of California's private land claims. *Geographical Review, 69*, 434–448.

House, F. N. (1936). *The development of sociology*. New York: McGraw-Hill.

Hoyt, H. (1939). *The structure and growth of residential neighborhoods in American cities*. Washington, DC: U.S. Government Printing Office.

Hudson, W. H. (1908). *Herbert Spencer*. London: Archibald, Constable and Company.

Hufferd, J. (1980). Toward a transcendental human geography of places. *Antipode, 12*, 18–23.

Huntington, E., & Cushing, S. W. (1934). *Principles of human geography*, (4th ed.). New York: John Wiley & Sons.

Innis, D. (1958). *Human ecology in Jamaica*. Unpublished doctoral dissertation, University of California, Berkeley.

Isaac, E. (1964). God's acre—Property in land: A sacred origin. *Landscape, 14*, 28–32.

Isajiw, W. (1974). Definitions of ethnicity. *Ethnicity, 1*, 111–124.

Isbister, J. (1977). Agriculture, balanced growth, and social change in central Canada since 1850: An interpretation. *Economic Development and Cultural Change, 25*, 673–692.

Ittelson, W. H., Proshansky, H. M., Rivlin, L. G., and Winkel, G. H. (1974). *An introduction to environmental psychology*. New York: Holt, Rinehart and Winston.

Jackson, J. B. (1970). *Landscape: Selected writings of J. B. Jackson*. Amherst: University of Massachusetts Press.

Jackson, J. B. (1984). *Discovering the vernacular landscape*. New Haven, CT: Yale University Press.

Jackson, P. (1984). Social geography: Culture and capital. *Progress in Human Geography, 8*, 105–122.

Jackson, P. (1985). Social geography: Race and racism. *Progress in Human Geography, 9*, 99–108.

Jackson, P. (1986). Social geography: The rediscovery of place. *Progress in Human Geography, 10*, 118–124.

Jackson, P., & Smith, S. J. (1981). Introduction. In P. Jackson & S. J. Smith (Eds.), *Social interaction and ethnic segregation* (pp. 1–17). New York: Academic Press.

Jackson, P., & Smith, S. J. (1984). *Exploring social geography*. London: Allen & Unwin.

Jackson, R. H, & Henrie, R. (1983). Perception of sacred space. *Journal of Cultural Geography, 3,* 94–107.

Jakle, J. A., Brunn, S., & Roseman, C. C. (1976). *Human spatial behavior*. North Scituate, MA: Duxbury.

James, P. E. (1929). The Blackstone Valley. *Annals, Association of American Geographers, 19,* 67–109.

James, P. E., & Martin, G. J. (1981). *All possible worlds: A history of geographical ideas* (2nd ed.). New York: John Wiley & Sons.

Jeans, D. N. (1981). Mapping the regional patterns of Australian society: Some preliminary thoughts. *Australian Historical Geography Bulletin, 2,* 1–6.

Johnson, D. (1929). The geographic prospect. *Annals, Association of American Geographers, 19,* 167–231.

Johnson, J. H., Jr. (1983). The role of community action in neighborhood revitalization. *Urban Geography, 4,* 16–39.

Johnston, R. J. (1981). The state and study of social geography. In P. Jackson & S. J. Smith (Eds.), *Social integration and ethnic segregation* (pp. 205–222). New York: Academic Press.

Johnston, R. J. (1983a). *Geography and geographers: Anglo-American human geography since 1945* (2nd ed). London: Arnold.

Johnston, R. J. (1983b). *Philosophy and human geography: An introduction to contemporary approaches*. London: Arnold.

Johnston, R. J. (1985). Introduction: Exploring the future of geography. In R. J. Johnston (Ed.), *The future of geography* (pp. 3–26). London: Methuen.

Johnston, R. J. (1986). North America. In J. Eyles (Ed.), *Social geography in international perspective* (pp. 30–59). Totowa, NJ: Barnes and Noble.

Jones, E., & Eyles, J. (1977). *An introduction to social geography*. New York: Oxford University Press.

Jordan, T. G. (1966). *German seed in Texas soil*. Austin: University of Texas Press.

Jordan, T. G. (1973). *The European culture area: A systematic geography*. New York: Harper & Row.

Jordan, T. G. (1977). Land survey patterns in Texas. In R. C. Eidt, Singh, K. N., and Singh, R. P. B. (Eds.), *Man, culture and settlement* (pp. 141–146). New Delhi, India: Kalyani.

Jordan, T. G. (1978). Perceptual regions in Texas. *Geographical Review, 68,* 293–307.

Jordan, T. G. (1980). A religious geography of the hill country Germans of Texas. In F. C. Luebke (Ed.), *Ethnicity on the Great Plains* (pp. 109–128). Lincoln: University of Nebraska Press.

Jordan, T. G. (1982). *Texas graveyards: A cultural legacy*. Austin: University of Texas Press.

Jordan, T. G. (1983). A reappraisal of Fenno-Scandian antecedents for midland American log construction. *Geographical Review, 73,* 58–94.

Jordan, T. G. (1985). *American log buildings: An Old World heritage*. Chapel Hill: University of North Carolina Press.

Jordan, T. G., & Rowntree, L. C. (1986). *The human mosaic: A thematic introduction to cultural geography* (4th ed.). New York: Harper & Row.

Karan, P. P. (1984). Landscape, religion and folk art in Mithila: An Indian cultural region. *Journal of Cultural Geography, 5*, 85–102.

Katz, P. (1974). Adaptations to crowded space: The case of Taos Pueblo. In M. Richardson (Ed.), *The human mirror* (pp. 300–316). Baton Rouge: Louisiana State University Press.

Kaups, M. (1966). Finnish place names in Minnesota: A study in cultural transfer. *Geographical Review, 56*, 377–397.

Kay, G. (1971). Stages of technology and economic development: An approach to the study of human geography. *Proceedings, Geographical Assocation of Rhodesia, 4*, 3–14.

Kearns, K. C. (1974). Resuscitation of the Irish Gaeltacht. *Geographical Review, 64*, 82–110.

Kelly, K. (1974). The changing attitude of farmers to forest in nineteenth century Ontario. *Ontario Geography, 8*, 64–77.

Kesby, J. D. (1977). *The cultural regions of East Africa*, London: Academic Press.

Kirk, W. (1951). Historical geography and the concept of the behavioral environment. *Indian Geographical Journal, 25*, 152–160.

Kirk, W. (1963). Problems in geography. *Geography, 48*, 357–371.

Kirk, W. (1975). The role of India in the diffusion of early cultures. *Geographical Journal, 14*, 19–34.

Kniffen, F. (1932). Lower California studies III: The primitive cultural landscape of the Colorado Delta. *University of California Publication in Geography, 5*, 43–66.

Kniffen, F. (1936). Louisiana house types. *Annals, Association of American Geographers, 26*, 179–193.

Kniffen, F. (1937). The lower Mississippi. *Annals, Association of American Geographers, 27*, 162–167.

Kniffen, F. (1951). The American covered bridge. *Geographical Review, 41*, 114–123.

Kniffen, F. (1961). The American agricultural fair: Time and place. *Annals, Association of American Geographers, 41*, 42–57.

Kniffen, F. (1965). Folk housing: Key to diffusion. *Annals, Association of American Geographers, 55*, 549–557.

Kniffen, F. (1974). Material culture in the geographic interpretation of the landscape. In M. Richardson (Ed.), *The human mirror* (pp. 252–267). Baton Rouge: Louisiana State University Press.

Kollmorgen, W. M. (1969). The woodsman's assaults on the domain of the cattlemen. *Annals, Association of American Geographers, 59*, 215–239.

Krech, S. III (Ed.). (1981). *Indians, animals and the fur trade*. Athens: University of Georgia Press.

Kroeber, A. L. (1904). *Types of indian culture in California*. Berkeley: University of California Press.

Kroeber, A. L. (1917). The Superorganic. *American Anthropologist, 19*, 163–213.

Kroeber, A. L. (1928). Native cultures of the Southwest. *University of California Publications in American Archaeology and Ethnology, 23*, 375–398.

Kroeber, A. L. (1939). Cultural and natural areas of native North America. *University of California Publications in American Archaeology and Ethnology, 38*.

Lambert, A. M. (1985). *The making of the Dutch landscape: An historial geography of the Netherlands* (2nd ed.). New York: Academic Press.

Lamme, A. J. III, & Oldakowski, R. K. (1982). Vernacular areas in Florida. *Southeastern Geographer*, *22*, 100–109.

Lanegran, D. A. (1986). Enhancing and using a sense of place within urban areas: A role for applied cultural geography. *Professional Geographer*, *38*, 224–228.

Langton, J. (1975). Residential patterns in pre-industrial cities: Some case studies from seventeenth-century Britain. *Transactions, Institute of British Geographers*, *65*, 1–27.

Leaf, M. J. (1979). *Man, mind and science: A history of anthropology*. New York: Columbia University Press.

Leighly, J. (1937). Some comments on contemporary geographic method. *Annals, Association of American Geographers*, *27*, 125–141.

Leighly, J. (1954). Innovation and area. *Geographical Review*, *44*, 439–441.

Leighly, J. (1976). Carl Ortwin Sauer, 1889–1975. *Annals, Association of American Geographers*, *66*, 337–348.

Leighly, J. (1978). Town names of colonial New England in the West. *Annals, Association of American Geographers*, *68*, 233–248.

Leighly, J. (1979). Drifting into geography in the twenties. *Annals, Association of American Geographers*, *69*, 4–9.

Leonard, S. (1982). Urban managerialism: A period of transition. *Progress in Human Geography*, *6*, 190–215.

Lewin, K. (1936). *Principles of topological psychology*. New York: McGraw-Hill.

Lewin, K. (1951). *Field theory in social science: Selected theoretical papers*. D. Cartwright, (Ed.) New York: Harper.

Lewis, C. B. (1979). Cultural conservatism and pioneer Florida viticulture. *Agricultural History*, *53*, 622–636.

Lewis, K. E. (1984). *The American frontier: An archaeological study of settlement pattern and process*. New York: Academic Press

Lewthwaite, G. R. (1966). Environmentalism and determinism: A search for clarification. *Annals, Association of American Geographers*, *56*, 1–23.

Ley, D. (1974). *The black inner city as frontier outpost: Images and behavior of a Philadelphia neighborhood*. (Monograph Series No. 7). Washington, DC: Association for American Geographers.

Ley, D. (1977). Social geography and the taken-for-granted world. *Transactions, Institute of British Geographers*, *2*, 498–512.

Ley, D. (1981). Cultural/humanistic geography. *Progress in Human Geography*, *5*, 249–257.

Ley, D. (1983a). Cultural humanistic geography. *Progress in Human Geography*, *7*, 267–275.

Ley, D. (1983b). *A social geography of the city*. New York: Harper & Row.

Ley, D. (1987). Styles of the times: Liberal and neo conservative landscapes in inner Vancouver, 1868–1986. *Journal of Historical Geography*, *13*, 40–56.

Ley, D., & Cybriwsky, R. (1974). Urban graffiti as territorial markers. *Annals, Association of American Geographers*, *64*, 491–505.

Ley, D., & Samuels, M. S. (1978). Contexts of modern humanism in geography. In D. Ley & M. S. Samuels (Eds.), *Humanistic geography* (pp. 1–18). Chicago: Maaroufa Press.

Lovell, W. G. (1985). *Conquest and survival in colonial Guatemala*. Kingston, Canada: McGill-Queen's University Press.

Lowenthal, D. (1961). Geography, experience and imagination: Towards a geographical epistemology. *Annals, Association of American Geographers, 51*, 241–260.

Lowenthal, D. (1978). Finding valued landscapes. *Progress in Human Geography, 2*, 373–418.

Lowenthal, D., & Prince, H. C. (1964). The English landscape. *Geographical Review, 54*, 309–346.

Lowenthal, D., & Prince, H. C. (1965). English landscape tastes. *Geographical Review, 55*, 186–222.

Lowie, R. H. (1937). *History of ethnological theory*. New York: Farrar and Rinehart.

Luebke, F. C. (1984). Regionalism and the Great Plains: Problems of concept and method. *Western Historical Quarterly, 15*, 19–38.

Lynch, K. (1960). *The image of the city*. Cambridge, MA: MIT Press.

McCarty, J. W. (1973). Australia as a region of recent settlement in the nineteenth century. *Australian Economic History Review, 13*, 148–167.

McKee, J. O. (1971). The Choctaw Indians: A geographical study in culture change. *Southern Quarterly, 9*, 107–141.

McKenzie, R. D. (1926). The scope of human ecology. *20th Annual Meeting, American Sociological Society*, 1925, Papers and Proceedings, *20*, 141–154.

Mackenzie, S. (Ed.). (1986). *Humanism and geography* (Discussion Pap. No. 3). Ottawa, Canada: Carleton University, Department of Geography.

Mackinder, H. J. (1902). *Britain and the British Seas*. New York: D. Appleton and Company.

McQuillan, D. A. (1978). Farm size and work ethic: Measuring the success of immigrant farmers on the American grasslands, 1875–1925. *Journal of Historical Geography, 4*, 57–76.

Malin, J. C. (1967). *The grassland of North America: Prolegomena to its history with addenda and postscript* (rev. ed.). Gloucester, MA: Peter Smith.

Mannion, J. (1974). *Irish settlements in eastern Canada: A study of culture transfer and adoption* (Research Pub. No. 12). Toronto, Canada: University of Toronto, Department of Geography.

Marchand, J. P. (1982). Physical constraints and contemporary geography. In R. J Bennett (Ed.), *European progress in spatial analysis* (pp. 71–82). London: Pion.

Martin, C. (1978). *Keepers of the game: Indian-animal relationships and the fur trade*. Berkeley: University of California Press.

Mason, O. (1895). Influence of environment upon human industries and arts. *Annual Report of the Smithsonian Institution*, 639–665.

Massey, D. (1984). Introduction: Geography matters. In D. Massey & J. Allen (Eds.), *Geography matters! A reader* (pp. 1–11). New York: Cambridge University Press.

Matejko, J., & Matejko, A. (1978). Polish pioneers in the Canadian praires. *Ethnicity, 5*, 351–369.

Matley, I. M. (1977). The evaluation and preservation of the cultural landscape. In H. A Winters & M. K Winters (Eds.), *Applications of geographic research* (pp. 61–73). East Lansing: Michigan State University.

Mead, G. (1959). *Philosophy of the present*. Chicago: Open Court.

Meggers, B. J. (1954). Enviromental limitation on the development of culture. *American Anthropologist, 56*, 801–824.

Meigs, P. (1935). The Dominican mission frontier of lower California. *University of California Publications in Geography, 7*.

Meinig, D. W. (1965). The Mormon culture region: Strategies and patterns in the geography of the American West, 1847–1964. *Annals, Association of American Geographers, 55*, 191–220.

Meinig, D. W. (1969). *Imperial Texas: An interpretive essay in cultural geography.* Austin: University of Texas Press.

Meinig, D. W. (1972). American Wests: Preface to a geographical introduction. *Annals, Association of American Geographers, 62*, 159–185.

Meinig, D. W. (1978). The continuous shaping of America: A prospectus for geographers and historians. *American Historical Review, 83*, 1186–1217.

Meinig, D. W. (1979a). Reading the landscape: An appreciation of W. G. Hoskins and J. B. Jackson. In D. Meinig (Ed.), *The interpretation of ordinary landscapes* (pp. 195–244). Oxford, UK: Oxford University Press.

Meinig, D. W. (1979b). Symbolic landscapes. In D. W. Meinig (Ed.), *The interpretation of ordinary landscapes* (pp. 164–192). Oxford, UK: Oxford University Press.

Meredith, T. C. (1985). The Upper Columbia Valley 1900–20: An assessment of "Boosterism" and the "biography of landscape." *Canadian Geographer, 29*, 44–55.

Merrens, H. R. (1969). The physical environment of early America. *Geographical Review, 59*, 530–556.

Meyer, J. W. (1975). Ethnicity, theology and immigrant church expansion. *Geographical Review, 65*, 180–197.

Mikesell, M. W. (1967). Geographic perspectives in anthropology. *Annals, Association of American Geographers, 57*, 617–634.

Mikesell, M. W. (1969). The borderlands of geography as a social science. In M. Sherif & C. W. Sherif (Eds.), *Interdisciplinary relationships in the social sciences* (pp. 227–248). Chicago: Aldine.

Mikesell, M. W. (1977). Cultural geography. *Progress in Human Geography, 1*, 460–464.

Mikesell, M. W. (1978). Tradition and innovation in cultural geography. *Annals, Association of American Geographers, 68*, 1–16.

Miller, E. J. W. (1968). The Ozark culture region as revealed by traditional materials. *Annals, Association of American Geographers, 58*, 51–77.

Miller, G. J., & Parkins, A. E. (1928). *Geography of North America.* New York: John Wiley & Sons.

Miller, V. P., Jr. (1971). Some observations on the science of cultural geography. *Journal of Geography, 70*, 27–35.

Mills, W. J. (1982). Positivism reversed: The relevance of Giambattisto Vico. *Transactions, Institute of British Geographers, 7*, 1–14.

Mitchell, R. D. (1978). The formation of early American cultural regions. In J. R. Gibson (Ed.), *European settlement and development in North America (pp. 66–90).* Toronto, Canada: University of Toronto Press.

Mogey, J. (1971). Society, man and environment. In R. H. Buchanan, E. Jones, & D. McCourt (Eds.), *Man and his habitat* (pp. 79–92). New York: Barnes and Noble.

Moore, J. H. (1974). The culture concept as ideology. *American Ethnologist, 1*, 537–549.

Moran, E. F. (1982). *Human adaptability: An introduction to ecological anthropology.* Boulder, CO: Westview Press.

Morgan, W. B., and Moss, R. P. (1965). Geography and ecology: The concept of the community and its relationship to environment. *Annals, Association of American Geographers, 55,* 339–350.

Morrill, R. L. (1965). The Negro ghetto: Problems and alternatives. *Geographical Review, 55,* 339–361.

Morrill, R. L. (1979). On the spatial organization of the landscape. *Lund Studies in Geography B, 46.*

Morrill, R. L. (1986). Review of *Geographical Futures* by R. King (Ed.). *Geographical Review, 76,* 97–99.

Muller, E. K. (1978). Sharpening the focus on mid-nineteenth century urban life: A review essay. *Historical Geography Newsletter, 8,* 1–16.

NAS–NRC (1965), *The Science of Geography.* Washington: NAS–NRC.

Netting, R. McC. (1977). *Cultural ecology.* Menlo Park, CA: Cummings.

Newson, L. (1976). Cultural evolution: A basic concept for human and historical geography. *Journal of Historical Geography, 2,* 239–255.

Newton, M. (1974). Cultural preadaptation and the Upland South. *Geoscience and Man, 5,* 143–154.

Nisbet, R. (1980). *History of the idea of progress.* New York: Basic Books.

Noble, A. G. (1982). *Studies of the American Settlement landscape.* Unpublished manuscript, University of Akron, Akron, OH.

Noble, A. G., & Dhussa, R. C. (1983). The linguistic geography of Dumka, Bihar, India. *Journal of Cultural Geography, 3,* 73–81.

Norton, W. (1974). Some investigations of a growth model of innovation diffusion. *South African Geographer, 4,* 383–387.

Norton, W. (1976). Commentary: Frontier agriculture subsistence or commercial. *Annals, Association of American Geographers, 66,* 463–464.

Norton, W. (1981). Cultural analysis in geography: A course outline. *Journal of Geography, 80,* 46–51.

Norton, W. (1984a). *Historical analysis in geography.* London: Longman.

Norton, W. (1984b). The meaning of culture in cultural geography: An appraisal. *Journal of Geography, 83,* 145–148.

Norton, W. (1987). Humans, land and landscape: A proposal for cultural geography. *Canadian Geographer, 31,* 21–30.

Norton, W. (1988). Abstract cultural landscapes. *Journal of Cultural Geography, 8,* 67–80.

Norton, W., & Pouliot, D. F. (1984). A critical appraisal of contemporary human geography. *Geographical Perspectives, 52,* 64–66.

Norwine, J., & Anderson, T. D. (1980). *Geography as human ecology.* Lanham, MD: University Press of America.

Nostrand, R. C. (1970). The Hispanic American borderland: Delimitation of an American culture region. *Annals, Association of American Geographers, 60,* 638–661.

Ogilvie, P. G. (1952). The time element in geography. *Transactions, Insitute of British Geographers, 18,* 1–15.

Olwig, K. (1980). Historical geography and the society/nature "Problematic": The perspective of J. F. Schouw, G. P. Marsh and E. Reclus. *Journal of Historical Geography, 6,* 29–45.

Ortner, S. B. (1984). Theory in anthropology since the sixties. *Comparative Studies in Society and History, 26,* 126–166.

Ostergren, R. C. (1980). "Prairie bound: Migration patterns to a Swedish settlement on the Dakota frontier. In F. C. Luebke (Ed.), *Ethnicity on the Great Plains* (pp. 73–91). Lincoln: University of Nebraska Press.

Pahl, R. E. (1965). Trends in social geography. In R. J. Chorley & P. Haggett (Eds.), *Frontiers in geographical teaching.* (pp. 81–100). London: Methuen.

Pahl, R. E. (1969). Urban social theory and research. *Environment and Planning, 1,* 143–153.

Palmer, B. D. (1979). *A culture in conflict.* Montreal, Canada: McGill-Queen's University Press.

Park, R. E. (1915). The city: Suggestions for the investigation of human behavior in the city environment. *American Journal of Sociology, 20,* 577–612.

Park, R. E. (1952). Human communities: The city and human ecology. The collected papers of Robert Ezra Park (Vol. 2). Glencoe, IL.: Free Press.

Park, R. E, & Burgess, E. W. (1921). *Introduction to the science of sociology.* Chicago: Chicago University Press.

Parry, M. L. (1978). *Climatic change, agriculture and settlement.* Folkstone, England: Dawson.

Parsons, J. J. (1979). The later Sauer years. *Annals, Association of American Geographers, 69,* 9–15.

Peach, C. (1983). Ethnicity. In M. Pacione (Ed.), *Progress in urban geography* (pp. 103–127). London: Croom Helm.

Pelto, P. J. (1966). *The nature of anthropology.* Columbus, OH: Merrill.

Pfeifer, G. (1938). Regional geography in the United States since the war: A review of trends in theory and method. *Zeitschrift der Gesselschaft fur Erdkunde zu Berlin,* 93–125.

Phillips, A., & Williams, A. (1984). *Rural Britain: A social geography.* Oxford, UK: Blackwell.

Pickles, J. (1985). *Phenomenology, science and geography.* New York: Cambridge University Press.

Porter, P. W. (1965). Environmental potentials for economic opportunities: A background for cultural adaptation. *American Anthroplogist, 67,* 409–420.

Porter, P. W. (1978). Geography as human ecology. *American Behavioral Scientist, 22,* 15–39.

Pred, A. (1967). Postscript. In T. Hagerstrand, *Innovation diffusion as a spatial process* (A. Pred, Trans., pp. 299–324). Chicago: University of Chicago Press.

Pred, A. (1981a). Power, everyday practice and the discipline of human geography. *Lund Studies in Geography B, 48,* 30–55.

Pred, A. (1981b). Production, family and free-time projects: A time-geographic perspective on individual and societal change in nineteenth century U.S. cities. *Journal of Historial Geography, 7* 3–36.

Pred, A. (1984). Place as historically contingent process: Structuration and the time geography of becoming places. *Annals, Association of American Geographers, 74,* 279–297.

Pred. A. (1986). *Place practice and structure: social and spatial transformation in southern Sweden, 1750–1850.* Totowa, NJ: Barnes and Noble.

Pryce, W. T. R. (1975). Migration and the evolution of culture areas: Cultural and linguistic frontiers in north-east Wales, 1750 and 1851. *Transactions, Institute of British Geographers, 65,* 79–107.

Pyle, G. (1969). The diffusion of cholera in the United States in the nineteenth century. *Geographical Analysis, 1*, 59–75.

Quani, M. (1982). *Geography and Marxism*. Oxford, UK: Blackwell.

Quinn, J. A. (1950). *Human ecology*. New York: Prentice Hall.

Raby, S. (1973). Indian land surrenders in southern Saskatchewan. *Canadian Geographer, 17*, 36–52.

Raitz, K. B. (1973). Ethnicity and the diffusion and distribution of cigar tobacco production in Wisconsin and Ohio. *Tijdschrifte voor Economische en Sociale Geografie, 64*, 293–306.

Raitz, K. B. (1979). Themes in the cultural geography of European ethnic groups in the United States. *Geographical Review, 69*, 79–94.

Raitz, K. B., & Ulack, R. (1981). Appalachian vernacular regions. *Journal of Cultural Geography, 2*, 106–119.

Rappaport, R. A. (1963). Aspects of man's influence on island ecosystems: Alteration and control. In F. R. Fosberg, (Ed.), *Man's place in the island ecosystem* (pp. 155–174). Honolulu, HI: Bishop Museum Press.

Ray, A. J. (1971). *Indian exploration of the forest-grassland transition zone in western Canada, 1680–1850: A geographical view of two centuries of change*. Unpublished doctoral dissertation, University of Wisconsin.

Reed, J. G. (1976). The heart of Dixie: An essay in folk geography. *Social Forces, 54*, 925–939.

Rees, R. (1984). *Land of earth and sky: Landscape painting of western Canada*. Saskatoon, Canada: Western Producer Prairie Books.

Relph, E. C. (1976). *Place and placelessness*. London: Pion.

Relph, E. C. (1984). Seeing, thinking and describing landscapes. In T. F. Saarinen, D. Seamon, & J. L. Sell (Eds.), *Environmental perception and behavior* (Res. Pap. No. 209, pp. 209–223). Chicago: University of Chicago, Department of Geography.

Renfrew, C. (1981). Space, time and man. *Transactions, Institute of British Geographers, 6*, 257–278.

Reynolds, H. (1982). *The other side of the frontier: Aboriginal resistance to the European invasion of Australia*. Ringwood, Australia: Penguin.

Richardson, M. (1974a). The Spanish American (Colombian) settlement pattern as a societal expression and as a behavioral cause. *Geoscience and Man, 5*, 35–51.

Richardson, M. (1974b). The spatial configuration." In M. Richardson (Ed.), *The human mirror* (pp. 197–199). Baton Rouge: Louisiana State University Press.

Richardson, M. (1981). On "The superorganic in American cultural geography." *Annals, Association of American Geographers, 71*, 284–287.

Riddell, J. B. (1970). *The spatial dynamics of modernization in Sierra Leone: Structure, diffusion and response*. Evanston, IL: Northwestern University Press.

Robinson, D. J. (1979). Introduction to themes and scales. In D. J. Robinson (Ed.), *Social fabric and spatial structure in colonial Latin America* (Microfilms International, pp. 1–24). Syracuse: Syracuse University, Department of Geography.

Robson, B. T. (1969). *Urban analysis: A study of city structure with special reference to Sunderland*. Cambridge, UK: Cambridge University Press.

Rogers, E. M. (1962). *Diffusion of innovations*. New York: Free Press of Glencoe.

Rooney, J. R., Jr., Zelinsky, W., & Loudon D. R. (Eds.). (1982). *This remarkable continent: An atlas of United States and Canadian society and cultures.* College Station, TX: Texas A&M University Press.

Rossi, I., & O'Higgins, E. (1980). Theories of culture and anthropological methods. In I. Rossi (Ed.), *People in culture: A survey of cultural inquiry* (pp. 31–78). New York: Praeger.

Rowntree, L. C. (1986). Cultural/humanistic geography. *Progress in Human Geography, 10,* 580–586.

Rowntree, L. C., & Conkey, M. W. (1980). Symbolism and the cultural landscape, *Annals, Association of American Geographers, 70,* 459–474.

Roxby, P. M. (1930). The scope and aims of human geography. *Scottish Geographical Magazine, 46,* 276–299.

Rubin, B. (1979). Aesthetic ideology and urban design. *Annals, Association of American Geographers, 69,* 339–361.

Ruggles, R. I. (1971). The West of Canada in 1763: Imagination and reality. *Canadian Geographer, 15,* 235–261.

Russell, R. J., & Kniffen, F. B. (1951). *Culture worlds.* New York: Macmillan.

Saarinen, T. F. (1974). Environmental perception. In I. R. Manners & M. W. Mikesell (Eds.), *Perspectives on environment* (Pub. No. 13, pp. 252–289. Washington: Association of American Geography, Commission on College Geography.

Sahlins, M. D. (1958). *Social stratification in Polynesia.* (Monograph No. 29). Seattle: Washington University Press, American Ethnological Society.

Sahlins, M. D., & Service, E. R. (Eds.). (1960). *Evolution and culture.* Ann Arbor: University of Michigan Press.

Salamon, S. (1985). Ethnic communities and the structure of agriculture. *Rural sociology, 50,* 323–340.

Salter, C. (Ed.). (1971). *The cultural landscape.* Belmont, CA: Duxbury.

Salter, C. (1977). Learning through landscape. *The California Geographer, 17,* 1–9.

Samuels, M. S. (1978). Existentialism and human geography. In D. Ley & M. S. Samuels (Eds.), *Humanistic geography* (pp. 22–40). Chicago: Maaroufa Press.

Samuels, M. S. (1979). The biography of landscape: Cause and culpability. In D. W. Meinig (Ed.), *The interpretation of ordinary landscapes* (pp. 51–88). New York: Oxford University Press.

Sauer, C. O. (1924). The survey method in geography and its objectives. *Annals, Association of American Geographers, 14,* 17–33.

Sauer, C. O. (1925). The morphology of landscape. *University of California Publications in Geography, 2,* 19–53.

Sauer, C. O. (1927). Recent developments in cultural geography. In E. C. Hayes (Ed.), *Recent developments in the social sciences* (pp. 154–212). Philadelphia: J. B. Lippincott.

Sauer, C. O. (1931). Cultural geography. *In Encyclopedia of the Social Sciences* (Vol. 6, pp. 621–624). New York: Macmillan.

Sauer, C. O. (1940). *Culture regions of the world: Outline of lectures.* Berkeley: University of California, Department of Geography.

Sauer, C. O. (1941). Foreword to historical geography. *Annals, Association of American Geographers, 31,* 1–24.

Sauer, C. O. (1948). *Colima of New Spain in the sixteenth century.* Berkeley: University of California Press.

Sauer, C. O. (1952). *Agricultural origins and dispersals.* New York: American Geographical Society.

Sauer, C. O. (1962). Homestead and community on the middle border." *Landscape, 12,* 3–7.

Sauer, C. O. (1974). The fourth dimension of geography. *Annals, Association of American Geographers, 64,* 189–192.

Sauer, C. O., & Brand, D. (1932). Prehistoric settlements of Sonora, with special reference to Cerros de Triacheras. *University of California Publications in Geography, 5,* 67–148.

Sauer, C. O., & Leighly, J. B. (1924). *Syllabus for an introduction to geography* [Processed: later editions to 1932]. Ann Arbor, MI: Edwards Brothers.

Sayer, A. (1979). Epistemology and conceptions of people and nature in geography. *Geoforum, 10,* 19–43.

Sayer, A. (1982). Explanation in economic geography. *Progress in Human Geography, 6,* 68–88.

Schnore, L. F. (1961). Geography and human ecology. *Economic Geography, 37,* 207–217.

Schorr, T. S. (1974). The structure and stuff of rural violence in a north Andean valley. In M. Richardson (Ed.), *The human mirror* (pp. 269–299). Baton Rouge: Louisiana State University Press.

Seamon, D. (1979). *A geography of the lifeworld.* London: Croom Helm.

Seig, L. (1963). The spread of tobacco: A study in cultural diffusion. *Professional Geographer, 15,* 17–21.

Semple, E. (1903). *American history and its geographic conditions.* Boston: Houghton Mifflin.

Semple, E. (1911). *Influences of geographic environment.* New York: Henry Holt.

Shilhav, Y. (1983). Principles for the location of synagogues: Symbolism and functionalism in a spatial context. *Professional Geographer, 35,* 324–329.

Shortridge, J. R. (1976). Patterns of religion in the United States. *Geographical Review, 66,* 420–434.

Shortridge, J. R. (1977). A new regionalization of American religion. *Journal of the Scientific Study of Religion, 16,* 143–153.

Shortridge, J. R. (1980). Vernacular regions in Kansas. *American Studies, 21,* 73–94.

Simon, J. (1978). *Basic research methods in social science.* New York: Random House.

Sitwell, O. F. G., & Bilash, S. E. (1986). Analyzing the cultural landscape as a means of probing the non-material dimension of reality. *Canadian Geographer, 30,* 132–145.

Smith, A. (1971). *Theories of nationalism.* London: Duckworth.

Smith, M. G. (1969). Some developments in the analytical framework of pluralism. In L. Kuper & M. G. Smith (Eds.), *Pluralism in Africa* (pp. 415–458). Berkeley: University of California Press.

Smith, N., & O'Keefe, P. (1980). Geography, Marx and the concept of nature. *Antipode, 12,* 30–39.

Sopher, D. E. (1967). *Geography of religions.* Englewood Cliffs, NJ: Prentice Hall.

Sopher, D. E. (1981). Geography and religions. *Progress in Human Geography, 5,* 510–524.

Spate, O. H. K. (1952). Toynbee and Huntington: A study in determinism. *Geographical Journal, 118,* 406–428.

Spencer, C., & Blades, M. (1986). Pattern and process: A review essay on the relationship between behavioral geography and environmental psychology. *Progress in Human Geography*, *10*, 230–248.

Spencer, J. E. (1960). The cultural factor in "Underdevelopment": The case of Malaya. In N. Ginsburg (Ed.) *Geography and economic development* (Res. Pap. No. 62, pp. 35–48). Chicago: University of Chicago, Department of Geography.

Spencer, J. E. (1978). The Growth of cultural geography. *American Behavioral Scientist*, *22*, 79–92.

Spencer, J. E. (1982). Southeast Asia. *Progress in Human Geography*, *6*, 265–269.

Spencer, J. E., & Horvath, R. J. (1963). How does an agricultural region originate? *Annals, Association of American Geographers*, *53*, 74–92.

Spencer, J. E., & Thomas, W. L., Jr. (1973). *Introducing cultural geography*. New York: John Wiley & Sons.

Speth, W. W. (1967). Environment, culture and the Mormon in early Utah. *Yearbook, Association of Pacific Coast Geographers*, *29*, 53–67.

Stanislawski, D. (1946). The origin and spread of the the grid pattern town. *Geographical Review*, *36*, 105–120.

Steward, J. (1936). The economic and social basis of primitive bands. In R. H. Lowie (Ed.), *Essays in anthropology presented to A. L. Kroeber* (pp. 331–345). Berkeley: University of California Press.

Steward, J. (1938). *Basin-plateau aboriginal sociopolitical groups*. (No. 120). Washington, DC: Bureau of American Ethnology.

Steward, J. (1955). *Theory of culture change: The methodology of multilinear evolution*. Urbana: University of Illinois Press.

Stilgoe, J. R. (1982). *Common landscape of America, 1580 to 1845*. New Haven, CT: Yale University Press.

Stoddard, R. H., Blouet, B. W., & Wishart, D. J. (1986). *Human geography: People, places and cultures*. Englewood Cliffs, NJ: Prentice Hall.

Stoddart, D. R. (1965). Geography and the ecological approach. *Geography*, *50*, 242–251.

Stoddart, D. R. (1966). Darwin's impact on geography. *Annals, Association of American Geographers*, *56*, 683–698.

Stoddart, D. R. (1967). Organism and ecosystem as geographical models. In R. J. Chorley & P. Haggett (Eds.), *Models in geography* (pp. 511–548). London: Methuen.

Stoddart, D. R. (1986). *On geography*. Oxford, UK: Blackwell.

Stump, R. W. (1987). Introduction. *Journal of Cultural Geography*, *7*, 1–3.

Sutter, R. E. (1973). *The next place you come to: A historical introduction to communities in North America*. Englewood Cliffs, NJ: Prentice Hall.

Swierenga, R. P. (1982). Theoretical perspectives on the new rural history: From environmentalism to modernization. *Agricultural History*, *56*, 495–502.

Swierenga, R. P. (Ed.). (1984). *James C. Malin: History and ecology, studies of the grassland*. Lincoln: University of Nebraska Press.

Taafe, E. J. (1974). The spatial view in context, *Annals, Association of American Geographers*, *64*, 1–16.

Tampke, J. (Ed.). (1982). *Wunderbar country: Germans look at Australia, 1850–1914*. Sydney, Australia: Hale and Iremonger.

Tanaka, H. (1977). Geographic expression of Bhuddist pilgrim places on Shikoku Island, Japan. *Canadian Geographer*. *21*, 111–132.

Tanaka, H. (1984). Landscape expression of the evolution of Buddhism in Japan. *Canadian Geographer*, *28*, 240–257.

Tatham, G. (1951). Environmentalism and possibilism. In G. Taylor (Ed.), *Geography in the twentieth century* (pp. 128–162). New York: Philosophical Library.

Taylor, G. (1951). Introduction: The scope of the volume. In G. Taylor (Ed.), *Geography in the twentieth century* (pp. 3–27). New York: Philosophical Library.

Thomas, W. L., Jr., Sauer, C. O., Bates, M., Mumford, L. (Eds.). (1956). *Man's role in changing the face of the earth*. Chicago: University of Chicago Press.

Thomson, G. M. (1976). *The north-west passage*. London: Futura.

Thornthwaite, C. W. (1940). The relation of geography to human ecology. *Ecological Monograph*, *10*, 343–348.

Traugott, M. (1985). *Armies of the poor*. Princeton: Princeton University Press.

Trigger, B. G. (1982). Responses of native peoples to European contact. In G. M. Story (Ed.), *Early European settlement and exploitation in Atlantic Canada* (pp. 139–155). St. John's, Canada: Memorial University of Newfoundland.

Trigger, B. G. (1985). *Natives and newcomers: Canada's "heroic age" reconsidered*. Kingston, Canada: McGill-Queen's University Press.

Tuan, Y. F. (1968). Discrepancies between environmental attitude and behavior: Examples from Europe and China. *Canadian Geographer*, *12*, 176–191.

Tuan, Y. F. (1971). Geography, phenomenology, and the study of human nature. *Canadian Geographer*, *15*, 181–192.

Tuan, Y. F. (1978). Sacred space: Exploration of an idea. In K. W. Butzer (Ed.), *Dimensions of human geography: Essays on some familiar and neglected themes* (Res. Pap. No. 186, pp. 84–99). Chicago: University of Chicago Press, Department of Geography.

Tuan, Y. F. *Landscapes of fear*. Oxford, UK: Blackwell.

Tuan, Y. F. (1986). Strangers and strangeness. *Geographical Review*, *76*, 10–19.

Tyler, S. A. (Ed.). (1969). *Cognitive anthropology*. New York: Holt, Rinehart and Winston.

van der Laan L., & Piersma, A. (1982). The image of man: Paradigmatic cornerstone in human geography. *Annals, Association of American Geographers*, *72*, 411–426.

van Paassen, C. (1981). The philosophy of geography: From Vidal to Hagerstrand. *Lund Studies in Geography B*, *48*, 17–29.

Vayda, A. P., & Rappaport, R. A. (1968). Ecology, cultural and noncultural. In J. A. Clifton (Ed.), *Introduction to cultural anthropology* (pp. 477–497). Boston: Houghton Mifflin.

Wacker, P. O. (1968). *The Musconetcong Valley: A historical geography*. New Brunswick, NJ: Rutgers University Press.

Wacker, P. O. (1975). *Land and people: A cultural geography of pre-industrial New Jersey, origins and settlement patterns*. New Brunswick, NJ: Rutgers University Press.

Wagner, P. L. (1958). Remarks on the geography of language. *Geographical Review*, *48*, 86–97.

Wagner, P. L. (1972). *Environments and peoples*. Englewood Cliffs, NJ: Prentice Hall.

Wagner, P. L. (1974). Cultural landscapes and regions: Aspects of communication. *Geoscience and Man*, *5*, 133–142.

Wagner, P. L. (1975). The themes of cultural geography rethought. *Yearbook, Association of Pacific Coast Geographers, 37,* 7–14.

Wagner, P. L. (1977). The concept of environmental determinism in cultural evolution. In C. A. Reed (Ed.), *Origins of agriculture* (pp. 49–74). The Hague: Mouton.

Wagner, P. L., & Mikesell, M. W. (1962). The themes of cultural geography. In P. L. Wagner & M. W. Mikesell (Eds.), *Readings in cultural geography* (pp. 1–24). Chicago: University of Chicago Press.

Wallerstein, I. (1974). *The modern world system: capitalist agriculture and the origins of the European world economy in the sixteenth century.* New York: Academic Press.

Walmsley, D. J., & Lewis, G. J. (1984). *Human geography: Behavioral approaches.* London: Longman.

Watson, J. W. (1951). The sociological aspects of geography. In G. Taylor (Ed.), *Geography in the twentieth century* (pp. 463–499). New York: Philosophical Library.

Watson, R. A., & Watson, P. J. (1969). *Man and nature: An anthropological essay in human ecology.* New York: Harcourt, Brace and World.

Wessman, J. W. (1981). *Anthropology and Marxism.* Cambridge, MA: Schenkman.

White, C. L., & Renner, G. T. (1936). *Geography: An introduction to human ecology.* New York: Appleton, Century.

White, C. L., & Renner, G. T. (1948). *Human Geography: An ecological study of society.* New York: Appleton, Century, Crofts.

White, L. A. (1949). *The science of culture: A study of man and civilization.* New York: Grove Press.

White, L. A. (1959). *The evolution of culture.* New York: McGraw-Hill.

White, L. A. (1975). *The concept of cultural systems.* New York: Columbia University Press.

Whittlesey, D. (1929). Sequent occupance. *Annals, Association of American Geographers, 19,* 162–165.

Williams, C., & Smith, A. D. (1983). The national construction of social space. *Progress in Human Geography, 7,* 502–518.

Williams, M. (1983). The apple of my eye: Carl Sauer and historical geography. *Journal of Historical Geography, 9,* 1–28.

Williams, R. (1977). *Marxism and literature.* New York: Oxford University Press.

Williams, S. W. (1981). Realism, Marxism and human geography. *Antipode, 13,* 31–38.

Wilson, A. G. (1981). *Geography and the environment: Systems analytical methods.* New York: John Wiley & Sons.

Wishart, D. J. (1976). Cultures in co-operation and conflict: 1807–1840. *Journal of Historical Geography, 2,* 311–328.

Wisner, B. (1978). Does radical geography lack an approach to environmental relations? *Antipode, 10,* 84–95.

Wissler, C. (1917). *The American Indian: An introduction to the anthropology of the New World.* New York: McMurtie.

Wissler, C. (1926). *The relation of nature to man in aboriginal America.* New York: Oxford University Press.

Withers, C. J. (1981). The geographical extent of Gaelic in Scotland, 1698–1806. *Scottish Geographical Magazine, 97,* 130–139.

Wittfogel, K. A. (1968). The theory of oriental society. In M. Fried (Ed.), *Readings in anthropology* (Vol. 2, 2nd ed., pp. 179–198). New York: Crowell.

Wolf, E. R. (1964). *Anthropology*. Englewood Cliffs, NJ: Prentice Hall.

Worster, D. (1984). History as natural history: An essay on theory and method. *Pacific Historical Review, 53*, 1–19.

Wright, J. K. (1947). Terra incognitae: The place of imagination in geography. *Annals, Association of American Geographers, 37*, 1–15.

Wright, J. K. (1966). *Human nature in geography*. Cambridge, MA: Harvard University Press.

Wynn, G. (1983). Settler societies in geographical focus. *Historical Studies, 20*, 353–366.

Young, G. L. (1974). Human ecology as an interdisciplinary concept: A critical inquiry. *Advances in Ecological Research, 8*, 1–105.

Young, G. L. (1983a). Editor's comments on papers 1 through 6. In G. L. Young (Ed.), *Origins of human ecology* (pp. 12–19). Stroudsburg, PA: Hutchinson Press.

Young, G. L. (1983b). Introduction. In G. L. Young (Ed.), *Origins of human ecology* (pp. 1–9). Stroudsburg, PA: Hutchinson Press.

Zdorkowski, R. T., & Carney, G. O. (1985). This land is my land: Oklahoma's changing vernacular regions. *Journal of Cultural Geography, 5*, 97–106.

Zelinsky, W. (1961). An approach to the religious geography of the United States: Patterns of church membership; in 1952. *Annals, Association of American Geographers, 51*, 139–197.

Zelinsky, W. (1973). *Cultural geography of the United States*. Englewood Cliffs, NJ: Prentice Hall.

Zelinsky, W. (1980). North America's vernacular regions. *Annals, Association of American Geographers, 70*, 1–16.

Zimolzak, C. E., & Stansfield C. A., Jr. (1979). *The human landscape: Geography and culture*. Toronto, Canada: Merrill.

Index

Acculturation, 102
Adams, W. Y., 106
Agnew, John A., 117, 138
Agricultural origins, 157, 159
Alexander, Richard D., 21, 22
Alihan, M. A., 145
Allen, John L., 79
American Culture Association, 2
Anderson, Thomas D., 148
Antipode, 2
Arendt, Hannah, 166
Aschmann, Homer, 156
Asheim, B. T., 50
Association of American Geographers, 2, 43, 163

Baran, P. A., 135
Barker, R. G., 72
Barnett, J. R., 132
Barrell, John, 84
Barrows, Harlan H., 19, 39, 43, 63, 141, 147, 148, 164
Barth, Fredrik, 131, 145, 166
Bastian, Alfred, 25
Bates, M., 42
Bennett, J. W., 11, 19, 20, 150–51
Berdoulay, V., 36
Berlin Geographical Society, 25

Berry, J. W., 146, 150
Berry, Thomas M., 29
Bilash, S. E., 138
Billinge, Mark, 133
Billington, Ray A., 95
Binford, Lewis R., 103
Biswas, L., 129
Bjorklund, Elaine M., 123
Blades, M., 72, 75, 78
Blaut, James M., 47, 49, 51, 109, 133
Blouet, Brian W., 161
Boas, Franz, 13, 14, 15, 25, 63, 109
Bodin, Jean, 32, 63
Bolton, Herbert E., 36
Boorstin, Daniel J., 76
Boserup, Ester, 157
Boulding, Kenneth E., 19, 73, 154
Bourdieu, P., 115
Bourne, Larry S., 137
Bowden, Leonard W., 108
Bowen, E., 31
Bowen, E. H., 125
Brand, Donald, 97
Breisach, E., 30
Brigham, Albert P., 164
Broek, J. O. M., 28, 89, 91, 107
Brookfield, Harold C., 41, 74, 157

Browett, J., 51
Brown, I. W., 104
Brown, L. A., 106, 108, 109
Brown, M. A., 108
Bruhn, John G., 19
Brunger, Alan G., 132, 133
Brunhes, Jean, 35, 36, 47, 164
Brunn, S., 118, 133
Bryan, Patrick, 43
Bryson, Reid A., 59
Buckle, Henry T., 31
Bunkse, Edmunds V., 68, 84
Bunting, T. E., 74, 76
Burgess, Ernest W., 19, 142
Burgess, Rod, 48, 50
Burton, I., 74
Buttimer, A., 35
Butzer, Karl W., 138, 152

Cameron, James M. R., 78, 79–80
Carlstein, Tommy, 116, 117, 157–58
Carney, George O., 120, 121
Carol, Hans, 167
Carroll, Glenn R., 5
Carter, George F., 41, 43, 90, 157
Carter, H., 106, 125
Chamberlain, Houston Stewart, 132
Chappell, John E., Jr., 59
Chase, William G., 75–76, 78
Chi, Micheline T. H., 75–76, 78
Childe, V. Gordon, 21
Chisholm, Michael, 59
Chorley, Richard J., 59–60, 166
Christopher, A. J., 77, 96, 100
Church, Frederick E., 84
Clare, John, 84
Clarkson, James D., 39, 60, 156–57
Class, 49, 133
Claval, P., 47
Clout, Hugh, 118, 136, 148
Cognition, 74
Cohen, Anthony P., 166
Cohen, E., 127
Collingwood, Robert George, 53
Comte, August, 14, 16, 31, 63
Condorcet, 12
Conkey, M. W., 62
Corn Belt, 92–93, 121

Cosgrove, D., 2, 49, 55, 83, 84, 166
Craig, A. K., 110
Cromar, Peter, 133
Cronon, W., 146
Crowley, W. K., 107
Crush, J. S., 51
Cullen, I. G., 74
Cultural adaptation, 103, 110, 149–53
Cultural conservatism, 82–83
Cultural contact, 13, 101–5
Cultural determinism, 57–58, 62, 63. *See
    also* Social organism, superorganic
    concept
Cultural ecology, 12, 18–20, 61, 144,
    167; and adaptation, 146; examples of,
    156–57
Cultural geography: and the state, 134;
    approaches to, 65; definition of, 6–7,
    8, 161–62; development of, 65; inte-
    gration with social geography, 1, 6, 7,
    8, 47, 62, 83, 113, 115–19, 138–39,
    161–62; links with other disciplines,
    6
Cultural materialism, 20, 23
Cultural preadaptation, 110
Cultural regions, 16, 35, 38, 44, 47, 61,
    68, 90–97, 107; in Africa, 96–97; in
    Australia, 96; in Europe, 97; in the
    United States, 93–96, 121, 129; in the
    World, 91–92
Culture: as symbol of, 18, 44, 55–56,
    57–58, 113; concepts of, 63; definition
    of, 44, 57–58, 61–62; in landscape
    school, 38; interactionist view of, 55–
    56, 57–58; marxist view of, 23–24
Curtin, Phillip D., 76
Cushing, Sumner W., 164
Cybriwsky, R. A., 136, 137

Darby, H. Clifford, 59, 89
Darley, John M., 75, 85
Darwin, Charles, 12, 21, 23, 63, 142,
    143
Davidson, W. V., 98
Davis, William Morris, 42, 164
de Blij, H. J., 92
DeFreitas, C., 29
Denevan, William M., 60, 110, 152

Dennis, Richard J., 118, 136, 148
Denoon, D., 135
Dependency theory, 51
Dhussa, R. C., 126
Dickinson, Robert E., 88, 89, 90
Diffusion, 13–14, 93, 96, 101, 105–9;
  radical view of, 109
Diffusionism, 12–14, 61
Dilthey, Wilhelm, 46, 54
Dodge, S. D., 43
Downs, Roger, 75
Drakakis-Smith, David, 51, 134
Dunbar, Gary S., 89, 114
Duncan, James S., 6, 15, 36, 49, 55, 62,
  117, 123
Duncan, S. S., 48
Durham, William H., 22
Durkheim, Emile, 14, 17, 19, 20, 21–22,
  25, 36, 40, 41, 51, 58, 63, 114,
  116
Dyck, J. H. A., 166

Earman, J., 58
Eastern Canada, 81
Eastman, C., 126
Ecosystem, 153, 159
Edwards, J., 123, 126, 131
Elazar, Daniel J., 95
Elitist space, 121
Ellen, Roy, 11, 12, 23, 56
Energy, 17–18, 20
English, Paul W., 41, 153, 156
Ennals, Peter M., 101
Entrikin, J. N., 39, 54
Environmental determinism, 4, 14, 16,
  32–34, 37, 40–41, 43, 46, 57–58, 62,
  63, 65, 68, 88, 145
Environmental psychology, 72
Ericksen, E. Gordon, 60, 63, 145
Ethnicity, 47, 98, 99, 107, 131–33; and
  inequality, 132; and minorities, 132;
  and race, 131–32; and social interac-
  tion, 132–33; definition of, 131,
  133
Ethnoscience, 21
Evans, E. E., 89
Evernden, Neil, 84

Evolutionism, 12–14; general and special,
  110; new, 17–18
Existentialism, 45, 54, 65, 73
Exploratory images, 78–79
Eyles, John, 136

Fairweather, J. R., 135
Febvre, Lucien, 63, 164
Feldman, Douglas A., 12
Fenneman, N. M., 164
Firey, Walter, 115, 137, 145
First effective settlement, 94, 95, 124,
  135
Flinn, Mark V., 21, 22
Flora, J. L., 99
Florida, 82–83, 121
Flowerdew, R., 133
Foote, Don C., 154
Ford, Larry, 7
Formal region, 90, 98
Found, William C., 80
Francaviglia, Richard V., 100, 128,
  129
Freeman, Donald B., 109
French Canada, 94
Freud, Sigmund, 116
Friedl, J., 14, 25
Friesen, Richard J., 100
Functional region, 90
Functionalism, 16–17

Gade, Daniel W., 121
Gale, Donald T., 100, 129
Gastil, Raymond D., 95
Gay, John, 126
Geertz, Clifford, 21, 25, 57–58, 60, 62,
  63, 154
Geipel, R., 138
Genetic fallacy, 88
Geosophy, 69
Gerlach, Russel L., 99
Gerland, Georg, 32
Gestalt psychology, 71–73
Giddens, Anthony, 51, 116–17
Gilbert, Daniel T., 75, 85
Glacken, Clarence, 83
Gobineau, Joseph Arthur de, 132
Gold, John R., 2, 72, 74

Golledge, Reginald G., 75
Goodey, B., 2, 72, 74
Goodwin, Crauford P. V., 76
Gordon, Burton L., 156
Gould, P., 75
Gould, Stephen J., 22
Grano, Olavi, 28
Great Plains, 77, 95
Greer-Wooten, Bryn, 154
Gregory, D., 51, 118
Gregson, Nicky, 117
Grice, K., 134
Griffin, Ernst, 7
Gritzner, Charles F., 43–44, 59, 91
Grossman, Larry, 15, 16, 42, 152
Guatemala, 104–5
Guelke, Leonard, 2, 52–53, 74, 76

Habermas, Jurgen, 51
Haeckel, Ernst, 142
Hagerstrand, T., 93, 106–9, 113, 116
Haggett, Peter, 161
Hale, Ruth F., 120, 121
Halévy, Élie, 131
Hall, C. S., 73
Hamill, L., 83–84
Hansis, R., 152
Hanson, J., 115–16
Hardesty, D. L., 146, 151, 152, 154
Hardy, Thomas, 84
Harris, David R., 156
Harris, Marvin, 15, 16, 20, 23, 25, 146
Harris, R., 137
Harris, R. C., 29, 96, 135
Harriss, B., 2
Harriss, J., 2
Hartshorne, Richard, 40, 42, 88, 89, 90, 165
Harvey, David W., 50, 60, 88, 92
Hawley, Amos H., 145, 148
Haynes, R. M., 75
Heidegger, Martin, 73
Heidenreich, Conrad, 158
Henderson, John R., 103, 117
Henretta, James A., 135
Henrie, Roger, 121, 127, 128

Herder, Johann, 29, 30
Herskovits, J. N., 102
Hettner, Alfred, 34, 36, 88, 89
Heyer, P., 12, 14, 21, 23
Hillier, B., 115–16
Hoke, G. W., 114
Holtgrieve, Donald D., 100
Holt-Jensen, Arild, 28, 32, 60
Hornbeck, D., 100
Horvath, Ronald J., 92–93, 110
House, F. N., 145
Hoyt, Homer, 145
Hudson, W. H., 58
Hufferd, J., 55
Human ecology, 18–20, 34, 39, 43, 57, 59–60, 63, 65, 114, 115; and community, 148, 149; and systems analysis, 153–55; in an urban context, 155–56; in geography, 147–49; in other disciplines, 142–47; socialist, 49
Humanism, 46, 47, 49, 52–56, 65, 72–73, 83–84, 113, 143, 167
Humboldt, Alexander von, 28, 35, 63, 65, 68, 69, 84, 147
Huntington, Ellsworth, 16, 33, 42, 63, 164

Idealism, 30, 45, 46, 52–53, 54, 65, 73
Innis, Donald, 156
Isaac, Erich, 127
Isajiw, W., 131
Isbister, J., 135
Ittelson, W. H., 72

Jackson, John B., 84, 101, 127
Jackson, Peter, 2, 47, 49, 51, 54, 55–56, 62, 119, 125, 132, 133, 134, 143, 150
Jackson, Richard H., 121, 127, 128
Jakle, J. A., 118, 133
James, Preston E., 28, 30, 31, 33, 36, 38, 39, 43, 164
Jeans, Dennis N., 96
Jefferson, Thomas, 79
Johnson, D., 43, 168
Johnson, J. H. Jr., 137

Johnston, Ronald J., 3, 48, 53, 87, 134, 168
Jones, Emrys, 136
Jordon, Terry G., 8, 61, 89, 97, 99, 100, 101, 106, 107, 120, 121, 124, 129–30, 134, 163
Journal of Cultural Geography, 2

Kant, Immanuel, 28–29, 32, 34
Karan, P. P., 130
Katz, P., 152
Kaups, M., 125
Kay, George, 167
Kearns, K. C., 125
Kelly, K., 82
Kesby, John D., 96–97
Keynes, John Maynard, 59
Kirk, William, 55, 69, 107
Kniffen, Fred, 87, 91, 94, 98, 101, 106, 107, 109
Kollmorgen, Walter M., 77
Koroscil, Paul M., 100, 129
Krech S., III, 104
Kroeber, Alfred, 13, 14–16, 18, 25, 36–37, 38, 51, 58, 63, 90, 106, 143–44, 164
Kropotkin, Peter, 31, 63, 65

Lambert, Audrey M., 98
Lamme, Art J., III, 120, 121
Land policies, 100
Landscape: and region, 90–91, 164–65; approaches to, 2, 5; as symbol, 137–39; behavior in, 76–83; definition of, 2, 84, 91, 162, 166; evaluation of, 83–84, 88–90, 92–93, 97–101; evolution of, 3–5, 80–83, 166–67; school, 36–39, 40–41, 43, 46, 47, 162
Landschaft, 34, 36, 90
Lanegran, David A., 167
Langton, J., 136
Language, 47, 97, 123–26; and ethnicity, 124–25; and landscape, 125; and nationalism, 125; and religion, 124–25; and society, 125–26; families, 123–24
Law of Cultural Dominance, 60, 110
Le Play School, 114

Leaf, M. J., 12, 14, 17, 20, 25
Leighly, John, 36, 37, 38, 43, 93, 107
Leonard, Simon, 7, 54, 133, 137
Levine, G., 137
Levi-Strauss, Claude, 20–21, 25, 48
Lewin, Kurt, 19, 70–71, 85, 144, 146, 150
Lewis and Clark expedition, 79
Lewis, Carolyn B., 82
Lewis, G. J., 73, 74
Lewis, K. E., 167
Lewthwaite, G. R., 149
Ley, David, 25, 46, 47, 49, 52, 55, 62, 75, 132, 134, 136, 137, 148
Life space, 19
Lindzey, G., 73
Loudon, D. R., 2
Lovell, W. G., 105
Lowenthal, David, 55, 82, 138
Lowie, Robert, 13, 36–37, 38, 58, 63, 88, 106, 109, 164
Luebke, F. C., 95
Lynch, Kevin, 73, 75

McCarty, J. W., 135
McKee, J. O., 103
McKenzie, Roderick D., 142–43
Mackenzie, S., 52
Mackinder, H. J., 33
McQuillan, D. Aidan, 132
Malaya, 93, 156
Malin, James C., 135, 146, 149
Malinowski, Bronislaw, 17, 57
Mannion, J., 81
Marchand, J. P., 59
Marsh, George Perkins, 31, 42, 63, 65
Martin, C., 104
Martin, Geoffrey J., 28, 30, 31, 33, 36, 39
Marx, Karl, 12, 23–24, 29, 30, 31, 48–49, 59, 116, 166
Marxism, 4, 23–24, 45, 54, 57, 63; and humans and land, 48–50; and societies and individuals, 50–51
Mason, Otis, 16
Massey, D., 118

Matejko, A., 132
Matejko, J., 132
Matley, Ian M., 167
Mayfield, Robert C., 41, 153, 156
Mead, George, 63, 125
Meggers, Betty J., 145
Meigs, Peveril, 98
Meinig, Donald W., 84, 93, 95, 96, 97, 117, 128, 137, 138
Mental maps, 74–76
Mercer, J., 138
Meredith, T. C., 82
Merrens, H. Roy, 77
Meyer, J. W., 129
Migration, 101–9
Mikesell, Marvin W,. 16, 61, 62, 67, 148
Miller, E. Joan, 121
Miller, George J., 164
Miller, V. P., Jr., 168
Mills, W. J., 29
Minding, 18, 58
Mississippi, 103
Mitchell, R. D., 95–96
Mogey, J., 149–50, 152
Montesquieu, 12, 29, 32, 63
Moore, J. H., 25
Moran, Emilio F., 146
Morgan, Lewis, 13, 16, 109
Morgan, W. B., 148
Mormon region, 93–94, 99–100, 128, 129, 149
Morrill, Richard L., 108, 166, 168
Moss, R. P., 148
Muller, E. K., 136
Mumford, L., 42
Murray, Thomas J., 59

NAS-NRC, 3, 87
Netting, Robert, 146
New Jersey, 98
Newson, Linda, 60, 110
Newton, Milton, 110
Nisbet, Robert, 29
Noble, A. G., 62, 126
Norton, William, 29, 61, 82, 87, 95, 108, 161, 162, 167

Norwine, Jim, 148
Nostrand, R. C., 95

Ogilvie, P. G., 89
O'Higgins, Edward, 13
O'Keefe, Phil, 48
Oldakowski, Raymond K., 120, 121
Olwig, Kenneth, 31
Ortner, Sherry B., 24
Osborne, B. S., 137
Ostergren, Robert C., 132
Ozarks, 99

Pahl, Raymond E., 114, 137
Palmer, B. D., 133
Park, Robert E., 19, 39, 133, 142–43, 144
Parkins, Almon E., 164
Parry, Martin L., 59
Parsons, J. J., 36
Parsons, Talcott, 19
Peach, C., 132
Peebles, C. S., 110
Pelto, Pertti J., 14
Penck, Albrecht, 90
Perception, 40, 42, 68–69, 73–83, 119–22
Personality, geographic, 89, 91
Pfeifer, G., 164
Pfeiffer, J., 14, 25
Phenomenology, 45, 50, 53, 65, 73, 84
Philippines, 92–93
Phillips, A., 136
Piaget, Jean, 48
Pickles, John, 53, 163
Piersma, A., 46
Political economy, 24
Popular Culture Association, 2
Porter, Philip W., 60, 152, 159
Positivism, 45, 46, 52, 54, 63, 70, 83, 143
Possibilism, 34, 35–36, 43, 63, 65, 69, 145
Pouliot, D. F., 29
Pred, Allen, 51, 107, 116, 117, 133
Prince, Hugh C., 82
Probalism, 42, 43, 63, 65

Progress in Human Geography, 2, 47
Pryce, W. T. R., 97, 126
Pyle, G., 108

Quani, M., 30
Queen Charlotte Islands, 103
Quinn, James A., 148

Raby, Stewart, 104
Radcliffe-Brown, A. R., 17, 63
Radical methodologies, 47–52, 113, 133
Raitz, Karl B., 107, 120, 121, 131
Rappaport, R. Andrew, 20, 145, 146, 154
Ratzel, Friedrich, 16, 33, 63, 88, 116, 147, 164
Ray, Arthur J., 158
Reclus, Elisée, 31, 42, 63, 65, 114
Reed, John G., 120
Rees, Ronald, 84
Religion, 47, 98, 99–100, 126–31; and denominations, 128–29; and ecology, 130; and landscape, 129; and sacred space, 121–22, 127–28, 138; and social/economic change, 131–32
Relph, Edward C., 55, 167
Renfrew, C., 56
Renner, G. T., 148
Reynolds, Henry, 104
Richardson, Miles, 57, 58, 62, 118, 136
Richthofen, Ferdinand von, 34, 88
Riddell, J. B., 108
Ritter, Carl, 25, 28, 30–31, 63, 65, 116, 147
Robinson, David J., 118
Robson, B. T., 155
Rogers, Everett M., 106
Rooney, J. R., Jr., 2
Roseman, Curtis C., 118, 133
Rossi, I., 13
Roulston, P., 29
Rowntree, Lester C., 8, 52, 61, 62, 89, 107, 124, 130, 134, 163
Roxby, P. M., 114
Rubin, Barbara, 50

Ruggles, Richard I., 79
Russell, Richard J., 91

Saarinen, T. F., 68, 76
Sahlins, Marshall D., 18, 109, 110
Salamon, Sonya, 99
Salter, Christopher, 107, 167
Samuels, Marwyn S., 46, 52, 54, 82
Sauer, Carl O., 18, 27, 31, 36–39, 40–41, 42, 43, 52, 64, 68, 69, 87–88, 89, 90–91, 97–98, 110, 114, 148, 156, 157, 164, 165, 168
Sayer, Andrew, 7, 48–49, 50
Schluter, Otto, 36, 63, 65, 88, 89, 90
Schnore, Leo F., 148
Schorr, Thomas S., 151–52
Schouw, Joachim, 31, 63, 65
Schutz, Alfred, 53
Seamon, David, 55
Seig, L., 107
Semple, Ellen, 16, 33, 63, 164
Sequent occupance, 38, 40, 43, 65, 164
Service, Elman R., 109, 110
Shilhav, Y., 129
Shortridge, James R., 120, 128, 129
Simon, J., 120
Sitwell, O. F. G., 138
Smith, A., 125
Smith, Adam, 12
Smith, Anthony D., 134
Smith, Michael G., 132
Smith, Neil, 48
Smith, S. J., 49, 51, 54, 55–56, 62, 133, 143, 150
Social geography, 43, 63, 114–19; of settlements, 136–37; of the frontier, 134–35
Social organism, 14, 23, 62–63, 134. *See also* Cultural Determinism; Superorganic concept
Social scale of analysis, 7, 29, 41, 50–51, 53, 54, 55–56, 60, 62, 63, 81–83, 121–22, 133, 137–39, 151
Sociobiology, 21–22

Sopher, David, 126, 127, 129, 130, 138
Southern Ontario, 82
Spate, Oscar, H. K., 34, 41–42
Spencer, C., 72, 75, 78
Spencer, Herbert, 12, 14, 15, 16, 19, 23, 33, 58, 63, 109
Spencer, Joseph E., 2, 57, 61–62, 88, 89, 92–93, 107, 110, 167
Speth, William W., 149
Stanislawski, D., 106
Stansfield, C. E., Jr., 92, 124
Stea, David, 75
Steward, Julian, 18, 19, 20, 25, 109, 110, 144, 145, 146
Stilgoe, John R., 101
Stitz, J. M., 99
Stoddard, Robert H., 161
Stoddart, David R., 28, 33, 142, 153, 159
Stop and go determinism, 41, 43, 63, 65
Structural Marxism, 24, 49
Structuralism, 20–21, 45, 48, 56
Structuration, 51, 116–17, 133, 158
Stump, Roger W., 131
Superorganic concept, 4, 14–16, 20, 21, 23, 25, 36–37, 40–41, 134. *See also* Cultural determinism; social organism
Sutter, R. E., 166
Swan River Colony, 78
Swidden agriculture, 156
Swierenga, R. P., 135, 146, 149
Symbolic anthropology, 21
Symbolic interactionism, 55–58, 60, 62, 63, 118, 126, 134, 136

Taafe, E. J., 39, 165
Tampke, Jürgen, 76
Tanaka, H., 128, 129
Tansley, Arthur George, 153
Tatham, George, 31, 43
Taylor, Griffith, 34, 41
Texas, 95, 129
Thomas, William L., Jr., 42, 61–62, 89, 107
Thomson, G. M., 78
Thornthwaite, C. Warren, 148

Time geography, 116, 157–58
Toynbee, Arnold, 41–42
Traugott, M., 166
Trigger, B. G., 102, 103, 104
Tuan, Yi-fu, 53, 55, 127, 130, 165–66
Turner, Frederick Jackson, 95, 135
Tyler, Stephen A., 21
Tylor, Edward, 13, 25, 57, 63, 106, 109

Ulack, Richard, 120, 121
Urry, J., 118

van der Laan, Lambert, 46
van Paassen, C., 116
Varenius, Bernard, 28
Vayda, Andrew, 20, 145
Vernacular regions, 90, 119–22
Verstehen, 54
Vico, Giambattista, 29–30
Vidal de la Blache, Paul, 35, 36, 40, 41, 42, 43, 52, 59, 63, 65, 68, 69, 87, 89, 91, 114, 116, 164
Vidal school, 35, 39, 40, 41, 42, 45, 46, 47, 59, 162
Voltaire, 12

Wacker, Peter O., 98
Wagner, Philip L., 61, 62, 63, 109, 118, 124, 137, 157
Waibel, Leo H., 88
Wallerstein, Immanuel, 51
Walmsley, D. J., 73, 74
Watson, J. Wreford, 43, 114
Watson, Patty J., 12
Watson, Richard A., 12
Webb, J. W., 89, 91, 107, 146, 149
Webb, Walter Prescott, 135
Weber, Max, 51, 54, 63, 116, 130
Wessman, James W., 24
Western Canada, 79
Western, J., 137
White, C. L., 148
White, Leslie A., 12, 14, 17–18, 25, 58, 59, 60, 62, 63, 109, 110
White, R., 75

Whittlesey, Derwent, 38, 63, 164
Williams, A., 136
Williams, Colin, 134
Williams, Michael, 38
Williams, Raymond, 24
Williams, S. W., 50
Wilson, Alan G., 154
Wirth, Louis, 142
Wishart, David J., 104, 161
Wisner, Ben, 49, 51
Wissler, Clark, 13, 16, 43, 57, 63, 90, 143, 164
Withers, C. J., 126

Wittfogel, Karl A., 23, 146
Wolf, E. R., 17
World-systems, 51
Worster, Donald, 23, 146
Wright, John K., 69, 127
Wynn, Graeme, 135

Young, Gerald L., 19, 20, 142, 144

Zdorkowski, R. Todd, 120, 121
Zelinsky, Wilbur, 2, 59, 94, 96, 120, 121, 128, 134
Zimolzak, C. E., 92, 124

About the Author

WILLIAM NORTON is Professor of Geography and Department Head, the University of Manitoba. His publications include *Historical Analysis in Geography*, together with numerous articles and book chapters on topics in historical and cultural geography.